MOUNTAINS-TO-SEA TRAIL GUIDE

Mountains

MOUNTAINS-TO-SEA TRAIL GUIDE

MOUNTAINS

GREAT SMOKY MOUNTAINS TO STONE MOUNTAIN STATE PARK

Compiled by Friends of the Mountains-to-Sea Trail
Guidebook Editor: Jim Grode

Foreword by Allen de Hart

P.O. Box 10431
Raleigh, NC 27605
www.MountainstoSeaTrail.org

FRIENDS OF THE
MOUNTAINS
-to-SEA TRAIL
NORTH CAROLINA

Design and layout by The Roberts Group
Maps and elevation profiles by Curtis Belyea

Table of Contents

Foreword

Whether you are just being introduced to the Mountains-to-Sea Trail (MST) or are a veteran hiker, this guide will be one of the most important pieces of your hiking "equipment."

I have been involved with the MST for almost 40 of my 90 years. I have seen the dreamers, planners, organizers, and trail-oriented enthusiasts of North Carolina who are responsible for the planning and development of the trail. Some were volunteer leaders and workers involved in specific locations. Others were staff members of local, state, and national government agencies.

Together we saw the potential for a trail that ran from the Appalachian Mountains to the Atlantic Ocean. Our efforts have brought the trail to where it is today and hopefully will inspire current and future volunteers and officials to continue the dream of providing a way to walk across the state from the high-elevation Appalachian Trail to the highest sand dune on the east coast.

I was an interested party when the North Carolina Trails System Act was enacted in 1973. It called for a system of trails around the state, although it did not specifically mention a long distance trail across the state.

I was present when Howard Lee, then secretary of the North Carolina Department of Natural Resources and Community Development, addressed the Fourth National Trails Symposium in 1977, saying "I think the time has come for us to consider the feasibility of establishing a state trail between the mountains and the seashore in North Carolina."

I was active with the North Carolina Trails Committee and the North Carolina Trails Association as both groups worked diligently to plan and construct a "flagship trail" passing through as many federal, state, county, and city parks as possible and through as many North Carolina counties as feasible.

I was a trail leader for the first MST "trek" across the state in 1982, which served "to promote awareness of trails in North Carolina, to motivate local areas to build trails, and to make people conscious of the Mountains-to-Sea Trail."

In 1977, Alan Householder and I were the first to hike the entire length of the MST corridor proposed by the Division of Parks and Recreation. I have traversed the route many times since then for planning or construction purposes. I continue to enjoy every mile of the MST.

When state government staff showed less interest in the MST during the mid-1990s, I retired from the North Carolina Trails Committee to form a new organization incorporated in 1997. Our new board of directors named it Friends of the Mountains-to-Sea Trail. Among its purposes were to "encourage, sponsor, promote, publicize, and increase public awareness of the Mountains-to-Sea Trail."

In 2000, I authored *Hiking North Carolina's Mountains-to-Sea Trail*. The book's 371 pages gave a history of the trail, a description of the routing, and background about the sites along the way. The book also included maps and photographs. Also in 2000, the North Carolina General Assembly passed bills that directed the Division of Parks and Recreation to support "a continuous trail across the State." In the first years after that legislation was passed, we had four to five trail crews. We now have 24, with over 1,000 volunteers. As Trail Counsel and Director Emeritus, I continue to be active in the management of Friends' Task Forces and other aspects of Friends' activities.

With the publication of this series of trail guides, Friends has taken a big step in making the trail more accessible to the hiker. By using this book to hike the MST, you are benefitting from all this history and all the effort and vision of those who have been on the trail before you.

No one appreciates the beauty and the power of the MST more than I do. Experience hiking or, even better, participate in the activities of Friends as they build and maintain the trail, and you will understand my passion.

As I have worked with the various Task Force leaders along the trail, I have told most of them that their section was the most beautiful of the MST. In each case I was being truthful. Any hiking, including along the MST, is focused on the present. You are not thinking about what you did yesterday and you are not worrying about what you will do tomorrow. You are focused on the trail you are walking that day—through mountains and forests; along streams, rivers, and lakes. Be a hiker. Live in the moment. Enjoy the Mountains-to-Sea Trail.

Allen de Hart, September 2016
Allen passed away Oct. 14, 2016, after writing this Foreword.

NORTH CAROLINA'S MOUNTAINS-TO-SEA TRAIL

Introduction

The Mountains-to-Sea Trail (MST) provides an extraordinary way to explore North Carolina—one step at a time. This book, one of three regional guidebooks that cover the entire MST, is written by Friends of the Mountains-to-Sea Trail (Friends). We hope you will use this and our other guides to plan your hikes on the MST—whether on a section near your home for a day trip, for a weekend trip to explore new parts of North Carolina, or for a challenging, inspiring trek of the entire trail.

The Mountains-to-Sea Trail

The MST is a 1,150-mile trail that crosses North Carolina from Clingmans Dome in Great Smoky Mountains National Park near the Tennessee line to Jockey's Ridge State Park on the Outer Banks. It passes through 37 counties, 4 national parks, 3 national forests, 2 national wildlife refuges,

Current Trail Route

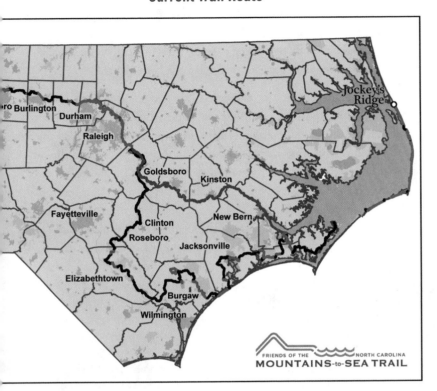

10 state parks, 4 state game lands, 1 state forest, 1 state historic site, and numerous local parks and protected areas, and alongside several lakes and reservoirs.

Ultimately, the trail will be a continuous footpath designated by the North Carolina Division of Parks and Recreation (State Parks) as a unit of the State Parks system. Until that goal is reached, Friends has laid out a continuous route that follows 680 miles of trail and forest road, much of it officially designated as MST by State Parks, with connecting routes on backroads and rivers. This guide provides hiking directions for that "current MST route" across North Carolina.

In 1973, the North Carolina Trails System Act expressed the need for abundant trails throughout the state "to provide for the ever-increasing outdoor recreation needs of an expanded population and . . . promote public access to, travel within, and enjoyment and appreciation of the outdoor, natural and remote areas of the State." One of the provisions of the act created the North Carolina Trails Committee (NCTC) to work with State Parks "on all matters directly or indirectly pertaining to trails, their use, extent, location, and the other objectives and purposes" of the Trail Systems Act.

As a result of the consultation between State Parks and NCTC, in September 1977, Howard N. Lee, then the secretary of the Department of Natural Resources and Community Development, gave a speech in which he proposed "establishing a state trail between the mountains and the seashore in North Carolina." He envisioned that the trail would cross land owned by the national park system, national forest system, state parks, city and county governments, and willing private landowners interested in providing "a legacy to future generations." The idea was to give hikers "a real feel for the sights, sounds, and people of the state" not simply to create a trail through the woods. The concept anticipated that costs would be shared among local, state, and federal agencies; private owners would donate land rights; and a strong volunteer organization would help promote, construct, and maintain the trail.

State Parks took a strong interest in the MST from its beginnings, but it was not until 2000 that it was officially incorporated into the North Carolina State Park System by a vote of the legislature. Since that time, State Parks has helped develop regional plans for the trail route and supported construction and maintenance of the trail through grants and bond funding. When trail along the planned route is opened to the public, State Parks officially dedicates it as part of the MST.

Volunteer efforts in support of the MST were first led by the North Carolina Trails Association (NCTA), which was informally created in 1977 and chartered in 1982 to "promote the establishment and conservation of a system of scenic, recreational, and historic trails . . . [t]o work with federal, state, and local agencies and trail related organizations, landowners, and individuals in planning, acquisition, development, maintenance and proper use of trails and trail related facilities." This organization worked actively with the NCTC until the late 1980s. One of its biggest accomplishments was the establishment of volunteer Task Forces charged with the construction and maintenance of sections of the trail.

In an effort to revitalize MST efforts after the demise of the NCTA, Friends of the Mountains-to-Sea Trail was formed in 1997 "to pursue the concept, research and provide information, advocate cooperative efforts among allied government offices and citizens, and support task forces and trail organizations for the benefit of a cross-state trail known as the Mountains to the Sea Trail."

As it was with NCTA, support for Task Forces is a primary part of the Friends mission. The number of Task Forces has grown from 4 to 24 today, and these groups are responsible for maintaining more than 500 miles of the MST. Construction and maintenance efforts are often carried out through associated trail organizations, such as the Carolina Mountain Club, High Peaks Trail Association, Elkin Valley Trails Association, Sauratown Trails Association, Friends of the Sauratown Mountains, and Carteret County Wildlife Association. In some areas, construction and maintenance are carried out by local or county government agencies.

Over the last 20 years, Friends has developed into a strong advocate of the MST. Friends is the primary source of information about the trail and how to hike it. It coordinates efforts with State Parks as well as with more than 40 other local, state, and federal agencies.

The Mountain Guide

This guide and its two companion guides for the Piedmont and coastal areas of the MST describe the trail in 18 segments, two of which have an alternate route. The segments were created so that each highlights a part of North Carolina with unique natural and historic features.

This Mountain guide covers Segments 1 through 5, including two alternate routes for Segment 1. These segments cover the route of the trail from Clingmans Dome in Great Smoky Mountains National Park to Devil's Garden Overlook on the Blue Ridge Parkway near Stone Mountain State Park and Sparta.

Here are descriptions of what you will encounter along the way in each segment:

Segment 1, "Peak to Peak," leads hikers from Clingmans Dome, the highest peak in Great Smoky Mountains National Park, to Waterrock Knob, the highest peak in the Plott Balsam mountain range. Currently, there are two alternate routes for this MST segment while studies are underway to determine the ultimate route for the trail in this area.[1] On Segment 1A, "The Great Smoky Mountains Route," hikers get a beautiful wilderness experience on trails and park roads through Great Smoky Mountains National Park and the Blue Ridge Parkway. This route is long and rugged with difficult resupply. Hikers on Segment 1B, "The River Valley Route," not only experience trails in the Great Smoky Mountains National Park but also hike along the Tuckaseegee River in the only mountain river valley experience on the MST. This route has less overall elevation change than Segment 1A and provides easy resupply in the mountain towns of Dillsboro and Sylva.

Segment 2, "The Balsams," takes hikers through one of the most biodiverse areas of the world, including the nearly trackless expanse of the Middle Prong Wilderness. Streams and waterfalls provide delightful coolness even on the hottest summer day. This segment is also one of the least accessible parts of the MST but ends at Pisgah Inn on the Blue Ridge Parkway, a tourist haven with a famous restaurant.

Segment 3, "The High Peaks and Asheville," is the most travelled part of the MST in the mountains, because of its proximity to the vibrant city of Asheville and also because of its rugged beauty and points of interest including the Shut-In Trail, Rattlesnake Lodge, Craggy Gardens, the Folk Art Center, and Mount Mitchell, the highest peak in the eastern United States.

Segment 4, "Gorges, Peaks, and Waterfalls," is the most remote part of the MST and perfect for hikers looking for multi-day, wilderness backpacking experiences. The name of the segment gives a picture of what you will experience in this beautiful area. Highlights include spectacular views of Linville Gorge, impressive promontories including Shortoff and Table Rock Mountains, and waterfalls including Harper, Hunt Fish, and Gragg Prong Falls.

---

1 State Parks has envisioned that the MST will be built from the Oconaluftee Visitor Center in Great Smoky Mountain National Park through the town of Cherokee and then parallel to the Blue Ridge Parkway to Waterrock Knob. Studies are currently underway to determine if that route is environmentally feasible. If so, Friends will assist State Parks and the Blue Ridge Parkway to build that trail to serve as the ultimate route of the trail.

Segment 5, "The High Country," is a part of the MST to explore if you are looking for gorgeous views. The trail parallels the Blue Ridge Parkway for more than 90 miles and lets you see, up close, the Linn Cove Viaduct, Price Park, the Moses Cone estate, and Doughton Park.

We hope you will enjoy using this guide and its two companion guides for the Piedmont and coastal areas of the MST not only to explore the trail but also to learn more about this beautiful, fascinating state. You can purchase any of the guides, plus several others that cover only individual segments of the trail, on the Friends website or at bookstores, outdoor outfitters, and online vendors.

How to Use this Guide

Each segment chapter in this guide includes information about the following:

+ a general description of the hike
+ trail distances
+ whether any uses in addition to hiking are allowed on the trail
+ trail difficulty
+ camping information
+ food and water sources near the trail
+ lodging/supplies/services/post offices
+ hunting information
+ information on signs and blazing
+ primary parking locations with accompanying GPS coordinates
+ sources for maps and other information
+ elevation chart (west to east)
+ an overview map of the segment
+ eastbound and westbound point-to-point directions

Note that the point-to-point directions have icons to indicate locations for camping, lodging, parking, food, restrooms, supplies, water sources, and picnic areas. A key explaining the symbols appears at the bottom of each page of the directions.

We hope you will use this guide to plan day hikes, multi-day trips, and even cross-state treks. To plan your hike, decide what area of the state you want to visit and select the appropriate segment description. Use the point-to-point directions and parking/access information in the guides to determine your starting and ending points. The length of your hike depends on how much time you have (a few hours or several days or several months for an MST thru-hike), the difficulty of the trail you feel comfortable hiking, and the location of convenient drop-off and pickup parking areas. For multi-day trips, the availability of campsites and resupply points may be important.

Check the additional sources listed in the guide to find hiking maps and other information. If you have unanswered questions, feel free to contact the Friends office at info@MountainstoSeaTrail.org or 919-825-0297. Friends staff are happy to help connect you with people who are very knowledgeable about the part of the trail you plan to hike.

The parking location section of this trail guide provides GPS coordinates that you can enter into your navigation system just as you would an address. You can also use the interactive Google map on the Friends website at www.MountainstoSeaTrail.org/map to find and print directions to parking locations. Note that you may find drop-off and pickup points on the interactive map that are not listed in the guide because there is no good spot to leave a car in that location or because there are numerous parking locations in that area.

The interactive Google map is also a good resource for planning your hike. Once you identify the area you want to hike, you can use the map to help plan shuttle routes; find accommodations, supply points, and points of interest outside this guide's scope; develop a feel for the trail surroundings (for instance, whether a road is in a rural, suburban, or urban setting); and more.

Before you leave on your hike, check for any trail updates for the segment of the trail you plan to hike at www.MountainstoSeaTrail.org/updates.

This guide does not try to provide general information on hiking such as the risks involved in different types of terrain and the precautions to take; what hiking and safety equipment to use; water and food requirements for short or longer hiking; the need for hiking companions and for arranging to have outside contacts for safety and other reasons; or testimonials about the various types of enjoyment and well-being that hiking provides. This type of information may be found in outdoor recreation outlets and on the internet.

If you are planning to hike the entire MST, either as a thru-hike or over time, start your planning by reviewing these trail guides. Then visit www. MountainstoSeaTrail.org as a good second step. There you will find additional information and contacts to help you plan your trip. You will also find information about how to qualify for a completion award.

Friends presents awards at its annual meeting each year to any hiker who has completed the entire trail as a thru-hiker or in segments. For the purposes of these awards, where the MST route follows an off-road trail, Friends expects completers to hike that portion on foot. However, for sections of the "current trail" that are on backroads, Friends recognizes hiking, biking, and/or paddling options as credit towards completion of the trail.

Finally, Friends has tried to make this guide as accurate as possible and will update it regularly through the website updates page, but trail conditions constantly change and the guide may contain mistakes or outdated information. This, or any other, guide is no substitute for good judgment, maps, and route-finding skills. If you do find inaccuracies in the guide, please send any corrections to info@MountainstoSeaTrail.org.

Friends of the Mountains-to-Sea Trail

Friends is a nonprofit organization that brings together communities and volunteers to build a simple footpath connecting North Carolina's natural resources for the enjoyment and education of people. Its work is focused in four areas: 1) building and maintaining trail, 2) improving the trail route, 3) helping people hike the trail, and 4) advocating for the trail.

Building and maintaining trail, acquiring land, and raising awareness and support are important, ongoing jobs. You can become a "friend" of the Mountains-to-Sea Trail by making a donation or volunteering your time. Friends needs volunteers with a variety of skills and interests—some to build trail and some to help in other ways. To become a member and to learn more about volunteering, visit our website at www.MountainstoSeaTrail. org or contact the Friends office at info@MountainstoSeaTrail.org or 919-825-0297.

Conclusion

On the MST, you will experience North Carolina wilderness, wildlife, small towns, farms, and historic sites. You will enjoy rivers, islands, lakes and bays, urban greenways, ferries and forests, mountains and beaches. You will get a real feel for the sights, sounds, and people of North Carolina. Please share your experiences on the trail and comments on this guide with Friends at info@MountainstoSeaTrail.org. Enjoy!

In Memoriam

Allen de Hart

September 3, 1926–October 14, 2016
Founder, Visionary, Mentor, Friend

View from the Mountains-to-Sea Trail at Clingmans Dome
Photo by Danny Bernstein

Peak to Peak—MST Segment 1A

CLINGMANS DOME TO WATERROCK KNOB— ALTERNATE ROUTE A: THE GREAT SMOKY MOUNTAINS

By Danny Bernstein

Great Smoky Mountains National Park (GSMNP) straddles Tennessee and North Carolina. Newfound Gap Road (US 441), which travels north from Cherokee, North Carolina, to Gatlinburg, Tennessee, forms the backbone of the park and climbs to over 5,000 feet at Newfound Gap.

If national parks have specialties, the Smokies is known as a hiker's park. The scenery is diverse: mountain views, old-growth trees, waterfalls, streams, and more shades of green than a paint chart. Mile for mile, you'll find hiking in the park easier than in the neighboring national forests. Even though there are no blazes on Smokies trails, they are so well marked at every intersection that you can follow them with confidence. (Still, stop at GSMNP Visitor Center and pick up a Great Smoky Mountains Trail Map for $1.00. Note that this alternate route differs from the MST depicted on the map—see Eastbound Mile 21.5, Westbound Mile 47.4, in the directions below.)

The Smokies may be the most visited national park in the country but only the roads and parking lots are congested. With over 800 miles of trails, even popular trails are not very busy. The Smokies, in a temperate rain forest, have a great variety of wildflowers, from the first bloodroot in March to the last asters in October. But hikers will also see the richness of the community life that was here before the area became a national park in 1934.

The MST starts at the observation tower on top of Clingmans Dome in GSMNP, on "top of old Smoky" at the state boundary. This 68.9-mile section goes deep in the woods, crosses US 441, climbs up to an isolated mountain, and comes out to the Blue Ridge Parkway (BRP). The trails in the Smokies are well maintained and well marked. Hikers will appreciate that they're in a *national park*.

Many maps, including the GSMNP and National Geographic map #229, show a different route for the MST than the one detailed in this guide. The "ultimate" route for the MST is under discussion, and this route and the alternate "River Valley Route" are ways that you can use to complete Segment 1 of the MST now. The old route veers off this route at the intersection of Newton Bald Trail and Mingus Creek Trail. To follow the current route, stay on Newton Bald Trail.

This route is approximately 20 miles longer than the River Valley Route, with more elevation change and fewer opportunities for resupply, but also more off-road mileage. Overall elevation gain on this segment is estimated at 14,518 feet and elevation loss at 14,974 feet.

HIGHLIGHTS INCLUDE

- The observation tower on Clingmans Dome at 6,643 feet

- Walking along Deep Creek, with its cascades and rock falls

- Campsite #57, Horace Kephart's last camp and the historic millstone put up in his memory

- Lufty Baptist Church, a small church established in 1836 and reconstructed in 1912

- Chasteen Creek Falls

- Masonic marker on the Blue Ridge Parkway

Total Distance: 68.9 miles (50.3 trail, 9.1 unpaved road, 9.5 paved road)
Difficulty: Challenging. Requires full backpack. The trails are well maintained, are well marked, and use frequent switchbacks.

Trail Updates

When planning your trip using this guide, take a moment to see whether Friends of the Mountains-to-Sea Trail (Friends) has posted any updates about the trail route by visiting Friends' "Trail Updates" page at www. MountainstoSeaTrail.org/updates.

Shuttle Services

Danny Bernstein maintains a list of people who provide shuttle services between Heintooga Rd. (Segment 1A) and Black Mtn. Campground (the eastern end of Segment 3). See www.hikertohiker.net/hiking/mountains-sea-trail-heintooga-road-black-mountain-campground.

Frontcountry Camping

Eastbound (EB) Mile 25.8; Westbound (WB) Mile 42.9
Smokemont Campground. Each site has a picnic table and barbecue grill. Restroom buildings have sinks with cold water and flush toilets. Water pumps and trashcans are plentiful. Open year-round. Reserve a campsite online at www.recreation.gov or by phone at 877-444-6777. You can also take your chances and get a site when you arrive; it's a very large campground.

EB Mile 53.6; WB Mile 15.3
Balsam Mtn. Campground. Each site has a picnic table and barbecue grill. Restroom buildings have sinks with cold water and flush toilets. Water pumps and trashcans are plentiful. You can't reserve a site—it's first come, first serve. Opens in the spring. Check the schedule at www.nps.gov/grsm/planyourvisit/frontcountry-camping.htm.

EB Mile 62.0; WB Mile 6.9
Mile High Campground. This private campground, located 0.7 mile off the trail, offers cabins and tent sites. It has a bathhouse with showers. It's open from mid-May to mid-October. Check the schedule and amenities at campmilehigh.com.

Backcountry Camping

Camping permits, reservations, and fees are required for all backcountry campsites in the park. Call 865-436-1231 or visit the backcountry reservations website at www.nps.gov/grsm/planyourvisit/backcountry-camping. htm. Each backcountry campsite has a flat surface for tents, a bear cable system to hang your food, and access to water nearby.

EB Mile 3.7; WB Mile 65.2	Mt. Collins shelter, 0.5 mile west on Sugarland Mtn. Trail
EB Mile 9.1; WB Mile 59.8	Poke Patch backcountry campsite #53
EB Mile 11.7; WB Mile 57.2	Nettle Creek backcountry campsite #54
EB Mile 12.5; WB Mile 56.4	Pole Rd. Creek backcountry campsite #55 (horses allowed)
EB Mile 12.8; WB Mile 56.1	Burnt Spruce backcountry campsite #56
EB Mile 13.3; WB Mile 55.6	Bryson Place backcountry campsite #57 (horses allowed)
EB Mile 20.7; WB Mile 48.2	Newton Bald backcountry campsite #52
EB Mile 27.2; WB Mile 41.7	Loweer Chasteen Creek backcountry campsite #50
EB Mile 29.5; WB Mile 39.4	Upper Chasteen backcountry campsite #48
EB Mile 34.3; WB Mile 34.6	Enloe Creek backcountry campsite #47
EB Mile 37.0; WB Mile 31.9	McGee Spring backcountry campsite #44
EB Mile 47.1; WB Mile 21.8	Spruce Mtn. backcountry campsite #42

Special Note Regarding Bear Activity and Requirements

Because of aggressive bear activity, the US Forest Service requires all backpackers to carry bear canisters in the Shining Rock Wilderness Area and nearby Forest Service lands to the northwest of the BRP. This area encompasses parts of Segments 2 and 3 of the MST. As a practical matter for MST thru-hikers, this will probably require carrying canisters between

Cherokee (Segment 1A) or Sylva (Segment 1B) and Asheville (Segment 3), as these are the nearest resupply points. For more information, see www.fs.usda.gov/detail/nfsnc/alerts-notices/?cid=stelprd3832543.

Lodging/Food/Supplies/Services/Post Office

Near EB Mile 25.5; WB Mile 43.4

Town of Cherokee with full services 3 miles south on US 441. Note that you can only buy alcohol at the Cherokee Casino.

Water/Restrooms

All water taken from springs and rivers should be treated.

EB Mile 1.5; WB Mile 67.4	Spring 💧
EB Mile 6.1; WB Mile 62.8	Stream 💧
EB Mile 9.1; WB Mile 59.8	Deep Creek 💧
EB Mile 25.8; WB Mile 42.9	Smokemont Campground 🚻 💧
EB Mile 27.9; WB Mile 41.0	Chasteen Creek Falls 💧
EB Mile 31.7; WB Mile 33.6	Enloe Creek 💧
EB Mile 39.8; WB Mile 29.1	Round Bottom Bridge 💧
EB Mile 53.6; WB Mile 15.3	Balsam Mtn. Campground 🚻 💧
EB Mile 62.0; WB Mile 6.9	Mile High Campground 🚻 💧

Hunting

Hunting is not allowed on GSMNP or BRP land.

Signs/Blazing

In GSMNP, large wooden signs at every junction indicate the name of the trail and the mileage to each intersecting trail. The trails, other than the Appalachian Trail, are not blazed.

The familiar MST blazes—3-inch white circles—start at EB Mile 62.0; WB Mile 6.9 on BIA (Bureau of Indian Affairs) 434. There are no blazes on the BRP roadway.

🔺Camping 🛏Lodging ⓟ Parking 🍴Food 🚻Restrooms 🏪Supplies 💧Water 🏕Picnic

Special Considerations

The road to Clingmans Dome observation tower is open April 1 to November 30 but may be closed in bad weather. If the road is closed when you want to start your hike, you can access the observation tower by hiking south on the Appalachian Trail 7.9 miles from the parking area at Newfound Gap on US 441.

Heintooga Rd. is closed seasonally to cars, usually from the end of October to mid-May. Check seasonal closures at www.nps.gov/grsm/planyourvisit/temproadclose.htm and the latest road closures at twitter.com/SmokiesRoadsNPS.

Remember that GPS units and vehicle navigation systems may provide inaccurate information in the mountains. You're encouraged to use a trail map.

Hikers should be supplied for a full backpack (tent, sleeping bag . . .) and food for several days.

Dogs are not allowed on the trails in GSMNP. Elsewhere on this segment, dogs should be leashed at all times.

ADDITIONAL INFORMATION

Friends office: 919-825-0297 or info@MountainstoSeaTrail.org

Trail Maps

Google map of the entire MST: www.MountainstoSeaTrail.org/map

GSMNP trail map:
   www.nps.gov/grsm/planyourvisit/upload/GSMNP-Map_JUNE14-complete4-2.pdf

Park Websites

GSMNP: www.nps.gov/grsm

GSMNP road closures: twitter.com/SmokiesRoadsNPS

BRP: www.nps.gov/blri

BRP road closures: go.nps.gov/blri-roads

Helpful Websites for Trails Through GSMNP—Under "Plan Your Visit"

www.nps.gov/grsm/planyourvisit/index.htm

www.nps.gov/grsm/planyourvisit/backcountry-camping.htm

www.nps.gov/grsm/planyourvisit/frontcountry-camping.htm

Other Websites

Town of Cherokee: visitcherokeenc.com

Bryson City–Swain County Chamber of Commerce:
   www.greatsmokies.com

Jackson County Chamber of Commerce: www.mountainlovers.com

Mile High Campground: campmilehigh.com

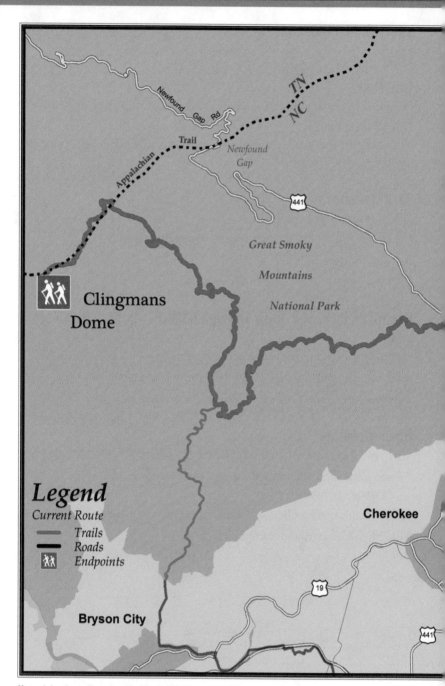

Map and elevation profile produced for Friends of the Mountains-to-Sea Trail by Curtis Belyea, 2016.

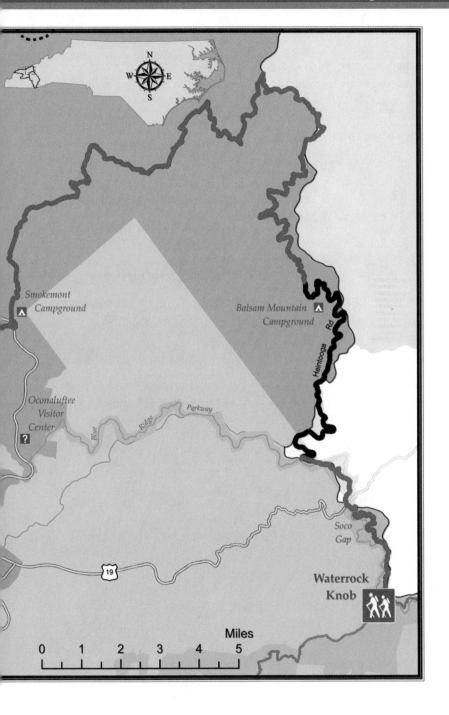

PRIMARY PARKING LOCATIONS

Clingmans Dome Parking Area, Western End of Segment 1B
EB Mile 0.0; WB Mile 68.9
Ⓟ 🚻
N35.55711, W83.49389

Smokemont Campground
EB Mile 25.5; WB Mile 43.4
Ⓟ 🚻 💧 ⛺
N35.56299, W83.31074

Round Bottom
EB Mile 39.8; WB Mile 29.1
Ⓟ 💧
N35.62230, W83.21128

Heintooga Ridge Picnic Area
EB Mile 53.1; WB Mile 15.8
Ⓟ 🚻 💧 🌲
N35.57290, W83.18001

Balsam Mtn. Campground
EB Mile 53.6; WB Mile 15.3
Ⓟ (when camping) ⛺
N35.56797, W83.17574

Polls Gap Parking
EB Mile 56.0; WB Mile 12.9
Ⓟ
N35.56330, W83.16153

Black Camp Gap Parking
EB Mile 58.4; WB Mile 10.5
Ⓟ
N35.53469, W83.17152

Mile High Overlook
EB Mile 60.7; WB Mile 8.2
Ⓟ
N35.51942, W83.17853

BRP at Wolf Laurel Gap (MP 458.2)
EB Mile 62.0; WB Mile 6.9
Ⓟ
N35.51044, W83.17895

Soco Gap Overlook (MP 455.5)
EB Mile 64.7; WB Mile 4.2
Ⓟ
N35.49434, W83.15567

Waterrock Knob Parking Area, Eastern End of Segment 1A (MP 451.2)
EB Mile 68.9; WB Mile 0.0
Ⓟ 🏪 🚻
N35.45999, W83.14132

Coordinates can be entered in your mapping software just like a street address.

Camping Lodging Parking Food Restrooms Supplies Water Picnic

Crossing Deep Creek
Photo by Danny Bernstein

HIKING DIRECTIONS, EASTBOUND

0.0   The MST and Segment 1A start at the Clingmans Dome observation tower at the western end of Clingmans Dome Rd. in GSMNP. From the Clingmans Dome parking area, walk up to the observation tower. *Note:* To reach the parking area, take US 441 west from Cherokee or east from Gatlinburg. At Newfound Gap, the NC/TN line, turn onto Clingmans Dome Rd. The road is closed November to April. If road is closed when you are hiking, you can access the observation tower by hiking south on the Appalachian Trail from the parking area at Newfound Gap in GSMNP. An information station and store managed by the Great Smoky Mountains Association is open in season. Ⓟ 🚻

🔺Camping 🛏️Lodging Ⓟ Parking 🍴Food 🚻Restrooms 🏪Supplies 💧Water 🪑Picnic

Segment 1A Eastbound

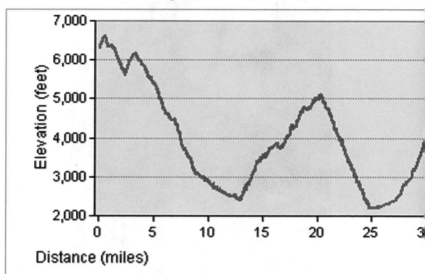

0.5 Just before the ramp to the observation tower, turn left at a sign marked "Appalachian Trail/Mountains-to-Sea Trail." After about 100 feet, turn right at the MST sign.

1.5 Continue straight at Old Buzzards Roost in a spruce-pine forest. A spring is on the right. 🔹

2.5 Continue straight at Mt. Collins Gap.

3.5 Continue straight to ascend the summit of Mt. Collins.

3.7 Continue straight through intersection with Sugarland Mtn. Trail. *Note:* Mt. Collins shelter is 0.5 mile to left on Sugarland Mtn. Trail. A permit is required to camp here, or at any backcountry site in GSMNP. See the "Backcountry Camping" section for this segment for information about fees and reservations. 🔺

4.0 Turn right and go 125 feet on spur trail to cross Clingmans Dome Rd., then continue straight on Fork Ridge Trail. *Note:* There is a small parking area at the trailhead. Ⓟ

4.5 Continue straight on Fork Ridge Trail, which descends 2,800 feet over the next 5.1 miles.

6.1 Cross a small stream. 🔹

9.1 Cross Deep Creek (there may or may not be a bridge). After crossing creek, turn right on Deep Creek Trail. *Note:* Poke Patch backcountry

Elevation Profile

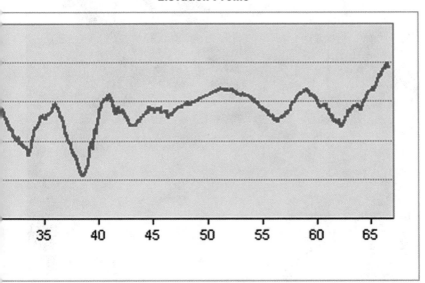

campsite #53 is at this junction. There are several significant creek crossings in the next 3.5 miles.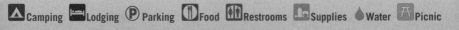

11.7 Continue straight past Nettle Creek backcountry campsite #54.

12.5 Continue straight past Pole Rd. Creek backcountry campsite #55, a horse campsite.

12.6 Pass Benton MacKaye Trail (Pole Rd. Creek Trail) on right. *Note:* Benton MacKaye Trail and MST continue on same trail to Mile 42.3 below.

12.8 Continue straight past Burnt Spruce backcountry campsite #56.

13.3 Pass Bryson Place backcountry campsite #57, a horse campsite, and turn left on Martins Gap Trail. *Note:* This is the last campsite of Horace Kephart (1862-1931), a writer and outdoor activist. If you continue on Deep Creek Trail for a couple of hundred feet and walk into a flat area on the right, you'll find a millstone put up by a Bryson City Boy Scout troop in his memory. The alternative "River Valley" route for Segment 1 of the MST continues straight ahead on Deep Creek Trail.

14.8 Turn left on Sunkota Ridge Trail.

19.7 Turn right on Thomas Divide Trail.

20.2 Turn left on Newton Bald Trail.

Chasteen Creek
Photo by Danny Bernstein

20.7 Pass Newton Bald backcountry campsite #52.

21.5 Turn left to stay on Newton Bald Trail. *Note:* Some GSMNP and National Geographic maps show the MST turning right on Mingus Creek Trail. This is not the current route of the trail so be sure to continue left on Newton Bald Trail.

25.5 Cross Newfound Gap Rd. and bridge across Oconaluftee River, then turn left toward Smokemont Campground. *Note:* There is a parking area on the right after the bridge. Walk straight up from the bridge to visit Lufty Baptist Church, which is always open. The town of Cherokee is about 3 miles down Newfound Gap Rd. with all services.

25.8 At Y-intersection, take right fork to enter Smokemont Campground and continue walking on right side of campground. *Note:* Register for a campsite if you wish to stay here. Each site has a picnic table and a barbecue grill. The campground has restroom buildings with cold water, sinks, and flush toilets. Water pumps and trashcans are plentiful, but there is no camp store.

Camping   Lodging   Parking   Food   Restrooms   Supplies   Water   Picnic

26.0 At the far back of section D of the campground, walk up Bradley Fork Trail.

27.2 Turn right on Chasteen Creek Trail. Lower Chasteen Creek backcountry campsite #50 is on the right almost immediately after you make the turn.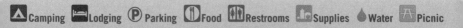

27.9 A short spur trail on the left takes you to Chasteen Creek Falls. Look for a hitching post for horses and continue toward the creek.

29.5 Pass Upper Chasteen backcountry campsite #48, situated between two creeks, on the left.

31.2 Turn left on Hughes Ridge Trail.

31.7 Turn right on Enloe Creek Trail. Water is available from small cascades and creeks for the next 2.6 miles.

34.3 Pass Enloe Creek backcountry campsite #47. The campsite is small and often muddy.

35.3 Turn left on Hyatt Ridge Trail.

37.0 Turn right on Beech Gap Trail II. *Note:* Follow side trail 0.9 mile one-way to the spacious and attractive McGee Spring backcountry campsite #44.

39.8 Turn left on Straight Fork Rd. at Round Bottom. Cross bridge. Walk across the parking area and take Beech Gap Trail I.

42.3 Turn right on Balsam Mtn. Trail. The MST now leaves the Benton MacKaye Trail.

44.6 At Pin Oak Gap, make a left on Balsam Mtn. Rd. This unpaved road is a one-way road going north, so you're walking against traffic. This road is closed to vehicles in winter from here until the BRP spur road.

45.3 Palmer Creek Trail takes off to the left. Stay straight.

47.1 Spruce Mtn. Trail takes off to the left. Stay straight. *Note:* Follow Spruce Mtn. Trail 1.1 miles one-way down to Spruce Mtn. backcountry campsite #42.

53.0 The road changes name to Heintooga Rd. The road is paved and two-way.

53.1 Pass Heintooga Ridge picnic area.

53.6 Pass Balsam Mtn. Campground, the highest campground in the park. The campground is first come, first served, with no reservations, and it is closed in winter.

View of the Smokies from Mile High Campground
Photo by Allen de Hart

56.0 Pass Polls Gap. Several trails start from here going to Hemphill Bald and the Cataloochee section of the Smokies. Ⓟ

57.2 Pass parking overlook with views of Flat Creek Falls when leaves are down. Ⓟ

58.4 Continue straight at Masonic Marker Trail, then pass Black Camp Gap parking area. The road leaves GSMNP and enters BRP. *Note:* The 250-foot Masonic Marker Trail leads to a huge Masonic monument, erected in 1938 with stones from 41 countries, which is worth the slight detour. Ⓟ

58.7 Pass Horsetrough Ridge parking area. Ⓟ

59.7 Pass Lake Junaluska Overlook. You can't really see the lake from here. Ⓟ

60.6 Pass Maggie Valley Overlook. Ⓟ

60.7 Pass Mile High Overlook with great views of Clingmans Dome and Mount LeConte. Ⓟ

62.0 Turn left on BIA 434 (dirt road). *Note:* If you continue straight a hundred feet or so, you'll reach BRP at Wolf Laurel Gap (MP 458.2). On the right, BIA 407 leads to Mile High Campground in 0.7 mile. Ⓟ 🏕 💧

🔺Camping 🛏Lodging Ⓟ Parking 🍴Food 🚻Restrooms 🏪Supplies 💧Water 🪑Picnic

62.7 Pass under BRP, then turn left on MST blazed footpath. Pass side trail to BRP on left.

64.6 Cross US 19. Walk up BRP access road to right at fork, then bear left onto trail.

64.7 Pass blue-blazed spur trail on right, then reach Soco Gap Overlook (MP 455.5) and turn right on BRP. Ⓟ

64.8 Turn left on old paved road at MST sign, then, after a bend in the road, turn left onto trail marked with MST blaze.

68.9 At T-intersection, turn right onto paved path. A few hundred feet later, reach a junction with a trail marked with the MST blaze. This is the eastern end of Segment 1A. To continue on Segment 2, turn left; to reach the Waterrock Knob Overlook (MP 451.2), continue straight down the paved path. *Note:* The overlook has parking, a visitor center with a small convenience store (open seasonally), and restrooms. There is no water. If you turn left onto the paved path, the summit of Waterrock Knob, with spectacular views, is 0.5 mile ahead. Ⓟ 🏪 🚻

Masonic Marker on the BRP
Photo by Danny Bernstein

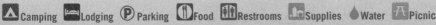
🔺Camping 🛏Lodging Ⓟ Parking 🍴Food 🚻Restrooms 🏪Supplies 💧Water ⛱Picnic

Hiking Directions, Westbound

0.0 Segment 1A begins at a trail junction just above the Waterrock Knob Overlook (BRP MP 451.2). If continuing a hike from Segment 2, turn right from the trail onto the paved path. If beginning from the parking area, follow the paved path up to the junction, then continue straight. A few hundred feet later, turn left onto a trail marked with the MST blaze. *Note:* The overlook has parking, a visitor center with a small convenience store (open seasonally), and restrooms. There is no water. If you continue straight on the paved path, the summit of Waterrock Knob, with spectacular views, is 0.5 mile ahead. Ⓟ 🏪 🚻

4.1 Turn right on old road, then turn right on BRP.

4.2 Turn into Soco Gap Overlook (MP 455.5) and continue on trail marked with MST blaze, then pass blue-blazed spur trail on left. Ⓟ

4.3 Bear left on BRP access road, then cross US 19 and continue on trail.

6.2 Pass side trail to BRP on right. At T-intersection, turn right on BIA 434 (dirt road), then pass under BRP.

6.9 Turn right on Heintooga Rd. The road is paved and two-way. *Note:* If you turn left, in a hundred feet or so you'll reach BRP at Wolf Laurel Gap (MP 458.2). Straight ahead, BIA 407 leads to Mile High Campground in 0.7 mile. Ⓟ ⛺ 💧

8.2 Pass Mile High Overlook with great views of Clingmans Dome and Mt. LeConte. Ⓟ

8.3 Pass Maggie Valley Overlook. Ⓟ

9.2 Pass Junaluska Overlook. You can't really see the lake from here. Ⓟ

10.2 Pass Horsetrough Ridge parking area. Ⓟ

10.5 Pass Black Camp Gap parking area. The road leaves the BRP and enters GSMNP. Pass Masonic Marker Trail. *Note:* The 250-foot trail on the right leads to a huge Masonic monument, erected in 1938 with stones from 41 countries, which is worth the slight detour. Ⓟ

11.7 Pass parking overlook with views of Flat Creek Falls when leaves are down. Ⓟ

12.9 Pass Polls Gap. Several trails start from here going to Hemphill Bald and the Cataloochee section of the Smokies. Ⓟ

⛺ Camping 🛏 Lodging Ⓟ Parking 🍴 Food 🚻 Restrooms 🏪 Supplies 💧 Water ⛏ Picnic

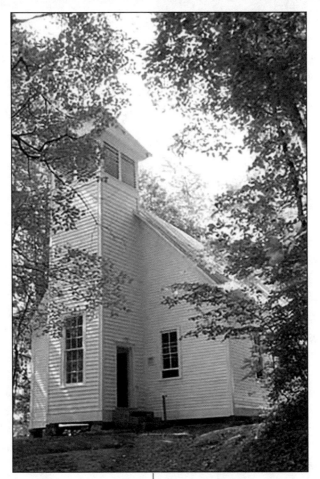

Lufty Baptist Church
Photo by Danny Bernstein

15.3 Pass Balsam Mtn. Campground, the highest campground in the park. The campground is first come, first served with no reservations and is closed in winter. ▲ Ⓟ 💧

15.8 Pass Heintooga Ridge picnic area. Ⓟ 🚻 🎋

15.9 The road changes name to Balsam Mtn. Rd. This unpaved road is a one-way road going north, so you're walking with traffic. This road is closed to vehicles in winter from here until the BRP spur road.

21.8 Spruce Mtn. Trail takes off to the right. Stay straight. *Note:* Follow Spruce Mtn. Trail 1.1 miles one-way down to Spruce Mtn. back-

▲Camping 🛏Lodging Ⓟ Parking 🍴Food 🚻Restrooms 🛒Supplies 💧Water 🎋Picnic

country campsite #42. A permit is required to camp here, or at any backcountry site in GSMNP. See the "Backcountry Camping" section for this segment for information about fees and reservations. ⛺

23.6 Palmer Creek Trail takes off to the right. Stay straight.

24.3 At Pin Oak Gap, make a left on Balsam Mtn. Trail.

26.6 Turn left on Beech Gap Trail I. *Note:* The Benton MacKaye Trail joins the MST from the right here and continues on the same trail to Mile 56.3 below.

29.1 Cross a bridge. Turn right on Straight Fork Rd. at Round Bottom. Walk across the parking area and take Beech Gap Trail II on the right. ⬥ ⓟ

31.9 Turn left on Hyatt Ridge Trail. *Note:* Follow side trail 0.9 mile one-way to the spacious and attractive McGee Spring backcountry campsite #44. ⛺

33.6 Turn right on Enloe Creek Trail. Water is available from small cascades and creeks for the next 2.6 miles. ⬥

34.6 Pass Enloe Creek backcountry campsite #47. The campsite is small and often muddy. ⛺

37.2 Turn right on Hughes Ridge Trail.

37.7 Turn right on Chasteen Creek Trail.

39.4 Pass Upper Chasteen backcountry campsite #48, situated between two creeks, on the right. ⛺

41.0 A short spur trail on the right takes you to Chasteen Creek Falls. Look for a hitching post for horses and continue toward the creek. ⬥

41.7 Turn left on Bradley Fork Trail. Lower Chasteen Creek backcountry campsite #50 is on the left just before you make the turn. ⛺

42.9 Walk into Smokemont Campground and take left fork to follow loop around campground. *Note:* Register for a campsite if you wish to stay here. Each site has a picnic table and a barbecue grill. The campground has restroom buildings with cold water, sinks, and flush toilets. Water pumps and trashcans are plentiful, but there is no camp store. ⛺ ⬥ 🚻

43.1 At T-intersection at end of campground loop, turn right.

43.4 Just before entering a parking area, turn right to cross bridge across Oconaluftee River, then cross Newfound Gap Rd. Turn right on

⛺ Camping 🛏 Lodging ⓟ Parking 🍴 Food 🚻 Restrooms 🏪 Supplies ⬥ Water 🏕 Picnic

Newton Bald Trail. *Note:* Turn left before the bridge to visit Lufty Baptist Church, which is always open. The town of Cherokee is about 3 miles down Newfound Gap Rd. with all services. Ⓟ 🛏️ 🍽️ 🏪

47.4 Turn right to stay on Newton Bald Trail. *Note:* Some GSMNP and National Geographic maps show the MST turning left on Mingus Creek Trail. This is not the current route of the trail so be sure to turn right on Thomas Divide Trail.

48.2 Pass Newton Bald backcountry campsite #52. ⛰️

48.7 Turn right on Thomas Divide Trail.

49.2 Turn left on Sunkota Ridge Trail

54.1 Turn right on Martins Gap Trail.

The millstone honoring Horace Kephart placed at his last camp
Photo by Danny Bernstein

Camping Lodging Ⓟ Parking Food Restrooms Supplies 💧Water 🏕️Picnic

55.6 Turn right on Deep Creek Trail and pass Bryson Place backcountry campsite #57, a horse campsite. *Note:* This is the last campsite of Horace Kephart (1862-1931), a writer and outdoor activist. If you go left on Deep Creek Trail for a couple of hundred feet and walk into a flat area on the right, you'll find a millstone put up by a Bryson City Boy Scout troop in his memory. The alternative "River Valley" route for Segment 1 of the MST merges here from the left on Deep Creek Trail. There are several significant creek crossings in the next 3.5 miles. ▲

56.1 Continue straight past Burnt Spruce backcountry campsite #56. ▲

56.3 Benton MacKaye Trail (Pole Rd. Creek Trail) splits off to left. Continue straight on Deep Creek Trail.

56.4 Continue straight past Pole Rd. Creek backcountry campsite #55, a horse campsite. ▲

57.2 Continue straight past Nettle Creek backcountry campsite #54. ▲

59.8 Turn left on Fork Ridge Trail, then cross Deep Creek (there may or may not be a bridge). *Note:* Poke Patch backcountry campsite #53 is at this junction. The trail ascends 2,800 feet over the next 5.1 miles. ▲ ◆

62.8 Cross a small stream. ◆

64.9 After crossing Clingmans Dome Rd., take spur trail 125 feet and turn left on the Appalachian Trail, which runs concurrently with the MST. *Note:* There is a small parking area at the trailhead. Ⓟ

65.2 Continue straight through intersection with Sugarland Mtn. Trail. *Note:* Mt. Collins shelter is 0.5 mile to right on Sugarland Mtn. Trail. ▲

65.4 Continue straight to ascend the summit of Mt. Collins.

66.4 Continue straight at Mt. Collins Gap.

67.4 Continue straight at Old Buzzards Roost in a spruce-pine forest. A spring is on the left. ◆

68.4 At the MST sign—the exact western end of the MST—turn left on a side trail. After about 100 feet you'll arrive at a paved path. The Clingmans Dome observation tower is on your left. Walk right (down) to the parking area, passing an information station and store managed by the Great Smoky Mountains Association, open in season.

▲ Camping   🛏 Lodging   Ⓟ Parking   🍴 Food   🚻 Restrooms   🛒 Supplies   ◆ Water   🪑 Picnic

68.9 Reach Clingmans Dome parking area and western end of Segment 1A and the MST. *Note:* To reach the parking area, take US 441 west from Cherokee or east from Gatlinburg. At Newfound Gap, the NC/TN line, turn onto Clingmans Dome Rd. The road is closed November to April. If road is closed when you are hiking, you can access the observation tower by hiking south on the Appalachian Trail from the parking area at Newfound Gap in GSMNP.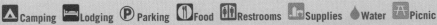

The Tuckaseegee River Valley
Photo by Steve Metcalf

Peak to Peak—MST Segment 1B

CLINGMANS DOME TO WATERROCK KNOB—
ALTERNATE ROUTE B: THE RIVER VALLEY ROUTE
By Kate Dixon and Jim Grode

From the temperate rainforest of Great Smoky Mountains National Park (GSMNP) to working farmland and small towns, from broad flat rivers to steep mountain streams, this 49.5-mile segment captures the variety of western North Carolina. It follows trails in GSMNP for approximately 19 miles before leaving the park at the Deep Creek campground near Bryson City. (Stop at GSMNP Visitor Center and pick up a Great Smoky Mountains Trail Map for $1.00. Note that this alternate route differs from the MST depicted on the map—see Eastbound (EB) Mile 13.3, Westbound

(WB) Mile 36.2, in the directions below.) Leaving the park, the route follows backroads along the Tuckaseegee River where Swain and Jackson Counties plan to build a greenway.

The trail then leads hikers through the small mountain towns of Dillsboro and Sylva and onward to the trail system in Sylva's Pinnacle Park to reach Waterrock Knob on the Blue Ridge Parkway (BRP) near Milepost 450.

Many maps, including the Great Smoky Mountains map and National Geographic map #229, show a different route for the MST than the one detailed in this guide. The "ultimate" route for the MST is under discussion, and this route and the alternate "Great Smoky Mountains" route are ways that you can use to complete Segment 1 of the Mountains-to-Sea Trail now.

This route is approximately 20 miles shorter than the "Great Smoky Mountains" route, with less elevation change and easy resupply. The most challenging parts of the hike are very steep climbs and descents at the beginning and end of the segment. Overall elevation gain on this segment is estimated at 9,396 feet and elevation loss at 9,851 feet.

HIGHLIGHTS INCLUDE:

- The observation tower atop Clingmans Dome, at 6,643 feet the highest point in GSMNP, where you can see seven states on a clear day (although, sadly, pollution often limits visibility to 20 miles or less)

- The deep forests of GSMNP, one of the most biodiverse places in the world, with more tree species than all of Europe

- The tumbling waters of Deep Creek, a favorite spot for tubers on hot summer days

- Campsite #57, Horace Kephart's last camp, and the historic millstone put up in his memory

- The broad but shallow Tuckaseegee River, where the train-wreck scene from the 1993 movie *The Fugitive* was filmed and props are still visible

- The galleries and artisan shops of downtown Dillsboro

- Downtown Sylva, presided over by the dome of the historic Jackson County courthouse, now repurposed as a library

- The 1.4-mile side hike to the Pinnacle, in Sylva's Pinnacle Park, with spectacular views of Sylva, the Scott Creek valley, and the surrounding mountains

Total Distance: 49.5 miles (24.3 on roads; 25.2 on trail)
Difficulty: Easy on-road sections to strenuous on trail

Trail Updates

When planning your trip using this guide, take a moment to see whether Friends of the Mountains-to-Sea Trail (Friends) has posted any updates about the trail route by visiting Friends' "Trail Updates" page at www. MountainstoSeaTrail.org/updates.

Shuttle Services

Danny Bernstein maintains a list of people who provide shuttle services between Heintooga Rd. (Segment 1A) and Black Mtn. Campground (the eastern end of Segment 3). See www.hikertohiker.net/hiking/mountains-sea-trail-heintooga-road-black-mountain-campground.

Camping
Great Smoky Mountains National Park

Camping permits, reservations, and fees are required for all backcountry campsites in the park. Call 865-436-1231 or visit the backcountry reservations website at www.nps.gov/grsm/planyourvisit/backcountry-camping.htm. Each backcountry campsite has a flat surface for tents, a bear cable system to hang your food, and access to water nearby.

EB Mile 3.7; WB Mile 45.8	Mt. Collins shelter, 0.5 mile west on Sugarland Mtn. Trail
EB Mile 9.1; WB Mile 40.4	Poke Patch backcountry campsite #53
EB Mile 11.7; WB Mile 37.8	Nettle Creek backcountry campsite #54
EB Mile 12.5; WB Mile 37.0	Pole Rd. Creek backcountry campsite #55 (horses allowed)
EB Mile 12.8; WB Mile 36.7	Burnt Spruce backcountry campsite #56
EB Mile 13.3; WB Mile 36.2	Bryson Place backcountry campsite #57 (horses allowed)
EB Mile 13.9; WB Mile 35.6	Nicks Nest Branch backcountry campsite #58

EB Mile 14.4; WB Mile 35.1	McCracken Branch backcountry campsite #59
EB Mile 16.8; WB Mile 32.7	Bumgardner Branch backcountry campsite #60
EB Mile 19.8; WB Mile 29.7	Deep Creek Campground, with 92 campsites. Registration and a fee are required on a first-come, first-served basis.

Sylva Pinnacle Park

Registration is required at the trailhead to camp within Pinnacle Park. For westbound hikers, this means continuing down to the trailhead at Mile 6.2 and then returning to your campsite.

EB Mile 44.0; WB Mile 5.5	Pinnacle Park Campsite No. 1
EB Mile 44.9; WB Mile 4.6	Pinnacle Park Campsite No. 2
EB Mile 45.2; WB Mile 4.3	Pinnacle Park Campsite No. 3, 0.6 mile west on Pinnacle Trail
EB Mile 47.8; WB Mile 1.7	Unmarked campsite. This campsite is not within Pinnacle Park and therefore is not subject to the permitting requirements.

Special Note Regarding Bear Activity and Requirements

Because of aggressive bear activity, the US Forest Service requires all backpackers to carry bear canisters in the Shining Rock Wilderness Area and nearby Forest Service lands to the northwest of the BRP. This area encompasses parts of Segments 2 and 3 of the MST. As a practical matter for MST thru-hikers, this will probably require carrying canisters between Cherokee (Segment 1A) or Sylva (Segment 1B) and Asheville (Segment 3), as these are the nearest resupply points. For more information, see www.fs.usda.gov/detail/nfsnc/alerts-notices/?cid=stelprd3832543.

Lodging

EB Mile 36.6; WB Mile 12.9

Best Western River Escape Inn and Suites, 248 WBI Dr., Dillsboro, 28725, 828-586-6060; www.bwriverescape.com. Rooms start at $89.99.

EB Mile 37.0; WB Mile 12.1
The Jarrett House, a historic inn in downtown Dillsboro, 100 Haywood Rd., Dillsboro, 28725, 828-586-0265; www.jarretthouse.com. Rooms start at $129/night.

EB Mile 38.4; WB Mile 11.1
Economy Inn, 940 W. Main St., Sylva, 28779, 828-586-2419.

EB Mile 38.6; WB Mile 10.9
Blue Ridge Inn, W. Main St., Sylva, 28779, 828-586-2123; www.facebook.com/blueridgeinnsylva.

Food/Supplies/Post Office

EB Mile 21.6; WB Mile 27.9	Downtown Bryson City, with restaurants and shops, is about 0.5 mile west of the intersection of E. Deep Creek Rd. and Old River Rd.
EB Mile 23.1; WB Mile 26.4	Just north of the intersection of Old River Rd. and Governor's Island Rd. is a community with water and supplies.
EB Mile 27.2; WB Mile 22.3	The town of Whittier, 0.3 mile north of the intersection of Old Bryson City Rd. and Thomas Valley Rd., has a general store with supplies and food.
EB Mile 33.3; WB Mile 16.2	Convenience store
EB Miles 37.0-37.4; WB Miles 12.1-12.5	Downtown Dillsboro, with shops, restaurants, and the Dillsboro post office
EB Mile 37.7; WB Mile 11.8	Harold's Supermarket
EB Miles 38.6-38.9; WB Miles 10.6-10.9	Downtown Sylva, with shops, including an outdoor-gear store, and restaurants
EB Mile 49.5; WB Mile 0.0	Waterrock Knob Visitor Center; small convenience store open seasonally

Water/Restrooms

In GSMNP and Pinnacle Park, water from streams is plentiful but must be treated before drinking. Bottled water is available at convenience and grocery stores along the route. Restrooms are available at the Clingmans Dome observation tower, Deep Creek Campground/picnic area, Bryson Park, and at stores along the route.

Hunting

Hunting is not allowed anywhere along Segment 1B.

Signs/Blazing

In GSMNP, large wooden signs at every junction indicate the name of the trail and the mileage to each intersecting trail. The trails, other than the Appalachian Trail, are not blazed. Within Pinnacle Park (EB Miles 43.3-49.2; WB Miles 0.3-6.2), the trail is marked with purple-and-gold blazes, along with a few double-blue blazes. There are no other blazes or signage in this segment.

Special Considerations

The road to Clingmans Dome observation tower is open April 1 to November 30 but may be closed in bad weather. If the road is closed when you want to start your hike, you can access the observation tower by hiking south on the Appalachian Trail 7.9 miles from the parking area at Newfound Gap on US 441.

Remember that GPS units and vehicle navigation systems may provide inaccurate information in the mountains. You're encouraged to use a trail map.

Watch for traffic and narrow shoulders on paved roads throughout the route. US 74 and Chipper Curve Rd., both near Sylva, are particularly difficult for cyclists; use extreme caution here.

Dogs are not allowed on the trails in GSMNP. Elsewhere on this segment, dogs should be leashed at all times.

ADDITIONAL INFORMATION
Friends office: 919-825-0297 or info@MountainstoSeaTrail.org

Trail Maps
Google map of the entire MST: www.MountainstoSeaTrail.org/map

GSMNP trail map:
www.nps.gov/grsm/planyourvisit/upload/GSMNP-Map_JUNE14-complete4-2.pdf

Pinnacle Park Map:
www.sylvanc.govoffice3.com/vertical/sites/%7B95F568B6-3344-493D-BB06-9C8755ED7CA2%7D/uploads/Pinnacle_Park_Map.pdf

Park Websites
GSMNP: www.nps.gov/grsm

GSMNP road closures: twitter.com/SmokiesRoadsNPS

BRP: www.nps.gov/blri

BRP road closures: go.nps.gov/blri-roads

Helpful Websites for Trails Through GSMNP—Under "Plan Your Visit"
www.nps.gov/grsm/planyourvisit/index.htm

www.nps.gov/grsm/planyourvisit/backcountry-camping.htm

www.nps.gov/grsm/planyourvisit/frontcountry-camping.htm

Tourism Websites
Bryson City–Swain County Chamber of Commerce:
www.greatsmokies.com

Jackson County Chamber of Commerce: www.mountainlovers.com

Visit Dillsboro: www.visitdillsboro.org

Main Street Sylva Association: www.mainstreetsylva.org

PRIMARY PARKING LOCATIONS

Clingmans Dome Parking Area, Western End of Segment 1B
Ⓟ 🚻
EB Mile 0.0; WB Mile 49.5
N35.55711, W83.49389

Deep Creek Trailhead Parking Area
Ⓟ 🚻
EB Mile 19.4; WB Mile 30.1
N35.46397, W83.43478

Pinnacle Park Parking Lot
Ⓟ
EB Mile 43.3; WB Mile 6.2
N35.42265, W83.19124

Waterrock Knob Parking Area, Eastern End of Segment 1B (BRP Milepost 451.2)
Ⓟ 🏪 🚻
EB Mile 49.5; WB Mile 0.0
N35.45999, W83.14132

Coordinates can be entered in your mapping software just like a street address.

Camping Lodging Parking Food Restrooms Supplies Water 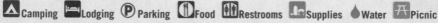Picnic

Hiking Directions, Eastbound

0.0 The MST and Segment 1B start at the Clingmans Dome observation tower at the western end of Clingmans Dome Rd. in GSMNP. From the Clingmans Dome parking area, walk up to the observation tower. *Note:* To reach the parking area, take US 441 west from Cherokee or east from Gatlinburg. At Newfound Gap, the NC/TN line, turn onto Clingmans Dome Rd. The road is closed November to April. If road is closed when you are hiking, you can access the observation tower by hiking south on the Appalachian Trail from the parking area at Newfound Gap in GSMNP. An information station and store managed by the Great Smoky Mountains Association is open in season. ℗ 🛆

Crossing Deep Creek in GSMNP
Photo by Susan Carpenter

Camping Lodging ℗ Parking Food Restrooms Supplies ◉Water Picnic

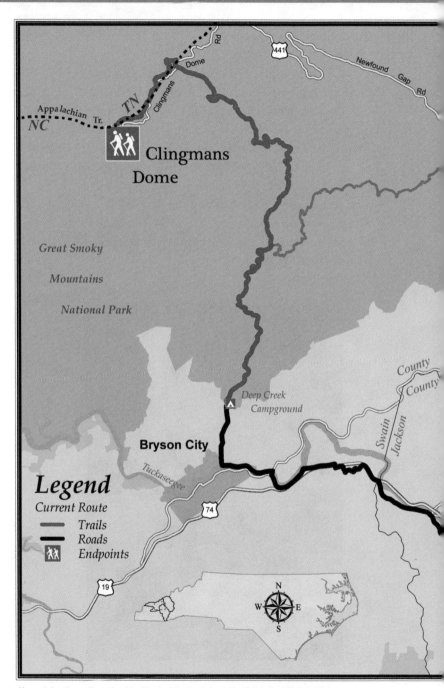

Map and elevation profile produced for Friends of the Mountains-to-Sea Trail by Curtis Belyea, 2016.

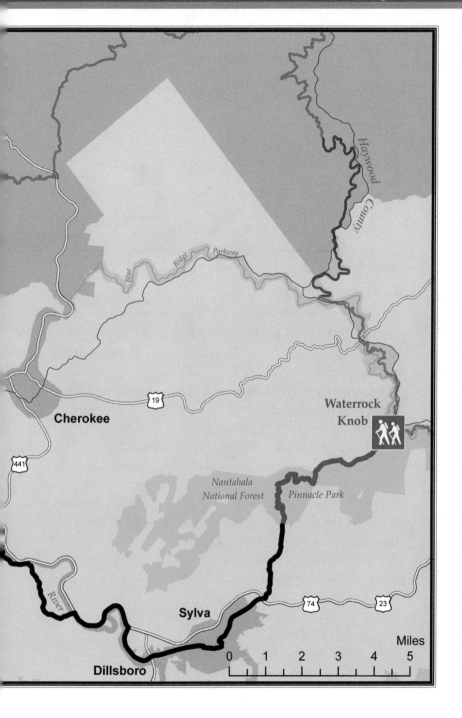

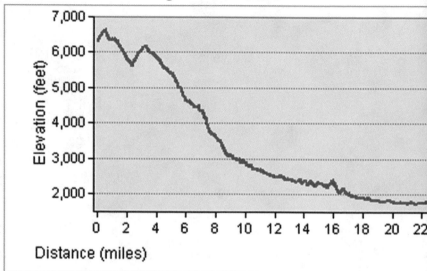

Segment 1B Eastbound

0.5 Just before the ramp to the observation tower, turn left at a sign marked "Appalachian Trail/Mountains-to-Sea Trail." After about 100 feet, turn right at the MST sign.

1.5 Continue straight at Old Buzzards Roost in a spruce-pine forest. A spring is on the right.

2.5 Continue straight at Mt. Collins Gap.

3.5 Continue straight to ascend the summit of Mt. Collins.

3.7 Continue straight through intersection with Sugarland Mtn. Trail. *Note:* Mt. Collins shelter is 0.5 mile to left on Sugarland Mtn. Trail. A permit is required to camp here, or at any backcountry site in GSMNP. See the "Camping" section for this segment for information about fees and reservations.

4.0 Turn right and go 125 feet on spur trail to cross Clingmans Dome Rd., then continue straight on Fork Ridge Trail. *Note:* There is a small parking area at the trailhead.

4.5 Continue straight on Fork Ridge Trail, which descends 2,800 feet over the next 5.1 miles.

6.1 Cross a small stream.

▲ Camping 🛏 Lodging Ⓟ Parking 🍴 Food 🚻 Restrooms 🛒 Supplies ◆ Water ⛱ Picnic

Elevation Profile

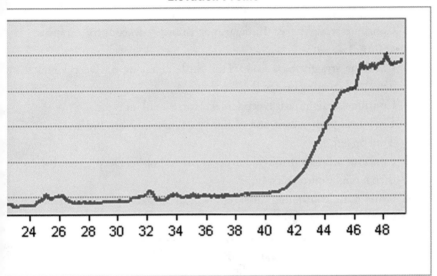

9.1 Cross Deep Creek (there may or may not be a bridge). After crossing creek, turn right on Deep Creek Trail. *Note:* Poke Patch backcountry campsite #53 is at this junction. There are several significant creek crossings in the next 3.5 miles. ▲ ⬤

11.7 Continue straight past Nettle Creek backcountry campsite #54. ▲

12.5 Continue straight past Pole Rd. Creek backcountry campsite #55, a horse campsite. ▲

12.6 Pass Benton MacKaye Trail (Pole Rd. Creek Trail) on right.

12.8 Continue straight past Burnt Spruce backcountry campsite #56. ▲

13.3 Continue straight on Deep Creek Trail past Bryson Place backcountry campsite #57 and junction with Martins Gap Trail on left. *Note:* This is the last campsite of Horace Kephart (1862-1931), a writer and outdoor activist. If you continue on Deep Creek Trail for a couple of hundred feet past the junction and walk into a flat area on the right, you'll find a millstone put up by a Bryson City Boy Scout troop. The alternative "Great Smoky Mountains" route for Segment 1 of the MST continues to the left on Martins Gap Trail. (Do not follow the MST sign here, which is for the Great Smoky Mountains route.) ▲

13.9 Continue straight past Nicks Nest Branch backcountry campsite #58. ▲

 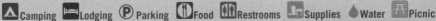

14.4 Continue straight past McCracken Branch backcountry campsite #59. ▲

16.8 Continue straight past Bumgardner Branch backcountry campsite #60. ▲ ◊

17.5 Continue straight past Loop Trail on left, staying on Deep Creek Trail and crossing bridge.

18.4 Continue straight past Deep Creek Horse Trail on right.

18.5 Cross bridge, then continue straight past junction with Indian Creek Trail on left.

19.3 Continue straight through cul-de-sac at end of W. Deep Creek Rd., then straight onto sidewalk.

19.4 Cross road, continuing on sidewalk next to parking area for Deep Creek Trailhead. Ⓟ ♦♦

19.5 At end of sidewalk continue on gravel trail toward parking area, then bear left into the picnic area. Ⓟ

19.6 Pass restrooms on right. ◊ ♦♦

19.7 Turn left at T-intersection, then take first left and cross bridge over Deep Creek.

19.8 After crossing bridge, turn right onto E. Deep Creek Rd. before entering Deep Creek Campground. *Note:* The Deep Creek Campground has 92 campsites. Registration and a fee are required to camp here. See the "Camping" section for this segment for more information. ▲

21.0 Pass Deep Creek Missionary Baptist Church on right.

21.6 At T-intersection, turn left on Old River Rd., a dirt road that goes over the railroad tracks. *Note:* If instead of turning left, you turn right, then left at the other end of the bridge, downtown Bryson City, with restaurants and shops, is about 0.5 mile away. ⑪ ▥

23.1 At T-intersection, turn right on Governor's Island Rd. to cross bridge over Tuckaseegee River. *Note:* Left on Governor's Island Rd. is community with water and supplies. ◊ ▥

23.2 Turn left on Walker Woody Rd. immediately after crossing bridge.

24.5 Continue straight across Hyatt Creek Rd. The road changes names to Old Bryson City Rd. here. *Note:* To your right at intersection with Hyatt Creek Rd. is the ramp to US 74.

25.4 Turn right on Old Bryson City Rd. at first intersection, then cross over highway bridge.

▲ Camping ▭ Lodging Ⓟ Parking ⑪ Food ♦♦ Restrooms ▥ Supplies ◊ Water ☗ Picnic

Downtown Sylva

25.5 Turn left after bridge crossing to continue on Old Bryson City Rd. *Note:* There is no road sign here for Old Bryson City Rd., but a sign for Owle Rd. is straight ahead. For the next 1.7 miles, you will be passing through the Cherokee Indian Reservation, and many road signs are printed in Cherokee as well as English.

27.2 At T-intersection at the Tuckaseegee River, turn right on Thomas Valley Rd. *Note:* If you turn left here instead, in 0.3 mile you will reach the town of Whittier. Across the bridge over the Tuckaseegee River is a general store for supplies and food.

31.0 Turn right to stay on Thomas Valley Rd. at Wilmot Missionary Baptist Church.

31.9 Pass Nations Creek Rd. on right.

32.4 Continue straight past Joe Branch Rd. on right.

33.1 Continue straight on Barkers Creek Rd. The road here is at the crest of a hill and ahead you can see the river, railroad, and US 74.

33.3 After crossing Tuckaseegee River, turn right on US 74. Walk along highway, facing traffic. Most of this section of US 74 has a concrete

barrier between the eastbound and westbound lanes. Carefully cross US 74 at the traffic turnaround 0.2 mile before reaching Haywood Rd. *Note:* There is a diner and convenience store directly across from the intersection. This section of US 74 is heavily traveled and more difficult on a bike than walking; use extreme caution here. 🍴 🛒

35.6 Turn right on Haywood Rd.

36.6 Pass Best Western River Escape Inn and Suites on the right. 🛏

37.0 Continue straight to cross US 23 into town of Dillsboro. *Note:* Restaurants and lodging are available here. 🍴 🛏

37.2 Continue straight past Dillsboro post office.

37.4 Cross bridge over Scott Creek.

37.6 Enter town of Sylva.

37.7 Pass Harold's Supermarket on left. 🍴 🛒

38.4 Pass Economy Inn on left. 🛏

38.5 Turn right on Keener Rd. at historic Jackson County courthouse, now a library. *Note:* There is no sign for Keener Rd. here, but there is a sign for Bicentennial Park.

38.6 Turn left on W. Main St. in Sylva. On immediate right (773 W. Main St.) is Jackson County chamber of commerce with tourism information. *Note:* Downtown Sylva has restaurants, an outdoor-gear store, and the Blue Ridge Inn, at this intersection. 🍴 🛒 🛏

38.9 Continue straight at intersection of W. Main and Mill Sts. Go straight toward NC 107.

39.1 Turn left on Chipper Curve Rd. This is a complicated intersection where three roads come together. Look for the firehouse on Municipal Dr. on your left. Chipper Curve Rd. is to the right of the firehouse. *Note:* This section of Chipper Curve Rd. is very narrow and winding, and is significantly more difficult on a bike than walking; use extreme caution here.

39.6 Pass Bryson Park (town of Sylva) on left. *Note:* The park has restrooms with running water open during daylight hours and a vending machine with drinks and water. 💧 🚻

39.9 Continue straight on Chipper Curve Rd. where Allen St. comes in from left.

40.2 Continue straight onto Skyland Dr.

41.0 Pass under US 74 overpass.

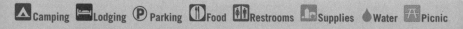

🏕 Camping   🛏 Lodging   Ⓟ Parking   🍴 Food   🚻 Restrooms   🛒 Supplies   💧 Water   ⛱ Picnic

West Fork Fisher Creek at Pinnacle Park
Photo by Jeff Clark   www.internetbrothers.org

41.1   Turn left on Fisher Creek Rd., the second left after the US 74 overpass.

42.1   At Y-intersection, stay right to continue on Fisher Creek Rd. past intersection with Dills Branch Rd.

43.3   Reach the parking lot of Pinnacle Park. Originally the town of Sylva's watershed, Pinnacle Park was opened to the public in 1991. The trail climbs steeply on a rocky old roadbed through rich hardwood cove forests to the summit ridge of the Plott Balsam Range. All hikers must register at the trailhead to enter the park. The trail is marked with purple-and-gold blazes and double-blue blazes all the way to Waterrock Knob, although they are infrequent on much of the trail. Ⓟ

43.6   At the junction of the West Fork and East Fork Trails, continue straight on the West Fork Trail.

43.8   This crossing of Fisher Creek is the last reliable source of water from here to Waterrock Knob. Although there are other small streams and seeps above here, they are not reliable as water sources. 💧

44.0   A side trail on the left leads to Campsite No. 1 less than 0.1 mile away. 🔺

44.9   A side trail on the right leads to Campsite No. 2. 🔺

Trailhead at Pinnacle Park
Photo by Jeff Clark www.internetbrothers.org

45.2 Continue straight on the West Fork Trail. *Note*: The 1.4-mile side trail to the left leads to the Pinnacle, which offers spectacular views of the Scott Creek valley, the town of Sylva, and the surrounding mountains. Campsite No. 3 is 0.6 mile along this trail.

45.7 Pass an old gate.

45.8 The East Fork Trail joins from the right. Continue straight towards Blackrock Mtn. The West Fork Trail ends here.

46.5 Make a sharp left turn, leaving the old roadbed, and continue up the steep singletrack trail through spruce-fir forest to Blackrock Mtn. *Note*: For the next mile or so, the trail is very rugged and at times difficult to follow. It involves minor scrambling over rocks and some wayfinding.

46.7 Although a large tree on the left is blazed, and there appears to be a trail in that direction, continue straight up here.

46.9 Take the left fork of the trail, then cross the 5,745-foot summit of Blackrock Mtn. The summit block is an excellent resting point and offers spectacular views.

47.0 The path crosses at the base of the rocks between the rock and tree, then up.

47.1 Cross an unnamed summit.

47.4 At the fork, follow the blazed trail to the right.

47.8 Pass a nice campsite on left. *Note*: This campsite is not within Pinnacle Park and therefore is not subject to the permitting requirements.

48.6 Cross the 6,032-foot summit of Yellow Face, an open bald covered with blackberries, passing faint trail on left near tree marked with blue blazes.

48.7 A short side trail leads to a viewpoint.

49.0 A short side trail leads to a viewpoint.

49.2 Turn right on BRP, then left on the road to Waterrock Knob.

49.5 Continue through the upper end of the Waterrock Knob Overlook parking lot (at BRP MP 451.2) onto a paved path. A few feet later, reach a junction with a trail to the right marked with the MST blaze, and the eastern end of Segment 1B. (Turn right to continue on Segment 2.) *Note*: The overlook has parking, a visitor center with a small convenience store (open seasonally), and restrooms. There is no water. If you continue straight on the paved path, the summit of Waterrock Knob, with spectacular views, is 0.5 mile ahead.

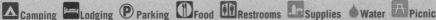

Road sign in English and Cherokee
Photo by Steve Metcalf

Hiking Directions, Westbound

0.0   Segment 1B begins at a trail junction just above the Waterrock Knob Overlook (BRP MP 451.2). If continuing a hike from Segment 2, turn left from the trail onto the paved path. If beginning from the parking area, return on the paved path to the parking area and continue down the road to the parkway. *Note:* The overlook has parking, a visitor center with a small convenience store (open seasonally), and restrooms. There is no water. If you continue straight up the paved path, the summit of Waterrock Knob, with spectacular views, is 0.5 mile ahead. Ⓟ 🏪 🚻

Camping Lodging Ⓟ Parking Food Restrooms 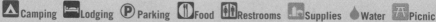Supplies 💧Water Picnic

0.3   Turn right on BRP and then almost immediately left on the trail heading into the trees. The trail is marked with purple-and-gold blazes and double-blue blazes all the way to Pinnacle Park Trailhead, although they are infrequent on much of the trail.

0.5   A short side trail leads to a viewpoint.

0.8   A short side trail leads to a viewpoint.

0.9   Cross the 6,032-foot summit of Yellow Face, an open bald covered with blackberries, passing faint trail on right near tree marked with blue blazes.

1.7   Pass a nice campsite on right. *Note:* This campsite is not within Pinnacle Park and therefore is not subject to the permitting requirements described below. For the next mile or so, the trail is very rugged and at times difficult to follow. It involves minor scrambling over rocks and some wayfinding.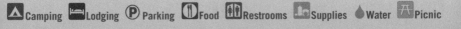

2.4   Cross an unnamed summit.

2.5   Scramble up the rocks here rather than following the trail below the base of the rocks, then go down the rocks and cross at the base of the rocks between the rock and tree.

2.6   Cross the 5,745-foot summit of Blackrock Mtn. The summit block is an excellent resting point and offers spectacular views. After leaving the summit, go down a steep trail a few yards, then scramble down a short rock face to continue on trail.

2.8   Although a large tree on the right is blazed, and there appears to be a trail in that direction, continue straight down here. The trail below here is not very well marked or developed, and generally simply follows drainage patterns.

3.0   Where the trail joins an old roadbed, turn right.

3.7   The East Fork Trail joins the trail from the left; continue straight onto the West Fork Trail.

3.8   Pass an old gate.

4.3   Continue straight on the West Fork Trail. *Note:* The 1.4-mile side trail to the right leads to the Pinnacle, which offers spectacular views of the Scott Creek valley, the town of Sylva, and the surrounding mountains. Campsite No. 3 is 0.6 mile along this trail. If you want to camp here, you will need to continue down to the trailhead to register.

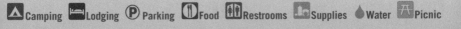

Camping   Lodging   P Parking   Food   Restrooms   Supplies   Water   Picnic

Old River Road
Photo by Steve Metcalf

4.6   A side trail on the left leads to Campsite No. 2. If you want to camp here, you will need to continue down to the trailhead to register. 🔺

5.5   A side trail on the right leads to Campsite No. 1 less than 0.1 mile away. If you want to camp here, you will need to continue down to the trailhead to register. 🔺

5.7   This crossing of Fisher Creek is the first reliable water coming down from Waterrock Knob. From here down to the trailhead, water is plentiful. 💧

5.9   At the junction of the West Fork and East Fork Trails, continue straight on the West Fork Trail. Stay on the old roadbed until you reach the Pinnacle Park parking area.

6.2   Reach Pinnacle Park parking lot. Originally the town of Sylva's watershed, Pinnacle Park was opened to the public in 1991. From the parking lot, continue straight down Fisher Creek Rd. Ⓟ

7.4   Continue straight on Fisher Creek Rd. where Dills Branch Rd. comes in from right.

8.4   At T-intersection, turn right on Skyland Dr.

🔺 Camping 🛏 Lodging Ⓟ Parking 🍴 Food 🚻 Restrooms 🛒 Supplies 💧 Water ⛱ Picnic

8.5 Pass under US 74 overpass.

9.3 Just beyond railroad crossing signs, at Y-intersection where Skyland Dr. continues to left, take right fork onto Chipper Curve Rd.

9.6 Continue straight on Chipper Curve Rd. where Allen St. goes up hill to right. *Note:* This section of Chipper Curve Rd. is very narrow and winding, and is significantly more difficult on a bike than walking; use extreme caution here.

9.9 Pass Bryson Park (town of Sylva) on right. *Note:* The park has restrooms with running water open during daylight hours and a vending machine with drinks and water. 💧 🚻

10.4 Just before firehouse on Municipal Dr., bear left through complicated intersection and turn right on W. Main St.

10.6 At Y-intersection where W. Main St. splits, hikers keep left to stay on W. Main and enter downtown Sylva. This is a one-way street the wrong way, so cyclists should keep right on Mill St., which parallels W. Main, and resume the main route at Mile 10.6, continuing straight there. *Note:* Downtown Sylva has restaurants, an outdoor-gear store, and two hotels noted later. Near the other end of downtown on the left (773 W. Main St.) is Jackson County chamber of commerce with tourism information. 🍴 🏪

10.9 At T-intersection in front of historic Jackson County courthouse, now a library, turn right on Keener St. *Note:* The Blue Ridge Inn is at this intersection. 🛏

11.0 At T-intersection, turn left on US Bus. 23.

11.1 Pass Economy Inn on right. 🛏

11.8 Pass Harold's Supermarket on right. 🍴 🏪

11.9 Enter town of Dillsboro.

12.1 Cross bridge over Scott Creek. *Note:* Food and lodging are available in downtown Dillsboro. 🍴 🛏

12.3 Continue straight past Dillsboro post office.

12.5 Continue straight across US 23.

12.9 Pass Best Western River Escape Inn and Suites on the left. 🛏

13.9 Turn left on US 74. Walk along highway facing traffic. This section of US 74 has a concrete barrier between the eastbound and westbound lanes. *Note:* This section of US 74 is heavily traveled and more difficult on a bike than walking; use extreme caution here.

▲ Camping 🛏 Lodging ℗ Parking 🍴 Food 🚻 Restrooms 🏪 Supplies 💧 Water ⛱ Picnic

16.2 Across from a diner and convenience store and just before Tuckasee-gee Outfitters, turn left on Barkers Creek Rd., then cross Tuckasee-gee River. 🍴 🏬

16.4 At Y-intersection, where left fork continues uphill and right fork goes down, bear right onto Thomas Valley Rd.

17.1 Continue straight past Joe Branch Rd. on left.

17.6 Pass Nations Creek Rd. on left.

18.5 Turn left to stay on Thomas Valley Rd. at Wilmot Missionary Baptist Church.

22.3 Just before crossing under a highway bridge, turn left on Old Bryson City Rd. *Note:* For the next 1.7 miles, you will be passing through the Cherokee Indian Reservation, and many road signs are printed in Cherokee as well as English. If you continue straight here instead of turning, in 0.3 mile you will reach the town of Whittier. Across the bridge over the Tuckaseegee River is a general store for supplies and food. 💧 🏬 🍴

24.0 At T-intersection, turn right to stay on Old Bryson City Rd., then cross over highway bridge. *Note:* There is no road sign for Old Bryson City Rd. here, but a sign for Owle Rd. is on your left.

24.1 At T-intersection, turn left to stay on Old Bryson City Rd.

25.0 Continue straight across Hyatt Creek Rd. The road changes names to Walter Woody Rd. here. *Note:* To your left at intersection with Hyatt Creek Rd. is the ramp to US 74.

26.3 At T-intersection, turn right on Governor's Island Rd. and immediately cross bridge over Tuckaseegee River.

26.4 After crossing bridge over Tuckaseegee River and just before railroad tracks, turn left on Old River Rd., a dirt road. *Note:* There is no sign for Old River Rd., but it is marked as SR 1336. Straight ahead on Governor's Island Rd. is community with water and supplies. 💧 🏬

27.9 Immediately after crossing the railroad tracks for the third time, turn right on E. Deep Creek Rd. This is the second of two parallel roads just before the bridge ahead of you. *Note:* If instead of turning right, you continue straight across the bridge, then turn left, downtown Bryson City, with restaurants and shops, is about 0.5 mile away. 🍴 🏬

28.5 Pass Deep Creek Missionary Baptist Church on left.

🔺 Camping   🛏 Lodging   Ⓟ Parking   🍴 Food   🚻 Restrooms   🏬 Supplies   💧 Water   ⛱ Picnic

29.7 After entering GSMNP, turn left at T-intersection and cross bridge over Deep Creek. *Note:* The Deep Creek Campground, on your right at this intersection, has 92 campsites. Registration and a fee are required to camp here. See the "Camping" section for this segment for more information. ▲

29.8 At T-intersection, turn right, then take first right into picnic area.

29.9 Pass restrooms on left. ⬤ 🚻

30.0 At parking area at the end of picnic area loop, continue straight onto gravel trail, then continue onto sidewalk. Ⓟ

30.1 Cross road, continuing on sidewalk next to parking area for Deep Creek Trailhead. Ⓟ 🚻

30.2 Continue straight, following sign to Deep Creek Trailhead, and then through gate onto Deep Creek Trail.

31.0 Continue straight past junction with Indian Creek Trail on right, then cross bridge.

31.1 Continue straight past Deep Creek Horse Trail on left.

32.0 After crossing bridge, continue straight past Loop Trail on right, staying on Deep Creek Trail.

32.7 Continue straight past Bumgardner Branch backcountry campsite #60. *Note:* A permit is required to camp here, or at any backcountry site in GSMNP. See the "Camping" section for this segment for information about fees and reservations. ▲ ⬤

35.1 Continue straight past McCracken Branch backcountry campsite #59. ▲

35.6 Continue straight past Nicks Nest Branch backcountry campsite #58. ▲

36.2 Continue straight on Deep Creek Trail past junction with Martins Gap Trail and Bryson Place backcountry campsite #57 on right. *Note:* This is the last campsite of Horace Kephart (1862-1931), a writer and outdoor activist. A couple of hundred feet before the junction, look for a flat area on the right where you'll find a millstone put up by a Bryson City Boy Scout troop in his memory. The alternative "Great Smoky Mountains" route for Segment 1 of the MST merges here from the right on Martins Gap Trail. There are several significant creek crossings in the next 3.5 miles. ▲

36.7 Continue straight past Burnt Spruce backcountry campsite #56. ▲

▲Camping 🛏Lodging Ⓟ Parking 🍴Food 🚻Restrooms 🛍Supplies ⬤ Water ⛺Picnic

Socked in at Clingmans Dome
Photo by William Dolling

36.9 Benton MacKaye Trail (Pole Rd. Creek Trail) splits off to left. Continue straight on Deep Creek Trail.

37.0 Continue straight past Pole Rd. Creek backcountry campsite #55, a horse campsite.

37.8 Continue straight past Nettle Creek backcountry campsite #54.

40.4 Turn left on Fork Ridge Trail, then cross Deep Creek (there may or may not be a bridge). *Note:* Poke Patch backcountry campsite #53 is at this junction. The trail ascends 2,800 feet over the next 5.1 miles.

43.4 Cross a small stream.

45.5 After crossing Clingmans Dome Rd., take spur trail 125 feet and turn left on the Appalachian Trail, which runs concurrently with the MST. *Note:* There is a small parking area at the trailhead. Ⓟ

Camping Lodging Ⓟ Parking Food Restrooms Supplies Water Picnic

45.8 Continue straight through intersection with Sugarland Mtn. Trail. *Note:* Mt. Collins shelter is 0.5 mile to right on Sugarland Mtn. Trail.

46.0 Continue straight to ascend the summit of Mt. Collins.

47.0 Continue straight at Mt. Collins Gap.

48.0 Continue straight at Old Buzzards Roost in a spruce-pine forest. A spring is on the left.

49.0 At the MST sign—the exact western end of the MST—turn left on a side trail. After about 100 feet you'll arrive at a paved path. The Clingmans Dome observation tower is on your left. Walk right (down) to the parking area, passing an information station and store managed by the Great Smoky Mountains Association, open in season.

49.5 Reach Clingmans Dome parking area and western end of Segment 1B and the MST. *Note:* To reach the parking area, take US 441 west from Cherokee or east from Gatlinburg. At Newfound Gap, the NC/TN line, turn onto Clingmans Dome Rd. The road is closed November to April. If road is closed when you are hiking, you can access the observation tower by hiking south on the Appalachian Trail from the parking area at Newfound Gap in GSMNP. (P)

Camping Lodging (P) Parking Food Restrooms Supplies ◆ Water Picnic

Rays and ridges from Waterrock Knob
Photo by Robert Stephens

The Balsams—MST Segment 2

WATERROCK KNOB TO PISGAH INN
By Jim Grode

This segment, located in one of the most biodiverse areas of the world, showcases that diversity. Nearly all the major plant communities of the southern Appalachians are represented, from spruce-fir forests typically found in Canada to rich cove forests, and from rhododendron thickets to heath balds—and even a little of the rare spray cliff community. Around every corner is a view greater than the one before it. And the myriad streams and waterfalls provide delightful coolness even on the hottest summer day.

This segment is also one of the least accessible parts of the MST—although it generally parallels the Blue Ridge Parkway (BRP). Segment

2 crosses a paved road only 7 times in the 52 miles between the US 74 crossing (Eastbound (EB) Mile 9.1, Westbound (WB) Mile 51.9) and its eastern end. The segment is also rugged: elevations range from over 5,800 feet to less than 3,500 feet in less than 10 miles, and there is almost 25,000 feet of climbing and descending over the entire length of the segment. The trail is often rocky, muddy, or indistinct, making travel sometimes difficult. Almost all of Segment 2 is on federally owned land, encompassing the Nantahala and Pisgah National Forests and the BRP. As a result, there is virtually no development and no opportunity for resupply on the segment.

HIGHLIGHTS INCLUDE

- The four-state views from Waterrock Knob, at 6,292 feet the highest point on Segment 2 and the third-highest point on the entire MST
- Skinny Dip Falls, a popular waterfall and swimming hole
- The nearly trackless expanse of the Middle Prong Wilderness Area
- The views over the ghost forest of Graveyard Fields
- The tourist haven of the Pisgah Inn, with its famous restaurant

Total Distance: 61.0 miles (57.4 on trail, 1.9 on gravel roads, and 1.7 on paved roads)
Difficulty: Strenuous, with significant elevation changes involving steep climbs and descents, difficult trail tread, and long stretches with no road crossings

Trail Updates

When planning your trip using this guide, take a moment to see whether Friends of the Mountains-to-Sea Trail (Friends) has posted any updates about the trail route by visiting Friends' "Trail Updates" page at www. MountainstoSeaTrail.org/updates.

Special Note Regarding Access

The BRP closes in winter, making large sections of this segment inaccessible except at major road crossings, which may be too far apart for day hikes. Wintertime hiking in this segment will require careful planning.

Shuttle Services

Danny Bernstein maintains a list of people who provide shuttle services between Heintooga Rd. (Segment 1A) and Black Mtn. Campground (the eastern end of Segment 3). See www.hikertohiker.net/hiking/mountains-sea-trail-heintooga-road-black-mountain-campground.

Primitive Camping

Camping is prohibited on all BRP property except in designated campgrounds. Except as noted below, primitive camping is allowed anywhere in the Pisgah and Nantahala National Forests. Before setting up a backcountry camp, please confirm that you are in a legal camping area.

Areas in Segment 2 where camping is allowed include:

EB Miles 19.8-33.8, 34.7-36.1, 36.3-43.3, 44.3-44.7, and 54.3-60.6.

WB Miles 0.4-6.7, 16.3-16.7, 17.7-24.7, 24.9-26.3, and 27.2-41.2.

Note: A number of the most obvious backcountry sites are noted in the hiking directions below, but there has been no attempt to completely catalog all suitable sites.

Rhododendron tunnel
Photo by PJ Wetzel, www.pjwetzel.com

Camping in the Middle Prong Wilderness Area (EB Miles 36.3-40.6; WB Miles 20.4-24.7) is limited to groups of 10 or fewer people and campfires are not permitted.

Special Note Regarding Bear Activity and Requirements

Because of aggressive bear activity, the US Forest Service requires all back-packers to carry bear canisters in the Shining Rock Wilderness Area and nearby Forest Service lands to the northwest of the BRP. This area encompasses parts of Segments 2 and 3 of the MST. As a practical matter for MST thru-hikers, this will probably require carrying canisters between Cherokee (Segment 1A) or Sylva (Segment 1B) and Asheville (Segment 3), as these are the nearest resupply points. For more information, see www.fs.usda.gov/detail/nfsnc/alerts-notices/?cid=stelprd3832543.

In addition, because of the bear activity, camping is currently prohibited in the Graveyard Fields area (EB Miles 44.7-51.1; WB Miles 9.9-16.3).

Campgrounds and Lodging

The only campground and hotel directly on the trail are listed below. Additional lodging is available in Waynesville, 7 miles northeast on US 74 from EB Mile 9.1; WB Mile 51.9.

EB Mile 61.0; WB Mile 0.0
Mt. Pisgah Campground, BRP Milepost (MP) 408.6, (828) 648-2644. The campground is open between late April and the end of October. The campground has water, restrooms, and showers, and sites are $16-$19/ night. For online reservations, go to www.recreation.gov and search for Mount Pisgah Campground.

EB Mile 61.0; WB Mile 0.0
Pisgah Inn, MP 408.6, 828-235-8228; www.pisgahinn.com. The inn is open April 1 to October 31; rooms range from $138 to $182 per night.

Food/Supplies/Post Office

There are almost no facilities on this segment. The nearest town is Waynesville, 7 miles northeast on US 74 from EB Mile 9.1; WB Mile 51.9.

EB Mile 0.0; WB Mile 61.0	The Waterrock Knob Visitor Center, open 10:00 AM-4:00 PM seasonally, has a small selection of snacks.
EB Mile 9.3; WB Mile 51.7	The Balsam post office is approximately 0.3 mile from the trail. To reach the post office, cross the railroad tracks, then turn left on the shoulder of US 74. Take the second left onto Candle Stick Ln. (there may not be a road sign), then the first left onto Cabin Flats Rd. The post office is on the left after you cross the railroad tracks again.
EB Mile 61.0; WB Mile 0.0	The Pisgah Inn has a convenience store with a wider selection of food and supplies, as well as a restaurant.

Water/Restrooms

Water is generally abundant in this segment, and this guide does not attempt to catalog every potential source, keeping in mind that a decent-sized stream in wet weather may completely stop flowing in dry periods. Only larger, named creeks; those useful for wayfinding; and water sources in areas where they are more widely scattered are listed here. **All surface water should be treated before drinking.**

In addition to surface water on the trail, water is available at the Pisgah Inn, which is the eastern end of this segment.

Hunting

Hunting is allowed throughout the Nantahala and Pisgah National Forests during the hunting season and is prohibited on BRP property. See www.ncwildlife.org/hunting.aspx for information about seasons and licenses.

Signs/Blazing

With the exception of the trail within the Middle Prong Wilderness Area, the MST in Segment 2 is generally well marked with the MST blaze—a 3-inch white circle—either painted on or affixed to trees or signposts. Within the Wilderness Area (EB Miles 36.3 to 40.6; WB Miles 20.4 to 24.7), there are no blazes because they are not permitted by wilderness law. Throughout this segment, the tread of the trail can be indistinct and difficult to follow in places.

Dogs

Dogs are allowed on this segment of the MST, but should be on leashes at all times.

ADDITIONAL INFORMATION

Friends office: 919-825-0297 or info@MountainstoSeaTrail.org

Walt Weber and the Carolina Mountain Club have published an excellent, highly detailed, set of maps and profiles for this segment of the MST entitled *Trail Profiles and Maps: From the Great Smokies to Mount Mitchell and Beyond.* The book is available on Amazon or through a number of outlets in the Asheville area.

Trail Maps

Google map of the entire MST: www.MountainstoSeaTrail.org/map

BRP map: www.nps.gov/blri/planyourvisit/upload/BLRImap1-1.pdf

National Geographic map 785 (Nantahala and Cullasaja Gorges) and map 780 (Pisgah Ranger District)

Federal Land Management Agency Sites

BRP: www.nps.gov/blri

National Forests in North Carolina: www.fs.usda.gov/nfsnc

Links for other points and organizations of interest

Pisgah Inn: www.pisgahinn.com

Carolina Mountain Club (trail maintainers in this segment): www.carolinamountainclub.org

Haywood County Tourism: visitncsmokies.com

Downtown Waynesville: www.downtownwaynesville.com

Biodiversity websites

highlandsbiological.org/nature-center/
    biodiversity-of-the-southern-appalachians

www.worldwildlife.org/ecoregions/na0403

For more detailed information about the plant communities of this area, Timothy P. Spira's *Wildflowers and Plant Communities of the Southern Appalachian Mountains and Piedmont* is an excellent and understandable resource.

PRIMARY PARKING LOCATIONS

Waterrock Knob (BRP Milepost [MP] 451.2)
EB Mile 0.0; WB Mile 61.0
Ⓟ 🏞️ 🚻
N35.45999, W83.14132

BRP Maintenance Area near US 74 Crossing
EB Mile 9.3; WB Mile 51.7
Ⓟ
N35.43263, W83.07851

Grassy Ridge Mine Overlook (MP 436.8)
EB Mile 16.9; WB Mile 44.1
Ⓟ
N35.40998, W83.045

MP 426.5
EB Mile 34.5; WB Mile 26.5
Ⓟ
N35.31348, W82.95407

NC 215 Crossing
EB Mile 40.6; WB Mile 20.4
Ⓟ
N35.30379, W82.9091

Black Balsam Rd. (FR 816) Crossing
EB Mile 44.7; WB Mile 16.3
Ⓟ
N35.32077, W82.87599

Graveyard Fields Parking Lot (MP 418.8; 0.4 Mile from Trail)
EB Mile 47.8; WB Mile 13.2
Ⓟ
N35.32004, W82.84718

Looking Glass Rock Overlook (MP 417.0)
EB Mile 49.7; WB Mile 11.3
Ⓟ
N35.32181, W82.82811

Cherry Cove Overlook (MP 415.7)
EB Mile 51.1; WB Mile 9.9
Ⓟ
N35.33598, W82.81518

US 276 Crossing
EB Mile 54.6; WB Mile 6.4
Ⓟ
N35.36601, W82.78956

Pisgah Inn (MP 408.6)
EB Mile 61.0; WB Mile 0.0
🍴 🏞️ 🛏️ 💧 Ⓟ 🚻 🏕️
N35.40360, W82.75425

Coordinates can be entered in your mapping software just like a street address.

Camping Lodging Ⓟ Parking Food Restrooms Supplies 💧Water Picnic

A foggy day on the trail
Photo by Jim Grode

Hiking Directions, Eastbound

0.0 Segment 2 begins at a trail junction just above the Waterrock Knob Overlook (BRP MP 451.2). If continuing a hike from Segment 1A, turn left from the paved path onto a trail marked with the MST blaze to begin Segment 2. If continuing a hike from Segment 1B or coming from parking at the overlook, follow the paved path up to the junction, then turn right. *Note*: The overlook has parking, a visitor center with a small convenience store (open seasonally), and restrooms. There is no water. If you continue straight up the paved path, the summit of Waterrock Knob, with spectacular views, is 0.5 mile ahead. Ⓟ 🏪 🚻

1.5 Cross a small stream. 💧

2.0 Cross a small stream. 💧

2.2 Reach BRP and turn left to walk alongside the road.

2.8 Enter woods on trail marked with signpost with white blaze and MST logo. The trail will begin climbing up switchbacks.

4.7 Cross footbridge over Woodfin Creek and then pass blue-blazed spur trail to BRP on right.

5.3 Cross small creek.

5.4 Emerge onto old roadbed and bear right.

5.5 Emerge onto a gravel road and bear right (downhill).

5.6 Pass through a gate.

5.8 Pass an overgrown track on left.

6.4 Continue straight where an old road comes in from left.

7.4 Continue straight where Rosemount Rd. comes in from left, then turn right at a signpost with white marker and arrow pointing right. You will cross to a parking lot, then turn right and go down the paved road. (P)

7.5 At T-intersection, turn left onto BRP. *Note:* For the next 0.9 mile, you will be on the shoulder of the BRP, so use caution.

8.0 Pass MP 444.

8.4 Just past gate, turn right into the woods at MST signpost.

9.1 Turn right onto BRP at Balsam Gap sign, then cross bridge over US 74.

9.2 Pass BRP MP 443 then, just before road to BRP maintenance facility, turn right on small trail.

9.3 At T-intersection, turn right on single-lane paved road then, just before crossing railroad tracks, bear left on grassy track into woods. *Note:* At the T-intersection, turn left up the hill to reach a parking area. The Balsam post office is approximately 0.3 mile from the trail at this point. See the "Food/Supplies/Post Office" section for this segment for directions. (P)

9.4 Cross wooden bridge.

10.4 Cross creek on log bridge.

10.7 Cross gravel road at a downhill angle, returning to the trail near a tree with a painted purple rectangle.

11.2 Cross a log bridge over a small seep.

11.5 Cross Redbank Branch.

12.0 Cross bridge over small stream, which may not always have water.

16.9 Pass short spur trail to Grassy Ridge Mine Overlook on right (MP 436.8). (P)

17.9 Cross log bridge over small gully.

▲ Camping 🏠 Lodging (P) Parking 🍴 Food 🚻 Restrooms 🛒 Supplies ◆ Water ⛺ Picnic

Segment 2 Eastbound

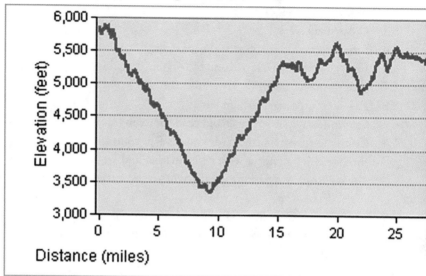

18.1 Pass short spur trail on left, leading to Licklog Gap Overlook (MP 435.7). ℗

18.7 At sign with white markers, continue straight past short spur trail on left to Doubletop Mtn. Overlook (MP 435.3). ℗

19.8 Bear right at MST sign, then continue straight onto an old roadbed (largely overgrown here, but it soon widens). *Note:* The trail to the left leads approximately 0.1 mile to a small parking area on the BRP at MP 434.2. As you continue on the MST, you are entering the Nantahala National Forest, where camping is allowed for the next 14 miles. ℗ ▲

20.2 Continue straight past clearing on left.

20.4 Just before reaching clearing, make sharp left onto another old roadbed.

20.5 Reach an open grassy area and continue on old roadbed straight past trail on left, then turn left at MST sign and return to woods.

20.9 Turn right at an open area that appears to be a former power-line cut, then turn left on old roadbed at post with white markers.

21.0 Turn sharply left onto a singletrack trail at post with white markers.

21.2 Cross Mull Creek. ◖

21.5 Continue straight onto an old roadbed.

▲ Camping 🏠 Lodging ℗ Parking 🍴 Food 🚻 Restrooms 🛒 Supplies ◖ Water 🏕 Picnic

Elevation Profile

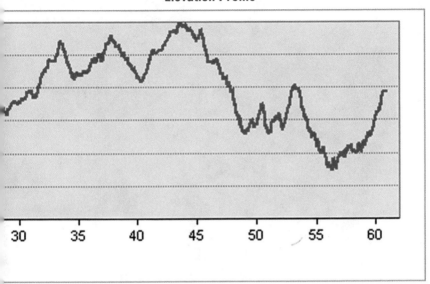

21.8 Pass a campsite on the right.

21.9 Turn left at T-intersection with white marker.

22.6 Pass a campsite on the right.

23.0 Continue straight onto singletrack trail. *Note:* The trail becomes much more rocky and difficult here; the next two miles are among the most difficult on the entire MST.

24.7 Continue straight onto old, mostly overgrown roadbed.

25.0 Cross Beechflat Creek, then continue straight where trail comes in from left.

25.6 Pass lean-to frame structure on right.

28.3 Where smaller trail appears to continue straight, take switchback to the left to stay on main trail.

28.6 Turn left at T-intersection.

29.1 At Y-intersection just before trail enters a deeply embanked section, bear left, then turn left at T-intersection.

29.4 Cross Birch Ridge Creek.

29.9 Continue straight onto an old roadbed joining the trail from the right.

30.1 Cross Piney Mtn. Creek.

30.3 Pass trail on the left to campsite with limited flat space.

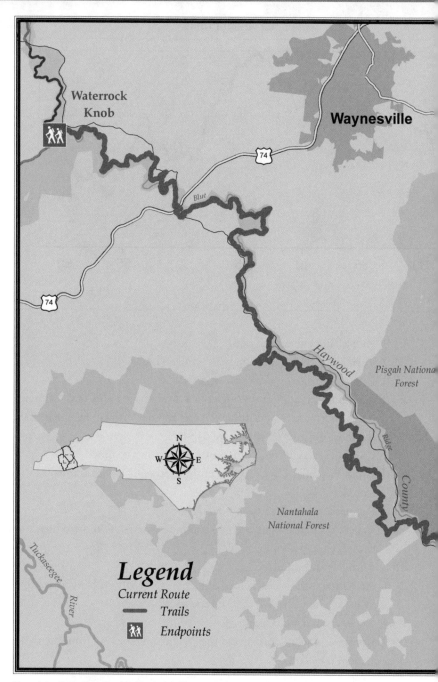

Map and elevation profile produced for Friends of the Mountains-to-Sea Trail by Curtis Belyea, 2016.

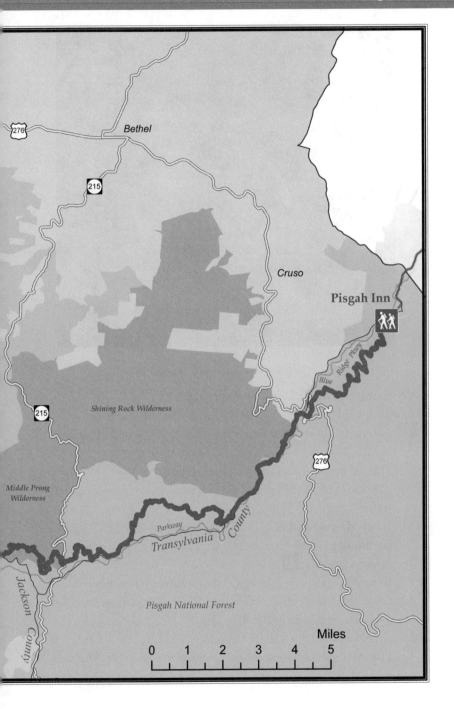

Butterfly on milkweed
Photo by PJ Wetzel, www.pjwetzel.com

31.6 Bear left at MST sign onto singletrack trail.

31.7 Turn left from singletrack trail to return to old roadbed.

32.4 Ascend to old road marked with MST sign and bear right onto the road.

32.5 Pass between the metal posts of an old gate.

32.9 Cross a set of "speed bumps" in the trail designed to discourage ATV traffic.

33.0 Reach clearing and turn left on trail marked with MST sign. *Note:* Continuing straight leads a few hundred feet to a campsite suitable for large groups. ▲

33.8 Enter BRP property (no sign), where camping is prohibited.

34.5 Cross BRP at a gravel parking area (MP 426.5), then turn right at T-intersection with MST sign. Ⓟ

34.7 Pass National Park Service Boundary Line sign. You are entering the Pisgah National Forest, where camping is allowed for the next 1.4 miles. ▲

36.1 Pass National Park Service Boundary Line sign. You are entering BRP property, where camping is prohibited.

36.3 Enter Middle Prong Wilderness Area; camping is allowed for the next 7 miles, but see the "Primitive Camping" section for this segment for restrictions. *Note:* The trail is not blazed through the wilderness area and can be difficult to follow.

37.2 Cross Buckeye Creek.

37.3 At Y-intersection, where trail narrows significantly, bear right (uphill), then pass trail to campsite on right.

37.4 Continue straight along lower edge of a heath bald.

37.8 Pass an MST sign, then cross logs over a boggy area.

37.9 Pass campsite on the left.

39.6 Reach the West Fork of the Pigeon River and cross a small tributary, keeping the main stream on your left, then return to the woods.

40.1 Pass through clearing with campsite on the left.

40.4 Pass unmarked trail on left just before MST sign, then pass campsite on right.

40.5 Cross Bubbling Spring Branch, then bear left.

40.6 Leave Middle Prong Wilderness Area, then cross NC 215.

40.7 Pass campsite on right.

41.0 At a tree marked with a double white blaze, turn left, looking for a tree 10 feet ahead with a single white blaze, then cross log bridge over creek.

42.2 Pass several campsites on the right and left.

42.4 Cross small stream on wooden bridge.

42.5 Pass wooden boardwalk, then pass Devil's Courthouse Connector Trail on right.

42.6 Cross two wooden bridges.

42.7 Pass Little Sam Trail on left and campsite on right.

43.0 Cross a pair of wooden bridges.

43.3 Enter BRP property (no sign), where camping is prohibited.

43.4 Pass side trail to rock outcrop overlook on right.

43.6 Pass Art Loeb Trail on right.

44.3 Enter the Pisgah National Forest (no sign), where camping is allowed for the next 0.4 mile.

44.5 Pass trail to campsite on left.

Camping Lodging Parking Food Restrooms Supplies Water 🏕 Picnic

Skinny Dip Falls
Photo by PJ Wetzel, www.pjwetzel.com

44.7 Cross Black Balsam Rd. (FR 816) and turn right just before Art Loeb Trail sign. At Y-intersection where the more obvious trail goes left, bear right into spruce forest, following white-painted blazes. *Note:* As noted in the introductory materials, the US Forest Service has prohibited camping in the Graveyard Fields area (Miles 44.7-51.1), which you are entering. Although these directions identify campsites in this area as wayfinding guides, do not camp there. Ⓟ

44.8 Cross the first in a series of 13 wooden bridges and boardwalks over a network of streams in the next 0.4 mile. 🌢

45.4 Bear right at top of rock outcropping.

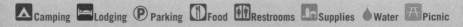

▲Camping 🛏Lodging Ⓟ Parking 🍴Food 🚻Restrooms 🛒Supplies 🌢Water ⛱Picnic

45.8 Begin descending a series of switchbacks.

46.2 Reach clearing with significant trail intersection and campsite. Continue straight, following MST blaze and sign toward "BRP MP 417 Looking Glass Overlook."

47.4 Continue straight past Graveyard Ridge Trail on right.

47.5 Pass campsite on right.

47.8 Turn left at T-intersection with sign to "BRP MP 417 Looking Glass Overlook." *Note:* If you turn right instead, you will reach the Graveyard Fields parking lot (MP 418.8) in 0.4 mile. Ⓟ

48.0 Pass campsite on right.

48.1 Bear left at Y-intersection where right fork is marked to campsites.

49.2 Pass campsite on left.

49.4 Cross wooden bridge over Yellowstone Prong just below Skinny Dip Falls, then ascend stairs and cross small stream on wooden bridge. ◍

49.7 Pass side trail on right to parking at Looking Glass Rock Overlook 400 feet away (MP 417). Ⓟ

50.0 At sign where Bridges Camp Gap Trail continues straight ahead, turn right.

50.3 Pass campsite on right.

51.1 Turn left on BRP at Cherry Cove Overlook (MP 415.7) and walk along shoulder. Ⓟ

51.2 Return to trail at Cherry Gap sign.

51.8 Cross BRP (with small parking area) at MP 415. Ⓟ

52.2 Continue straight past trail to viewpoint on right.

52.3 Turn right on BRP at Bennett Gap.

52.4 Cross BRP and return to trail at MST sign.

53.3 Pass through cleft in rocks, then pass between NPS benchmark on left and large boulder on right.

54.2 Cross BRP at Pigeon Gap (MP 412.5), near a power-line cut and small grassy parking area. Ⓟ

54.3 Enter the Pisgah National Forest (no sign), where camping is allowed for the next 6.3 miles. ▲

54.6 Cross US 276. *Note:* There is a small parking area 50 yards to the right. Ⓟ

55.0 Cross stream on log bridge. ◍

55.6 Cross creek on log bridge. ◍

▲Camping ▭Lodging Ⓟ Parking Ⓕ Food Ⓡ Restrooms Ⓢ Supplies ◍ Water Ⓟ Picnic

Indian Pipe
Photo by PJ Wetzel, www.pjwetzel.com

56.1 Turn left at T-intersection then cross stream on log. *Note:* The trail here becomes known as the Buck Spring Trail, which continues on your right as well. 💧

56.3 Continue straight past Barnett Branch Trail on right.

56.6 Cross Barnett Branch. 💧

57.8 Cross Poplar Creek. 💧

58.1 Pass campsite on left. 🔼

60.5 Begin ascending a series of switchbacks.

60.6 Enter BRP property (no sign), where camping is prohibited.

60.8 Continue onto grassy path.

60.9 At a seating area with a fence, turn left and go up the stairs, then turn right on the sidewalk next to the Pisgah Inn office.

61.0 Reach parking lot for the Pisgah Inn (MP 408.6) and eastern end of Segment 2. *Note:* The Pisgah Inn, open seasonally, has lodging, a restaurant, and a store with general supplies. The Mt. Pisgah Campground is nearby; to reach it, turn left on the BRP and walk approximately 0.1 mile to the entrance on the right. See the "Campgrounds and Lodging" section for this segment for more information. 🍴 🏪 🛏 💧 Ⓟ 🚻 🔼

🔼 Camping 🛏 Lodging Ⓟ Parking 🍴 Food 🚻 Restrooms 🏪 Supplies 💧 Water 🏕 Picnic

Hiking Directions, Westbound

0.0 Begin Segment 2 at parking lot for the Pisgah Inn (MP 408.6). From the back right corner of the parking lot (as viewed from the BRP), turn right on the sidewalk. Just beyond the inn office, turn left and go down a flight of stairs. *Note:* The Pisgah Inn, open seasonally, has lodging, a restaurant, and a store with general supplies. The Mt. Pisgah Campground is nearby; to reach it, turn left on the BRP and walk approximately 0.1 mile to the entrance on the right. See the "Campgrounds and Lodging" section for this segment for more information. 🍴 🏪 🛏️ 💧 🅿️ 🚻 ⛺

0.1 At a seating area with a fence, turn right onto the grassy path.

0.2 At end of grassy path, continue onto singletrack trail also known as the Buck Spring Trail.

0.3 Begin descending a series of switchbacks.

0.4 Enter the Pisgah National Forest (no sign), where camping is allowed for the next 6.3 miles. ⛺

2.9 Pass campsite on right. ⛺

3.2 Cross Poplar Creek. 💧

4.4 Cross Barnett Branch. 💧

4.7 Continue straight past Barnett Branch Trail on left.

4.9 Cross stream on log then turn right at sign where Buck Spring Trail continues straight. 💧

5.4 Cross creek on log bridge. 💧

6.0 Cross stream on log bridge. 💧

6.4 Cross US 276. *Note:* There is a small parking area 50 yards to the left. 🅿️

6.7 Enter BRP property (no sign), where camping is prohibited.

6.8 Cross BRP at Pigeon Gap (MP 412.5), near a power-line cut and small grassy parking area. 🅿️

7.7 Pass between NPS benchmark on right and large boulder on right, then down through cleft in rocks.

8.6 Turn right on BRP at Bennett Gap.

8.7 Return to trail at MST sign.

8.8 Continue straight past trail to viewpoint on left.

9.2 Cross BRP (with small parking area) at MP 415. 🅿️

In the Balsams
Photo by Danny Bernstein

9.8   Turn right on BRP at Cherry Gap and walk along shoulder.

9.9   Return to trail on right just beyond Cherry Cove Overlook (MP 415.7). Ⓟ

10.7 Pass campsite on left. *Note:* As noted in the introductory materials, the US Forest Service has prohibited camping in the Graveyard Fields area (Miles 9.9-16.3). Although these directions identify campsites in this area as wayfinding guides, do not camp there.

11.0 At T-intersection with MST marker, turn left. The trail on your right is the Bridges Camp Gap Trail.

🔺Camping ⬜Lodging Ⓟ Parking 🍴Food 🚻Restrooms 🏬Supplies 💧Water ⛲Picnic

11.3 Pass side trail on left to parking at Looking Glass Rock Overlook 400 feet away (MP 417). Ⓟ

11.6 Cross small stream on wooden bridge, then descend stairs and cross wooden bridge over Yellowstone Prong just below Skinny Dip Falls. 💧

11.8 Pass campsite on right.

12.9 Where trail to campsites comes in on left, continue straight along trail marked "Connector" and "Graveyard Fields Parking."

13.0 Pass campsite on right.

13.2 Turn right where sign points to Graveyard Fields parking lot straight ahead. *Note:* If you continue straight, you will reach the parking lot in 0.4 mile (MP 418.8). Ⓟ

13.5 Pass campsite on left.

13.6 Continue straight past Graveyard Ridge Trail on left.

14.8 Reach clearing with significant trail intersection and campsite. Continue straight, following MST blaze and sign toward "Black Bal. Rd. FSR 816." You will begin to ascend a series of switchbacks shortly.

15.6 Cross rock outcropping and head down a series of switchbacks.

15.8 Cross the first in a series of 13 wooden bridges and boardwalks over a network of streams in the next 0.4 mile. 💧

16.3 Continue straight past trail on right, then turn left at T-intersection, where the trail to the right is the Art Loeb Trail and cross Black Balsam Rd. (FR 816). *Note:* You are leaving the area the US Forest Service has closed to camping because of bear activity; camping is allowed for the next 0.4 mile. Ⓟ ⛺

16.5 Pass trail to campsite on right. ⛺

16.7 Enter BRP property (no sign), where camping is prohibited.

17.4 Pass Art Loeb Trail on left.

17.6 Pass side trail to rock outcrop overlook on left.

17.7 Enter the Pisgah National Forest; camping is allowed for the next 7 miles, but see the "Primitive Camping" section for this segment for restrictions. ⛺

18.0 Cross a pair of wooden bridges.

18.3 Pass Little Sam Trail on right and campsite on left. ⛺

18.4 Cross two wooden bridges. 💧

⛺ Camping 🛏 Lodging Ⓟ Parking 🍴 Food 🚻 Restrooms 🏬 Supplies 💧 Water ⛱ Picnic

18.5 Pass Devil's Courthouse Connector Trail on left, then cross wooden boardwalk.

18.6 Cross small stream on wooden bridge. 💧

18.8 Pass several campsites on the right and left. ⛺

20.0 Cross log bridge over creek. At faint T-intersection, turn right and go downhill. 💧

20.3 Pass campsite on left. ⛺

20.4 Cross NC 215 and enter Middle Prong Wilderness Area. *Note:* The trail is not blazed through the wilderness area and can be difficult to follow. Ⓟ

20.5 Cross Bubbling Spring Branch, then continue uphill, parallel to road. 💧

20.6 Pass campsite on left, then unmarked trail on right just after MST sign. ⛺

20.9 Pass through clearing with campsite on the right. ⛺

21.4 Reach the West Fork of the Pigeon River and cross a small tributary, keeping the main stream on your right, then return to the woods. 💧

22.4 Cross a stream then, less than 50 feet ahead, bear left at a faint Y-intersection (the right fork may be blocked by branches). 💧

23.1 Pass campsite on the right. ⛺

23.2 Cross logs over a boggy area, then bear right. If you look back at the end of the logs, you will see an MST sign.

23.6 Continue straight along lower edge of a heath bald.

23.7 Pass trail to campsite on left, then join wider trail. ⛺

23.8 Cross Buckeye Creek. 💧

24.7 Leave Middle Prong Wilderness Area. You are entering BRP property, where camping is prohibited.

24.9 Pass National Park Service boundary line sign. You are entering the Pisgah National Forest, where camping is allowed for the next 1.4 miles. ⛺

26.3 Pass National Park Service boundary line sign. You are entering BRP property, where camping is prohibited.

26.5 Turn left at MST sign, then cross BRP at a gravel parking area (MP 426.5). Ⓟ

27.2 Enter the Nantahala National Forest (no sign), where camping is permitted for the next 14 miles. ⛺

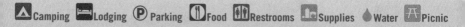

⛺Camping 🛏Lodging Ⓟ Parking 🍴Food 🚻Restrooms 🏪Supplies 💧Water 🏕Picnic

28.0 Turn right at T-intersection in clearing. *Note:* The left fork leads a few hundred feet to a campsite suitable for large groups.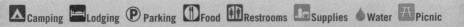

28.1 Cross a set of "speed bumps" in the trail designed to discourage ATV traffic.

28.5 Pass between the metal posts of an old gate.

28.6 Bear left at Y-intersection marked with MST sign.

29.3 Turn right off old roadbed onto singletrack trail.

29.4 Bear right at MST sign and return to old roadbed.

30.7 Pass trail on the right to campsite with limited flat space.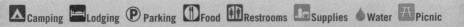

30.9 Cross Piney Mtn. Creek.

31.1 At Y-intersection, take right fork; the trail will soon narrow.

31.6 Cross Birch Ridge Creek.

31.9 At Y-intersection, where trail is deeply embanked, take right fork.

32.4 At trail intersection, where the trail continuing straight begins to descend, turn right to continue uphill.

32.7 Where smaller trail appears to go left, take switchback to the right to stay on main trail.

35.4 Pass lean-to frame structure on left.

36.0 Continue straight where trail comes in from right, then cross Beech-flat Creek.

36.3 Bear right off old roadbed (which by this point is mostly overgrown) onto singletrack trail at MST sign. *Note:* The tread of the trail will soon become much more rocky and difficult; the next two miles are among the most difficult on the entire MST.

38.0 Continue onto old roadbed.

38.4 Pass a campsite on the left.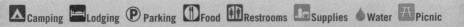

39.1 Turn right to continue on roadbed, heading uphill at white marker.

39.2 Pass a campsite on the left.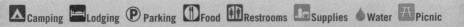

39.5 Leave the roadbed and continue straight on a singletrack trail.

39.8 Cross Mull Creek.

40.0 Turn sharply right onto an overgrown roadbed at post with white markers.

40.1 At open area that appears to be a former power-line cut, turn right at post with white marker to head uphill for about 100 feet, then bear left into woods. *Note:* The marker may be obscured by growth and somewhat difficult to see.

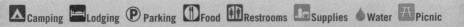

40.5 Bear right at open grassy area with MST sign, then continue on old roadbed straight past trail on right.

40.6 Just before reaching clearing, make sharp right onto another old roadbed.

40.8 Continue straight past clearing on right.

41.2 Bear left to leave roadbed just before earthen barrier, then take left fork at Y-intersection with MST sign. *Note:* The right fork leads approximately 0.1 mile to a small parking area on the BRP at MP 434.2. As you continue on the MST, you are entering BRP property, where camping is prohibited. Ⓟ

42.3 At sign with white markers, continue straight past short spur trail on right to Doubletop Mtn. Overlook (MP 435.3). Ⓟ

42.9 Pass short spur trail on right, leading to Licklog Gap Overlook (MP 435.7). Ⓟ

43.1 Cross log bridge over small gully.

44.1 Pass short spur trail to Grassy Ridge Mine Overlook on right (MP 436.8). Ⓟ

49.0 Cross bridge over small stream, which may not always have water. ◉

49.5 Cross Redbank Branch. ◉

49.8 Cross a log bridge over a small seep.

50.3 Cross gravel road at an uphill angle, aiming at a tree with a white blaze painted on it.

50.6 Cross creek on log bridge. ◉

51.6 Cross wooden bridge.

51.7 Turn right onto single-lane paved road paralleling railroad tracks. Just before reaching T-intersection, turn left onto trail and cross over stone footbridge. *Note:* Continue straight up the hill to reach a parking area. The Balsam post office is approximately 0.3 mile from the trail at this point. See the "Food/Supplies/Post Office" section for this segment for directions. Ⓟ

51.8 Turn left on BRP and pass MP 443.

51.9 Just after crossing bridge over US 74 at Balsam Gap, turn left into woods at MST signpost.

52.6 Turn left on BRP and go through the gate. *Note:* For the next 0.9 mile, you will be on the shoulder of the BRP, so use caution.

53.0 Pass MP 444.

▲ Camping 🛏 Lodging Ⓟ Parking 🍴 Food 🚻 Restrooms 🏪 Supplies ◉ Water 🏕 Picnic

53.5 Just beyond "Overlook Ahead" sign, turn right at MST signpost onto road with yield sign and single yellow stripe.

53.6 When you reach a parking lot, turn right onto a small path through the woods at the lower end of the parking lot, leading to a gravel road. Turn left on the gravel road, then stay left on Greenspire Dr. at a Y-intersection with Rosemount Rd. Ⓟ

54.6 Continue straight where an old road heads up to the right.

55.2 At Y-intersection with overgrown track, stay left on main road.

55.4 Pass through a gate.

55.5 At a hairpin turn in the gravel road, head into the woods on a trail marked with a white-blazed signpost.

55.6 Where the roadbed you are traveling on becomes overgrown, bear left onto trail heading slightly downhill.

55.7 Cross small creek. ◉

56.3 Pass blue-blazed spur trail to BRP on left, then cross footbridge over Woodfin Creek. ◉

58.2 Reach BRP and turn right to walk along the road.

58.8 Turn right into the woods at the white-blazed signpost just before Fork Ridge Overlook.

59.0 Cross a small stream. ◉

59.5 Cross a small stream. ◉

61.0 Reach the western end of Segment 2 at a T-intersection with a paved path. Turn right to begin hiking Segment 1A, or turn left to begin hiking Segment 1B or reach the Waterrock Knob parking lot (at MP 451.2). *Note:* The overlook has parking, a visitor center with a small convenience store (open seasonally), and restrooms. There is no water. If you turn right onto the paved path, the summit of Waterrock Knob, with spectacular views, is 0.5 mile ahead. Ⓟ ▣ ▣

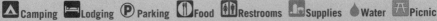

Approaching Blackstock Knob
Photo by Jeff Clark www.internetbrothers.org

The High Peaks and Asheville—MST Segment 3

PISGAH INN TO BLACK MOUNTAIN CAMPGROUND
By Jim Grode

Segment 3 is where Asheville comes to play. It is the most heavily used part of the MST within the mountains, and you are likely to encounter hikers, dog walkers, and trail runners at any time throughout the year. Virtually all of it is easily accessible from the Blue Ridge Parkway (BRP), and there are road crossings every few miles for most of the length.

Don't let its accessibility and popularity fool you, however: With elevations ranging from 2,000 feet at the French Broad River to over 6,600 feet at the summit of Mount Mitchell, this segment is quite rugged. Indeed, the section just west of Asheville hosts the infamous Shut-In Ridge Trail Run, an 18-mile trail run that annually humbles racers from around the country.

Complementing the natural beauty of the Blue Ridge Mountains in this area is the vibrancy of Asheville, a city of 80,000 nestled in the French Broad River valley, which regularly makes lists of the top 10 cities in the United States. Crammed with restaurants, shops, art galleries, and breweries, Asheville offers something for nearly everyone and is well worth a layover in your hiking schedule.

HIGHLIGHTS INCLUDE

- The views atop 6,684-foot Mount Mitchell, the highest point east of the Mississippi River

- The Shut-In Trail, which follows the old carriage road from the Biltmore House to George Vanderbilt's hunting lodge on Mount Pisgah (which no longer stands, but a few remnants of which are still visible)

- The cultural and scientific displays at the Blue Ridge Parkway Visitor Center & Headquarters near Asheville

- The fine collection of southern art and crafts at the Folk Art Center also near Asheville. Outside the Folk Art Center, look for the bronze plaque honoring Arch Nichols, who worked tirelessly as a volunteer leader of the Carolina Mountain Club and as a United States Forest Service employee to complete the MST from Mount Pisgah to Mount Mitchell.

- The ruins of Rattlesnake Lodge, a summer lodge built in 1903-4 by Asheville physician Chase Ambler

- In early summer, the azalea and rhododendron displays at Craggy Gardens

- In the fall, brilliant color displays that attract people from all over the country

Total Distance: 67.7 miles (all on trail except incidental stretches on the BRP, mostly on bridges at highway crossings)
Difficulty: Strenuous, with significant elevation changes involving steep climbs and descents and difficult trail tread

Trail Updates

When planning your trip using this guide, take a moment to see whether Friends of the Mountains-to-Sea Trail (Friends) has posted any updates about the trail route by visiting Friends' "Trail Updates" page at www.MountainstoSeaTrail.org/updates.

Special Note Regarding Access

The BRP closes in winter except for the section through Asheville, making large sections of this segment inaccessible except at major road crossings, which may be too far apart for day hikes. Wintertime hiking in this segment will require careful planning.

Shuttle Services

Danny Bernstein maintains a list of people who provide shuttle services between Heintooga Rd. (Segment 1A) and Black Mtn. Campground (the eastern end of Segment 3). See www.hikertohiker.net/hiking/mountains-sea-trail-heintooga-road-black-mountain-campground.

Camping and Lodging

Camping is prohibited on all BRP property, on the Bent Creek Experimental Forest, and in Mt. Mitchell State Park except in designated campgrounds. Primitive camping is allowed anywhere in the Pisgah National Forest, which surrounds the BRP for much of this segment east of Asheville. Before setting up a backcountry camp, please confirm that you are in a legal camping area. *Note:* A number of the most obvious backcountry sites are noted in the hiking directions below, but there has been no attempt to completely catalog all suitable sites.

EB Mile 0.0; WB Mile 67.7

Mt. Pisgah Campground, BRP Milepost (MP) 408.6, 828-648-2644. Open between late April and the end of October, this campground has water, restrooms, and showers, and sites are $16-$19/night. For online reservations, go to www.recreation.gov and search for Mount Pisgah Campground.

EB Mile 0.0; WB Mile 67.7

Pisgah Inn, MP 408.6, 828-235-8228; www.pisgahinn.com. The inn is open April 1 to October 31 and has rooms ranging from $138 to $182 per night.

EB Miles 17.8 to 31.0; WB Miles 36.7 to 49.9

Asheville. There are numerous camping and lodging options in Asheville, from small bed-and-breakfasts to large motels and luxury hotels. None are within a mile's walk of the MST, but taxis are readily available. See the "Additional Information" section for this segment for tourism information about Asheville.

EB Mile 61.7; WB Mile 6.0

Mt. Mitchell State Park Campground, 2338 NC 128, Burnsville, 28714. Open May 1-October 31 with full facilities (restrooms and water), year-round with limited facilities. Camping is $17/night; make reservations at www.ncparks.gov (there is a $3.00 surcharge for this option) or by calling 877-722-6762.

EB Mile 67.7; WB Mile 0.0

Black Mtn. Campground, 50 Black Mtn. Campground Road, Burnsville, 28714, 828-675-5616. Open April-October, primitive sites, with water, restrooms, and showers. Camping is $22/night, first come, first serve.

Special Note Regarding Bear Activity and Requirements

Because of aggressive bear activity, the US Forest Service requires all back-packers to carry bear canisters in the Shining Rock Wilderness Area and nearby Forest Service lands to the northwest of the BRP. This area encompasses parts of Segments 2 and 3 of the MST. As a practical matter for MST thru-hikers, this will probably require carrying canisters between Cherokee (Segment 1A) or Sylva (Segment 1B) and Asheville (Segment 3), as these are the nearest resupply points. For more information, see www.fs.usda.gov/detail/nfsnc/alerts-notices/?cid=stelprd3832543.

Food/Supplies/Post Office

EB Mile 0.0; WB Mile 67.7	Pisgah Inn restaurant and convenience store
EB Miles 17.8-31.0; WB Miles 36.7-49.9	Numerous restaurants and stores in Asheville
EB Mile 23.2; WB Mile 44.5	Commercial development along US 70, mostly 0.5 mile or more from the trail, including an Ingles supermarket
EB Mile 30.4; WB Mile 37.3	Commercial development along Hendersonville Rd., mostly 0.5 mile or more from the trail, including a Walmart
EB Mile 46.4; WB Mile 21.3	Craggy Gardens Visitor Center gift shop
EB Mile 61.8; WB Mile 5.9	Mt. Mitchell summit parking area concession stand open seasonally; restaurant, also open seasonally is approximately 1.6 miles away on NC 128
EB Mile 67.7; WB Mile 0.0	Black Mtn. Campground office

Water/Restrooms

Water is generally abundant in this segment, and this guide does not attempt to catalog every potential source, keeping in mind that a decent-sized stream in wet weather may completely stop flowing in dry periods. Only larger, named creeks; those useful for wayfinding; and water sources in areas where they are more widely scattered are listed here. **All surface water should be treated before drinking. Water in the Asheville area may be impacted by urban pollution, and we do not recommend drinking it, even treated.**

In addition to surface water on the trail, water and restrooms are available at a few developed locations:

EB Mile 0.0; WB Mile 67.7	Pisgah Inn restaurant and convenience store ◆ 🚻
EB Miles 17.8 -31.0; WB Miles 36.7-49.9	Numerous restaurants and stores in Asheville ◆ 🚻
EB Mile 28.4; WB Mile 39.3	BRP Visitor Center & Headquarters ◆ 🚻
EB Mile 30.8; WB Mile 36.9	Folk Art Center ◆ 🚻
EB Mile 45.6; WB Mile 22.1	Craggy Gardens Picnic Area 🚻
EB Mile 46.4; WB Mile 21.3	Craggy Gardens Visitor Center gift shop ◆ 🚻
EB Mile 61.8; WB Mile 5.9	Mt. Mitchell summit ◆ 🚻
EB Mile 67.7; WB Mile 0.0	Black Mtn. Campground office ◆ 🚻

Hunting

Hunting is allowed throughout the Pisgah National Forest during the hunting season but is prohibited on Blue Ridge Parkway property and in Mt. Mitchell State Park. See www.ncwildlife.org/hunting.aspx for information about seasons and licenses.

Signs/Blazing

The MST in Segment 3 is generally well marked with the MST blaze—a 3-inch white circle—either painted on or affixed to trees or signposts. Within Mt. Mitchell State Park, the trails are also blazed for the state park trail system, and there are informative signs at all the major trail junctions.

Dogs

Dogs are allowed on this segment of the MST, but should always be leashed.

🔺 Camping   🛏 Lodging   Ⓟ Parking   🍴 Food   🚻 Restrooms   Supplies   ◆ Water   ⛺ Picnic

ADDITIONAL INFORMATION

Friends office: 919-825-0297 or info@MountainstoSeaTrail.org

Walt Weber and the Carolina Mountain Club have published an excellent, highly detailed, set of maps and profiles for this segment of the MST entitled *Trail Profiles and Maps: From the Great Smokies to Mount Mitchell and Beyond.* The book, available on Amazon or through a number of outlets in the Asheville area, also includes historical information about, as well as photos and diagrams of, George Vanderbilt's Buck Spring Lodge and Chase Ambler's Rattlesnake Lodge; the ruins of both of these sites are on the MST in Segment 3.

Trail Maps

Google map of the entire MST: www.MountainstoSeaTrail.org/map

BRP map: www.nps.gov/blri/planyourvisit/upload/BLRImap1-1.pdf

Mt. Mitchell State Park map:
www.ncparks.gov/sites/default/files/ncparks/maps-and-brochures/
mount-mitchell-park-map.pdf (*Note:* This map incorrectly shows the route of the MST as following the Commissary Trail at the shortcut described at EB Mile 60.8, WB Mile 4.3 of this guide; the route described in this guide and on signs in the park is correct.)

National Geographic map 785 (Nantahala and Cullasaja Gorges) and
map 779 (Linville Gorge, Mt. Mitchell)

State and Federal Land Management Agency Sites

BRP website: www.nps.gov/blri

National Forests in North Carolina website: www.fs.usda.gov/nfsnc

Mt. Mitchell State Park website:
www.ncparks.gov/mount-mitchell-state-park

Links for other points and organizations of interest

Pisgah Inn website: www.pisgahinn.com

Carolina Mountain Club website (trail maintainers in this segment):
www.carolinamountainclub.org

North Carolina High Peaks Trail Association and Friends of Mt. Mitchell State Park website: nchighpeaks.org

Tourism links

Asheville Convention & Visitors Bureau website:
www.exploreasheville.com

Romantic Asheville website: www.romanticasheville.com

Yancey County Chamber of Commerce website: yanceychamber.com

Pink Turtlehead
Photo by PJ Wetzel, www.pjwetzel.com

PRIMARY PARKING LOCATIONS

**Pisgah Inn (BRP Milepost
[MP] 408.6)**
EB Mile 0.0; WB Mile 67.7

N35.40360, W82.75425

**BRP Stony Bald Overlook
(MP 402.6)**
EB Mile 6.4; WB Mile 61.3
Ⓟ
N35.45385, W82.69383

**BRP Sleepy Gap Parking Area
(MP 397.3)**
EB Mile 12.7; WB Mile 55.0
Ⓟ
N35.46579, W82.6294

**BRP Access Road at French Broad
River (MP 393.7)**
EB Mile 17.8; WB Mile 49.9
Ⓟ
N35.50059, W82.59353

**BRP at Hendersonville Rd.
(MP 388.9)**
EB Mile 23.1; WB Mile 44.6
Ⓟ
N35.51806, W82.52976

BRP at US 74A (MP 384.8)
EB Mile 27.7; WB Mile 40.0
Ⓟ
N35.56209, W82.49373

BRP Visitor Center (MP 384)
EB Mile 28.4; WB Mile 39.3
💧 🚻 Ⓟ
35.56518, W82.48720

Folk Art Center (MP 382)
EB Mile 30.7; WB Mile 37.0
Ⓟ
N35.59292, W82.48099

BRP at Craven Gap (MP 377.4)
EB Mile 35.9; WB Mile 31.8
Ⓟ
N35.64801, W82.49166

**BRP at Tanbark Ridge Tunnel
(MP 376.7)**
EB Mile 39.9; WB Mile 27.8
Ⓟ
N35.66548, W82.46185

**Craggy Gardens Picnic Area
(MP 367.6)**
EB Mile 45.6; WB Mile 22.1
Ⓟ 🚻 🏕
N35.69959, W82.39165

**Craggy Gardens Visitor Center
(MP 364.5)**
EB Mile 46.4; WB Mile 21.3
💧 🚻 🏬 Ⓟ
N35.69979, W82.37983

Coordinates can be entered in your mapping software just like a street address.

Camping Lodging Parking Food Restrooms Supplies Water 🏕Picnic

PRIMARY PARKING LOCATIONS (Continued)

**BRP Walker Knob Overlook
(MP 359.8)**
EB Mile 52.6; WB Mile 15.1
ⓟ
N35.74842, W82.33402

NC 128 Crossing
EB Mile 57.4; WB Mile 10.3
ⓟ
N35.72585, W82.28308

Mt. Mitchell Summit Parking Area
EB Mile 61.8; WB Mile 5.9
ⓟ 💧 🚻 🍴
N35.76622, W82.26525

Black Mtn. Campground Trailhead
EB Mile 67.7; WB Mile 0.0
ⓟ ⛺ 💧 🚻
N35.75110, W82.22024

Coordinates can be entered in your mapping software just like a street address.

Camping Lodging Parking Food Restrooms Supplies Water Picnic

Segment 4 Eastbound

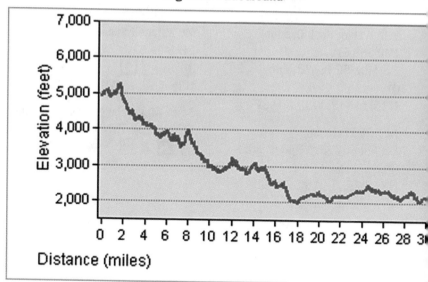

Distance (miles)

Hiking Directions, Eastbound

0.0   Begin Segment 3 at parking lot for the Pisgah Inn (MP 408.6). Continue to the back left corner of the parking lot (as viewed from the BRP), then go up stone stairs at MST signpost and kiosk for Mt. Pisgah Trail System. *Note:* The Pisgah Inn, open seasonally, has lodging, a restaurant, and a store with general supplies. The Mt. Pisgah Campground is nearby; to reach it, turn left on the BRP and walk approximately 0.1 mile to the entrance on the right (see the "Camping and Lodging" section for this segment for more information).

0.3   Continue straight past side trail on right, which leads to overlook.

0.7   Continue straight past junction with Pilot Rock Trail on right.

0.8   Continue straight past junction with Laurel Mtn. Trail on right.

1.0   Continue through clearing with wooden benches on the right and a spectacular view. *Note:* This is the former site of George Vanderbilt's Buck Spring Lodge. Walt Weber's book *Trail Profiles and Maps: From the Great Smokies to Mount Mitchell and Beyond* provides an interesting look at the history and current condition of the lodge site.

Camping   Lodging   Ⓟ Parking   Food   Restrooms   Supplies   Water   Picnic

Elevation Profile

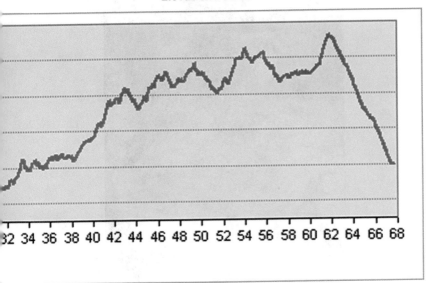

1.1 Continue straight across parking area at Buck Springs Gap Overlook (MP 407.6). Ⓟ

1.3 Reach road at parking area for Mt. Pisgah Trailhead (to your left) and walk along shoulder, then return to trail at stairs and sign for "Shut-In Trail." The trail from here to the French Broad River generally follows the path of, and is sometimes on the bed of, the old carriage road built by George Vanderbilt to connect Biltmore House to Buck Spring Lodge. *Note:* At this parking area (MP 407.6), you are crossing directly over the BRP's Buck Springs Tunnel, so the next time you reach the BRP, it will be from the other side. Ⓟ

3.1 Reach BRP at its junction with NC 151 and turn left to walk along the shoulder of BRP approximately 75 yards, then cross BRP and return to trail at white-blazed signpost. *Note:* There is a small gravel parking area at this junction (MP 405.5). Ⓟ

4.3 Cross parking area at Mills River Valley Overlook (MP 404.5) and continue on trail at far side of parking area. Ⓟ

5.3 Reach clearing and continue up wooden steps toward MST signpost and Big Ridge Overlook (MP 403.6), then cross BRP and continue on trail at white-blazed signpost. Ⓟ

▲ Camping 🛏 Lodging Ⓟ Parking 🍴 Food 🚻 Restrooms 🛒 Supplies 💧 Water �picnic Picnic

Pink Lady's Slippers
Photo by Sharon McCarthy

5.8 Cross BRP.

6.4 Reach Stony Bald Overlook (MP 402.6) and cross BRP at far end of overlook, returning to trail at white-blazed signpost. Ⓟ

7.3 Reach Beaver Dam Gap Overlook (MP 401.7) and walk across the back of parking lot to continue on the trail at far side. Ⓟ

8.0 Cross 4,064-foot Ferrin Knob just below remains of old fire tower on right.

8.4 Bear right where trail comes in from left. *Note:* Just down the other trail is a small stream that could be usable as a water source during high-flow periods. ◍

9.2 At Y-intersection, bear left down steps.

9.3 Cross gravel road leading into Bent Creek Experimental Forest.

9.4 Continue straight where trail heads uphill on right.

11.5 Continue straight past Chestnut Cove Trail on left.

11.8 At Y-intersection, take right fork.

11.9 At intersection with blue-blazed spur trail to BRP, turn left to stay on the MST. *Note:* The spur trail leads approximately 75 yards to parking at the Chestnut Cove Overlook (MP 398.3). ⓟ

12.5 Begin descending a series of switchbacks.

12.7 Where Sleepy Gap Parking Area (MP 397.3) is visible on right, continue on marked trail behind parking area. ⓟ

13.3 At Y-intersection, take right fork.

14.4 Continue straight past short spur trail to BRP on right.

15.6 At T-intersection, continue to right on gravel road. *Note:* There is a gravel parking area on the BRP (MP 359) just to the right of this point. ⓟ

15.7 Turn off gravel road, following white-blazed signpost up a set of concrete-and-wood stairs.

17.3 Cross creek. 💧

17.4 Pass through gate in chain-link fence. You are now entering the North Carolina Arboretum property.

17.5 Just before the trail in front of you enters a rhododendron thicket, make a sharp right turn to continue on the MST.

17.6 Cross small stream, then go through gate in chain-link fence to leave Arboretum property.

17.8 Turn right on BRP access road. *Note:* Parking is available along the shoulder of the access road. ⓟ

18.0 Turn left on BRP, then cross bridge over French Broad River.

18.2 At parking area (MP 393.4), turn right into the woods at MST signpost, then bear left. ⓟ

18.7 Continue straight where trail comes in from right.

18.9 Continue straight across dirt road that passes under BRP.

19.6 Cross BRP.

19.8 Turn left on BRP, then cross bridge over I-26.

19.9 Just past the bridge, turn right on trail marked with MST signpost.

20.2 Continue straight past trail on the right.

20.3 Continue straight past intersection with closed trail, then past another trail on the right.

20.9 Cross footbridge over small creek, then continue straight across gravel road with padlocked gate just to your right.

🔺 Camping   🛏 Lodging   ⓟ Parking   🍴 Food   🚻 Restrooms   🛒 Supplies   💧 Water   🪧 Picnic

21.0 At T-intersection with MST signpost, turn left then bear right and cross footbridge over Dingle Creek.

22.0 Continue straight across gravel road.

22.6 Cross footbridge over Fourmile Branch, then cross smaller footbridge over swampy area.

22.8 Descend stairs, cross trail intersection, then climb stairs on other side.

23.0 Bear right at Y-intersection.

23.1 Turn right on BRP and cross bridge over Hendersonville Rd. *Note:* There is a parking area just across the road from the trail (MP 388.9). Ⓟ

23.2 Turn left onto trail with MST signpost. *Note:* The access road across the BRP leads to Hendersonville Rd., a major thoroughfare in Asheville. Turning left (south) at the bottom of the ramp leads to a number of shopping options, including a Walmart approximately 0.5 mile away. To the right (north) are historic Biltmore Village and downtown Asheville, about 4 and 6 miles away, respectively, along with numerous smaller shopping centers. 🍴 🏬 🛏

23.4 Turn left on BRP, then cross bridge over railroad tracks.

23.5 Turn left onto trail with MST signpost.

23.9 Turn left on BRP, then cross bridge over Sweeten Creek Rd.

24.0 After the bridge, continue on shoulder of BRP for 50 yards, then turn left onto trail with MST signpost.

24.2 Cross footbridge over a small stream.

24.4 Continue straight past trail on the right.

24.5 At Y-intersection with fainter trail leading to BRP, bear left.

24.7 At T-intersection, turn right and follow MST markings.

25.0 Continue straight where larger trail joins from left.

25.1 Continue straight past old roadbed on right, then cross two small streams.

25.5 Cross a small stream.

25.8 Bear right at Y-intersection, then cross small creek.

26.2 Continue straight across old road.

26.3 Cross a small stream.

27.1 Cross a power-line cut.

27.2 Cross a small stream.

🔺 Camping 🛏 Lodging Ⓟ Parking 🍴 Food 🚻 Restrooms 🏬 Supplies 💧 Water ⛰ Picnic

27.3 Continue straight past trail on right.

27.7 Turn left on BRP at gravel parking area (MP 384.8), then cross bridge over US 74A. (P)

27.8 Just beyond end of bridge, turn right on trail with white MST signpost.

28.2 Continue straight past small unmarked spur trail to BRP on left.

28.4 At Y-intersection, take right fork signposted to Folk Art Center. *Note:* The left fork leads 0.3 mile to the BRP Visitor Center & Headquarters (MP 384), which has exhibits about the natural and cultural heritage of the BRP area as well as restrooms and water. It is open from 9 AM to 5 PM daily year-round. ⬤ 🚻 (P)

29.1 Continue straight through power-line cut.

29.3 Go down a flight of stairs, then turn left on dirt road and immediately go through tunnel under I-40.

29.4 After leaving tunnel, cross railroad tracks and continue straight on paved road to cross bridge over Swannanoa River, then at T-intersection continue straight over stile with white blaze and follow white blazes on BRP viaduct across field.

29.5 Cross stile at end of field.

30.1 Turn left on the shoulder of BRP, then cross bridge over US 70.

30.2 After crossing bridge, immediately turn left onto trail marked with MST signpost.

30.4 Continue straight across BRP access road. *Note:* The access road leads to US 70, with heavy strip development in both directions, including an Ingles supermarket approximately 0.5 mile to the right (west). 🍴 🏪

30.7 Continue straight on sidewalk at Folk Art Center parking lot (MP 382). (P)

30.8 Pass plaque on left honoring long-time Carolina Mountain Club volunteer Arch Nichols. Then continue to follow MST signs across access road and turn right onto gravel trail (a self-guided nature trail). *Note:* Continue straight instead to reach the Folk Art Center, which exhibits fine art and crafts from around the Southern Appalachians and has restrooms and water. It is open daily from 9 AM to 6 PM April-December and 9 AM to 5 PM January-March. ⬤ 🚻

30.9 Continue straight past trail on left.

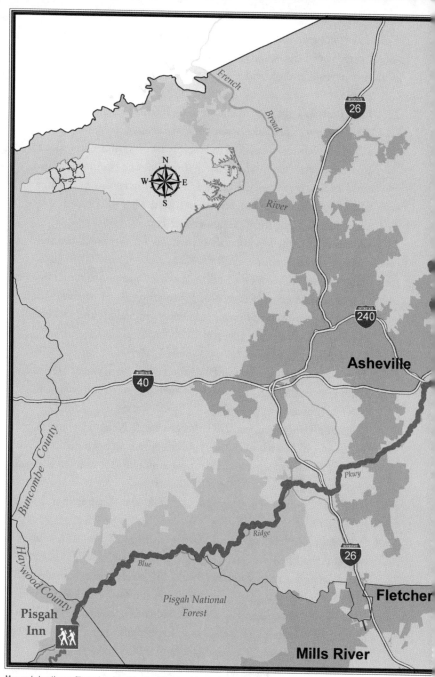

Map and elevation profile produced for Friends of the Mountains-to-Sea Trail by Curtis Belyea, 2016.

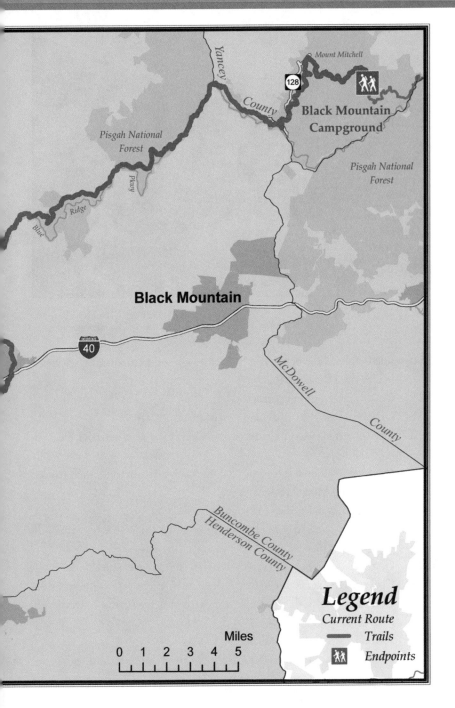

Mount Mitchell

Black Mountain
Campground

Yancey County

Pisgah National
Forest

Pisgah National
Forest

Pkwy

Ridge

Blue

Black Mountain

INTERSTATE
40

McDowell

County

Buncombe County
Henderson County

Miles

0 1 2 3 4 5

Legend

Current Route
— Trails
  Endpoints

Hiking in the Black Mountains
Photo by Jeff Clark www.internetbrothers.org

31.0 Just before a blue blaze on a tree, bear right off nature trail, then cross bridge over Riceville Rd.

31.6 Continue straight past trail on left.

31.8 Cross BRP at gravel parking lot (MP 381.2). Ⓟ

32.7 Pass blue-blazed spur trail to gravel parking area on BRP on left (MP 380.3). Ⓟ

33.1 Pass spur trail on left leading to rock, known locally as "Lunch Rock," overlooking Haw Creek Valley.

34.0 Continue straight onto old roadbed.

34.1 Pass spur trail to gravel parking area on the BRP on the left (MP 379). Ⓟ

34.7 Continue straight past trail on right in sharp curve of MST.

35.9 Cross BRP at Craven Gap, then turn right at T-intersection *Note:* there is parking at the access road a few yards to your left (MP 377.4). Ⓟ

36.7 Ascend a short set of stairs.

37.0 Cross stream, then take the left fork at the Y-intersection. 💧

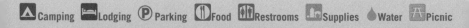

37.6 Continue straight across Elk Mtn. Scenic Hwy. at gravel parking area. Ⓟ

38.0 Pass trail on left, leading to gravel parking area on Ox Creek Rd. Ⓟ

38.3 Continue straight past spur trail on left, leading to Bull Gap gravel parking area on Ox Creek Rd. Ⓟ

38.4 Begin ascending a series of switchbacks.

39.7 Continue straight past the ruins of Rattlesnake Lodge, a summer home built by Asheville physician Chase Ambler in 1903-4. *Note: The trail leading down to your right is the first of two trails leading to a parking area on the BRP at Tanbark Ridge Tunnel (MP 376.7) approximately 0.5 mile away.* Ⓟ

39.9 At remains of an old fireplace, cross second trail on right leading to BRP parking area approximately 0.5 mile away, then cross small stream. Ⓟ

40.1 Turn left at a hairpin turn.

40.5 Cross a small stream—note the springhead on the right—then, at Y-intersection, take right fork (left fork has blue blaze). ◖

43.1 Descend ladder.

43.3 Ascend ladder.

44.4 Turn left on BRP and walk along shoulder approximately 100 yards before returning to trail at MST signpost at edge of grassy clearing.

45.0 At Y-intersection, take left fork.

45.1 Continue straight across Craggy Gardens picnic area access road (MP 367.6). Ⓟ

45.6 Continue straight past short spur trail on left leading to Craggy Gardens picnic area, with restrooms, parking, and picnic facilities. *Note: To reach the trail from the top of the parking area, follow the trail marked with a blue blaze and the MST logo, then turn left on the MST.* Ⓟ 🚻 🛤

45.7 Where trail comes in at sharp angle from left, follow white arrow to right.

46.2 Continue straight through old CCC shelter.

46.4 Turn left where trail is signed to Douglas Falls, then turn right at T-intersection. *Note: Continuing straight leads about 100 yards to the Craggy Gardens Visitor Center (MP 364.5), with water, restrooms, a gift shop, and parking.* ◖ 🚻 🏪 Ⓟ

47.4 Pass Douglas Falls Trail on left.

48.7 Continue straight onto paved road next to building.

48.8 Leave paved road where trail heads into woods on left.

48.9 Cross BRP.

49.0 Continue straight through Graybeard Mtn. Overlook (MP 363.4). Ⓟ

51.3 Continue straight through Glassmine Falls Overlook (MP 361.2). Ⓟ

52.6 Cross BRP at Walker Knob Overlook (MP 359.8), then continue past yellow-blazed trail on left and follow MST sign onto trail parallel to and on right of road. You will soon begin ascending a long series of switchbacks. Ⓟ

53.4 Reach summit ridge and turn right.

54.1 Cross 6,320-foot summit of Blackstock Knob.

55.8 Begin descending a series of switchbacks.

56.2 Cross a small stream that may not have water during dry seasons. ◐

56.4 Continue through clearing with nice lunch rock on right overlooking city of Asheville's water-supply reservoir, then turn left at T-intersection. *Note:* The trail to the right leads to a rock outcrop with views.

57.4 Pass through stile, then cross NC 128 at gravel parking area (which can be easy to miss in a car), pass by trail on right and merge onto wider trail, which is the Buncombe Horse Range Trail. Ⓟ

57.5 Cross stream, then continue straight at sign toward Camp Alice. ◐

57.6 Cross Right Prong of South Toe River. ◐

58.4 Cross South Fork of Upper Creek. ◐

60.5 Cross Lower Creek. ◐

60.8 Turn sharply left onto Commissary Trail at the sign marked with orange diamonds as well as MST white circles. Then pass a second sign to enter Mt. Mitchell State Park. *Note:* If you continue straight, which is also the Commissary Trail, you can avoid the 1.4-mile-long, 900-vertical-foot climb to the summit of Mt. Mitchell. If you choose this alternative, walk 0.5 mile then return to the MST at Mile 63.4.

61.0 Continue straight past gravel road on right.

61.1 Cross Lower Creek, then turn right at sign onto Camp Alice Trail. From this point, you will climb steeply through spruce-fir forest on a trail that is marked with blue squares as well as the MST white circles. *Note:* If you continue straight here, the Mt. Mitchell State Park office is 1.2 miles ahead. ◐

▲ Camping 🛏 Lodging Ⓟ Parking 🍴 Food 🚻 Restrooms 🛒 Supplies ◐ Water ⛱ Picnic

61.5 At sign, pass trail on left and continue on Old Mitchell Trail, marked with yellow circles as well as white circles, then almost immediately take a switchback up the hill. *Note:* The trail to the left is also the Old Mitchell Trail and leads down 1.5 miles to the park office.

61.6 Switchback left where the trail straight ahead is blocked with branches, then switchback right.

61.7 At T-intersection with sign, turn right to stay on Old Mitchell Trail. *Note:* The trail to the left (the Campground Spur Trail) leads 0.3 mile to the Mt. Mitchell State Park Campground. See the "Camping and Lodging" section for this segment for information about camping here.

61.8 At T-intersection, turn right on paved trail. *Note:* Turn left on the paved trail and walk 100 yards to reach the Mt. Mitchell parking lot, with water, restrooms, and a concession stand. The Mt. Mitchell State Park restaurant is approximately 1.6 miles away on the road from the parking lot.

61.9 Pass Mt. Mitchell State Park Environmental Education Center on left, then turn left off paved trail onto Balsam Nature Trail. *Note:* Continue straight on the paved trail for 500 feet to reach the summit of Mt. Mitchell.

62.2 Continue straight past Balsam Nature Trail on left, then pass sign marked "Black Mountain Campground 5.5 miles."

62.6 Pass state-park boundary sign.

63.4 Turn left at T-intersection in clearing with power-line cut, turn left to continue on Mt. Mitchell Trail and MST. *Note:* In the next 0.4 mile, you will cross this power-line cut 5 times while descending a long series of switchbacks.

63.5 Pass campsite on right, then bear right onto Mt. Mitchell Trail at Y-intersection where Buncombe Horse Range Trail continues to left.

63.8 Cross power-line cut for the last time in this series.

64.0 Pass campsite on left.

64.5 Pass campsite on left.

64.7 Bear right at Y-intersection with Mt. Mitchell Trail. *Note:* A few yards down the Mt. Mitchell Trail is Setrock Creek, a good water source.

Camping   Lodging   Parking   Food   Restrooms   Supplies   Water   Picnic

65.2 Pass campsites on right and left.

65.3 Cross Setrock Creek. 💧

65.4 Cross power-line cut.

65.9 Continue straight past Old Mt. Mitchell Trail on left (this is a different trail than the Old Mitchell Trail you followed a few miles ago).

67.4 Cross wooden bridge over Little Mtn. Creek.

67.5 Continue straight across road, turn left at T-intersection, then bear right at Y-intersection.

67.6 At T-intersection, turn right on road.

67.7 Turn right at camp office, cross bridge over South Toe River, and reach parking area on South Toe River Rd. near Black Mtn. Campground and end of Segment 3. *Note:* To reach the parking area by car from the BRP, take NC 80 (at MP 344) toward Burnsville. After the small community of Busick, turn left onto South Toe River Rd. This road will eventually turn to gravel and follow the river. At the gravel road intersection, turn right and continue to follow the road right. The parking area is on your left just before a bridge and the entrance to the Black Mtn. Campground on the right. See the "Camping and Lodging" section for this segment for information about camping at the Black Mtn. Campground. Ⓟ 💧 🚻

Hiking Directions, Westbound

0.0   Turn left out of the parking area on South Toe River Rd. near Black Mtn. Campground to begin Segment 3, then cross bridge over South Toe River and turn left at sign pointing to Mt. Mitchell. *Note:* To reach the parking area by car from the BRP, take NC 80 (at MP 344) toward Burnsville. After the small community of Busick, turn left onto South Toe River Rd. This road will eventually turn to gravel and follow the river. At the gravel road intersection, turn right and continue to follow the road right. The parking area is on your left just before a bridge and the entrance to the Black Mtn. Campground on the right. See the "Camping and Lodging" section for this segment for information about camping at the Black Mtn. Campground. Ⓟ ⛺ 💧 🚻

0.1   Bear left at Y-intersection with trail to Briar Bottom Group Camping.

0.2   Continue straight past trail on right, turn right at signpost for Mt. Mitchell Trail, then continue straight across road.

0.3   Cross wooden bridge over Little Mtn. Creek.

1.8   Bear left at Y-intersection to follow Higgins Bald Trail.

2.3   Cross power-line cut.

2.4   Cross Setrock Creek. 💧

2.5   Pass campsites on right and left. ⛺

3.0   Continue straight past Mt. Mitchell Trail on right. *Note:* A few yards down the Mt. Mitchell Trail is Setrock Creek, a good water source. 💧

3.2   Pass campsite on right. ⛺

3.7   Pass campsite on right and begin ascending a long series of switchbacks. ⛺

3.9   Cross power-line cut. *Note:* In the next 0.4 mile, you will cross this power-line cut 5 times.

4.2   Continue straight past trail on right marked Buncombe Horse Range (the trail you are continuing on is also called the Buncombe Horse Range Trail), then pass campsite on left. ⛺

4.3   Reach the power-line cut for the last time at a well-marked junction and turn right onto the Mt. Mitchell Trail, which is marked with

⛺ Camping   🛏 Lodging   Ⓟ Parking   🍴 Food   🚻 Restrooms   🏬 Supplies   💧 Water   ⛱ Picnic blue diamonds as well as the MST white circles. *Note:* If you continue straight, you will be on the Commissary Trail, which avoids the 1.1-mile-long, 900-vertical-foot climb to the summit of Mt. Mitchell. If you choose this alternative, walk 0.5 mile then return to the MST at mile 6.9.

5.1 Pass state-park boundary sign.

5.5 Pass sign marked "Black Mtn. Campground 5.5 miles" (in the other direction), then pass Balsam Nature Trail on right.

5.8 Continue straight onto paved trail, then pass Mt. Mitchell State Park Environmental Education Center on right. *Note:* Turn left on the paved trail and walk 500 feet to reach the summit of Mt. Mitchell.

5.9 Turn left onto Old Mitchell Trail at sign. *Note:* Continuing straight on the paved trail for 100 yards leads to the Mt. Mitchell parking lot, with water, restrooms, and a concession stand. The Mt. Mitchell State Park restaurant is approximately 1.6 miles away on the road from the parking lot. Ⓟ 💧 🚻 🍴

6.0 Turn left at sign to stay on Old Mitchell Trail. *Note:* The trail straight ahead (the Campground Spur Trail) leads 0.3 mile to the Mt. Mitchell State Park Campground. See the "Camping and Lodging" section for this segment for information about camping here. 🔺

6.1 Make two quick switchbacks, left then right. At the second one, a trail from the left is blocked.

6.2 At sign, pass trail on right and continue on Camp Alice Trail, marked with blue squares as well as white circles. *Note:* The trail to the right is the continuation of the Old Mitchell Trail and leads down 1.5 miles to the park office.

6.6 Turn left on gravel road, then cross Lower Creek. *Note:* If you turn right here, the Mt. Mitchell State Park office is 1.2 miles ahead. 💧

6.7 Continue straight past gravel road on left.

6.9 Pass sign to leave Mt. Mitchell State Park, then make a sharp right turn onto the Buncombe Horse Range Trail just before a small stream.

7.2 Cross Lower Creek. 💧

9.3 Cross South Fork of Upper Creek. 💧

10.1 Cross Right Prong of South Toe River. 💧

🔺Camping 🛏Lodging Ⓟ Parking 🍴Food 🚻Restrooms 🏪Supplies 💧Water 🏕Picnic

Sunlight filtering through clouds over Asheville
Photo by Matt Mutel

10.2 Continue straight past sign marked for Buncombe Horse Range Trail, South Toe River Rd., and Camp Alice, then cross stream.

10.3 At Y-intersection, take right fork with white marker, then cross NC 128 at gravel parking area (which can be easy to miss in a car) and pass through a stile. *Note:* If you continue straight until you reach the road, you went too far but can turn right on the road and go 100 yards to the correct crossing, marked with MST signs. Ⓟ

11.3 At Y-intersection, take right fork then continue through clearing with nice lunch rock on left overlooking city of Asheville's water-supply reservoir. *Note:* The left fork leads to a rock outcrop with views.

11.5 Cross a small stream that may not have water during dry seasons, then begin ascending a series of switchbacks.

13.6 Cross 6,320-foot summit of Blackstock Knob.

14.3 Just before trail straight ahead almost disappears, turn left and head down a steep hill. You soon begin descending a long series of switchbacks.

15.1 Continue past yellow-blazed trail on right, then cross BRP at Walker Knob Overlook (MP 359.8). Ⓟ

16.4 Continue straight through Glassmine Falls Overlook (MP 361.2). Ⓟ

18.7 Continue straight through Graybeard Mtn. Overlook (MP 363.4). Ⓟ

18.8 Cross BRP.

▲ Camping 🛏 Lodging Ⓟ Parking 🍴 Food 🚻 Restrooms 🏪 Supplies 💧 Water 🧺 Picnic

18.9 Bear right on paved road.

19.0 At building on your right, continue straight onto trail.

20.3 Pass Douglas Falls Trail on right.

21.3 Turn left, then right at T-intersection. *Note:* Going left at the second turn will take you about 100 yards to the Craggy Gardens Visitor Center (MP 364.5), with water, restrooms, a gift shop, and parking. 🌢 🚻 🏪 Ⓟ

21.5 Continue straight through old CCC shelter.

22.0 At Y-intersection, take left fork.

22.1 Continue straight past short spur trail on right leading to Craggy Gardens picnic area (MP 367.6), with restrooms, parking, and picnic facilities. The unmarked trail is between two signs noting that the MST is closed to horses and bicycles. *Note:* To reach the trail from the top of the parking area, follow the trail marked with a blue blaze and the MST logo, then turn right on the MST. Ⓟ 🚻 🏕

22.6 Continue straight across Craggy Gardens picnic area access road, continuing on trail to left of gravel road. Ⓟ

22.7 Turn right at T-intersection.

23.3 Turn right on BRP and walk along shoulder approximately 100 yards before returning to trail at MST signpost.

24.4 Descend ladder.

24.6 Ascend ladder.

27.2 Pass blue-blazed trail on right, then cross a small stream—note the springhead on the left. 🌢

27.6 Turn right at a hairpin turn.

27.8 Cross a small stream, then, at remains of old chimney, cross trail marked with blue blaze. The trail to the left is the first of two trails leading to the parking area on the BRP at Tanbark Ridge Tunnel (MP 376.7) approximately 0.5 mile away. Ⓟ

28.0 Continue straight past second trail to BRP parking area and ruins of Rattlesnake Lodge, a summer home built by Asheville physician Chase Ambler in 1903-4. Ⓟ

29.2 Begin descending a series of switchbacks.

29.4 At Y-intersection, take left fork. *Note:* The right fork leads to Bull Gap gravel parking area on Ox Creek Rd. Ⓟ

29.7 Pass trail on right leading to gravel parking area on Ox Creek Rd. Ⓟ

🏕 Camping 🛏 Lodging Ⓟ Parking 🍴 Food 🚻 Restrooms 🏪 Supplies 🌢 Water 🏕 Picnic

30.1 Continue straight across Elk Mtn. Scenic Hwy. at gravel parking area. Ⓟ

30.7 Cross stream. ◢

31.0 Descend a short set of stairs.

31.8 Just before a Y-intersection, where the left trail passes a blue-blazed tree, take steps down and to the left as shown by a white arrow, then cross the BRP. *Note:* Continuing straight leads to parking area at Craven Gap (MP 377.4). Ⓟ

33.0 Continue straight past trail on left in sharp curve of MST.

33.6 Pass spur trail to gravel parking area on the BRP on the right (MP 379). Ⓟ

33.7 Where roadbed is blocked by brush pile, bear right up wooden steps.

34.6 Pass spur trail on right leading to rock, known locally as "Lunch Rock," overlooking Haw Creek Valley.

35.0 Pass blue-blazed spur trail to gravel parking area on BRP on right (MP 380.3). Ⓟ

35.9 Cross BRP at gravel parking lot (MP 381.2). Ⓟ

36.1 Continue straight past trail on right.

36.7 Cross bridge over Riceville Rd., then, at T-intersection where tree on the left has a double white blaze, turn left. This is beginning of the Folk Art Center's self-guided nature trail.

36.8 Continue straight past trail on left.

36.9 At sidewalk, turn right and cross access road to pick up sidewalk around parking lot. Then pass plaque on right honoring long-time Carolina Mountain Club volunteer Arch Nichols. *Note:* Turn left instead to reach the Folk Art Center (MP 382), which exhibits fine art and crafts from around the Southern Appalachians and has restrooms and water. It is open daily from 9 AM to 6 PM April-December and 9 AM to 5 PM January-March. ◢ ⊞

37.0 At end of parking lot, bear left onto trail marked with MST signpost. Ⓟ

37.3 Continue straight across BRP access road. *Note:* The access road leads to US 70, with heavy strip development in both directions, including an Ingles supermarket approximately 0.5 mile to the right (west). ⊞ ⊟

Evening at Bee Tree Gap, Great Craggy Mountains
Photo by Stephen Schoof

37.5 Turn right onto BRP shoulder and immediately cross bridge over US 70.

37.6 Turn right into the woods at MST signpost.

38.2 Cross stile with white blaze, then follow white blazes under BRP viaduct across field.

38.3 Cross stile at end of field, continue straight on bridge over Swannanoa River towards railroad tracks, then cross railroad tracks and pass through tunnel under I-40.

38.4 At end of tunnel, turn right on white-blazed trail, then go up stairs.

▲ Camping 🛏 Lodging Ⓟ Parking 🍴 Food 🚻 Restrooms 🏬 Supplies 💧 Water ⛱ Picnic

38.6 Continue straight through power-line cut.

39.3 Where trail to the BRP Visitor Center comes in from right, bear left towards US 74. *Note:* The BRP Visitor Center & Headquarters (MP 384) is 0.3 mile down the trail on the right. It has exhibits about the natural and cultural heritage of the BRP area as well as restrooms and water. It is open from 9 AM to 5 PM daily year-round. ◆ 🚻 Ⓟ

39.5 Continue straight past small unmarked spur trail to BRP on right.

39.9 Turn left on BRP, then cross bridge over US 74A.

40.0 At parking area at end of bridge (MP 384.8), turn right onto trail marked with MST signpost. Ⓟ

40.4 Continue straight past trail on left.

40.5 Cross a small stream.

40.6 Cross a power-line cut.

41.4 Cross a small stream.

41.5 Continue straight across old road.

41.9 Cross small creek, then continue straight past trail on right.

42.2 Cross a small stream.

42.6 Cross two small streams, then continue straight past old roadbed on left.

42.7 At Y-intersection where larger trail continues down to the right, bear left on smaller trail.

43.0 Bear left at Y-intersection.

43.2 Continue straight past fainter trail leading to BRP on left.

43.3 Continue straight past trail on the left.

43.5 Cross footbridge over a small stream.

43.7 Turn right on BRP, then cross bridge over Sweeten Creek Rd.

43.8 At end of bridge, turn right onto trail with MST signpost.

44.2 Turn right on BRP, then cross bridge over railroad tracks.

44.3 Cross bridge over railroad tracks, then turn right on trail with MST signpost.

44.5 Turn right onto BRP, then cross bridge over Hendersonville Rd. *Note:* The access road across the BRP leads to Hendersonville Rd., a major thoroughfare in Asheville. Turning left (south) at the bottom of the ramp leads to a number of shopping options, including a Walmart approximately 0.5 mile away. To the right (north) are historic Biltmore Village and downtown Asheville, about 4 and 6

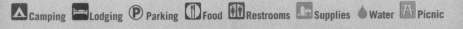

miles away, respectively, along with numerous smaller shopping centers. 🍴 🛒

44.6 After passing access road, and just before gate, turn left on trail marked with MST signpost. *Note:* There is a parking area just across the road from the trail (MP 388.9). Ⓟ

44.7 Continue straight past trail coming in from right.

44.9 Descend stairs, cross trail intersection, then climb stairs on other side.

45.1 Cross small footbridge over swampy area, then larger footbridge over Fourmile Branch.

45.7 Continue straight across gravel road.

46.7 Cross footbridge over Dingle Creek, bear left and slightly uphill, then turn right at MST signpost.

46.8 Cross gravel road with padlocked gate just to your left, then cross footbridge over small creek.

47.4 At Y-intersection, bear right, then continue straight past intersection with closed trail.

47.5 Continue straight past trail on the left.

47.8 Turn left on BRP, then cross bridge over I-26.

47.9 Just past the bridge, turn right on trail marked with MST signpost.

48.1 Cross BRP.

48.8 Continue straight across dirt road that passes under BRP.

49.0 At Y-intersection, where left trail is marked with a blue diamond with an arrow, continue straight as shown on MST signpost.

49.5 Bear right at a Y-intersection, come out to parking area (MP 393.4), then turn left on BRP and cross bridge over French Broad River. Ⓟ

49.7 Just after crossing bridge, turn right on BRP access road.

49.9 Just past road gate, turn left on trail marked with white-blazed signpost and informational sign titled "Shut-In Trail." The trail from here to the Mt. Pisgah Trailhead parking area generally follows the path of, and is sometimes on the bed of, the old carriage road built by George Vanderbilt to connect Biltmore House to Buck Spring Lodge, his hunting lodge on Mt. Pisgah. *Note:* Parking is available along the shoulder of the access road. Ⓟ

50.1 Pass through gate in chain-link fence, then cross small stream. You are now entering the North Carolina Arboretum property.

△ Camping 🛏 Lodging Ⓟ Parking 🍴 Food 🚻 Restrooms 🛒 Supplies 💧 Water ⛺ Picnic

Mt. Mitchell summit
Photo by Jake Blood

50.2 At T-intersection, turn left.

50.3 Pass through gate in chain-link fence to leave the Arboretum property.

50.4 Cross creek. 💧

52.0 Turn left on an old gravel road.

52.1 At open area showing signs of erosion, leave gravel road to the left and follow white-blazed signpost up the trail. *Note:* There is a gravel parking area on the BRP (MP 359) just to the left of this point. Ⓟ

53.3 Continue straight past short spur trail to BRP on left.

54.4 Where a trail comes in at a sharp angle from below on the right, continue straight on MST.

55.0 Where Sleepy Gap Parking Area is visible on right, continue on marked trail behind parking area, then begin climbing a series of switchbacks. Ⓟ

🔺Camping 🛏️Lodging Ⓟ Parking 🍴Food 🚻Restrooms 🏬Supplies 💧Water ⛱️Picnic

55.8 At intersection with blue-blazed spur trail to BRP, turn right towards MST signpost. *Note:* The spur trail leads approximately 75 yards to parking at the Chestnut Cove Overlook (MP 398.3). Ⓟ

55.9 Continue straight where trail comes in at sharp angle from right.

56.2 Continue straight past Chestnut Cove Trail on right.

58.3 Continue straight where trail heads uphill on left.

58.4 Cross gravel road leading into Bent Creek Experimental Forest.

58.5 Turn left at T-intersection.

59.3 At Y-intersection, bear left up trail marked "Shut-In Trail." *Note:* Just down the other trail is a small stream that could be usable as a water source during high-flow periods. ◆

59.7 Cross 4,064-foot Ferrin Knob just below remains of old fire tower on left.

60.4 Reach Beaver Dam Gap Overlook (MP 401.7) and walk across the back of parking lot to continue on the trail at far side. Ⓟ

61.3 Cross BRP, then walk through Stony Bald Overlook (MP 402.6) and return to trail at far right corner of parking area. Ⓟ

61.9 Cross BRP.

62.4 Cross BRP at Big Ridge Overlook (MP 403.6), then turn right at MST signpost at far right corner of parking area and follow trail down wooden stairs and into the woods. Ⓟ

63.4 Cross parking area at Mills River Valley Overlook (MP 404.5) and continue on trail at far side of parking area. Ⓟ

64.6 Turn left to walk on shoulder of BRP approximately 75 yards, then cross at the junction with NC 151 and enter woods on trail marked with white blazes and wooden vehicle barriers. *Note:* There is a small gravel parking area at this junction (MP 405.5). Ⓟ

66.4 Reach road at parking area for Mt. Pisgah Trailhead (to your right) and walk along shoulder approximately 50 yards, returning to the trail at white-blazed signpost. *Note:* At this parking area (MP 407.6), you are crossing directly over the BRP's Buck Springs Tunnel, so the next time you reach the BRP, it will be from the other side. Ⓟ

66.6 Continue straight across parking area at Buck Springs Gap Overlook (MP 407.6). Ⓟ

66.7 Continue through clearing with wooden benches on the right and a spectacular view. Note: This is the former site of George Vanderbilt's Buck Spring Lodge. Walt Weber's book *Trail Profiles and Maps: From the Great Smokies to Mt. Mitchell and Beyond* provides an interesting look at the history and current condition of the lodge site.

66.9 Continue straight past junction with Laurel Mtn. Trail on left.

67.0 Continue straight past junction with Pilot Rock Trail on left.

67.4 Continue straight past side trail on left, which leads to overlook.

67.7 Come down stone stairs to parking lot at the Pisgah Inn (MP 408.6) and the western end of Segment 3. *Note:* The Pisgah Inn, open seasonally, has lodging, a restaurant, and a store with general supplies. The Mt. Pisgah Campground is nearby; to reach it, turn left on the BRP and walk approximately 0.1 mile to the entrance on the right (see the "Camping and Lodging" section for this segment for more information).

Linville Gorge on a good day
Photo by William Dolling

Gorges, Peaks, and Waterfalls—MST Segment 4

BLACK MOUNTAIN CAMPGROUND TO BEACON HEIGHTS
By Robert Trawick

Hikers on this 75-mile segment through the Pisgah National Forest follow forested ridgelines, climb peaks to dramatic views, forge rivers, and meander along creeks that lead to stunning waterfalls and crashing whitewater. The segment is very remote, with long departures from roads and little access to amenities.

Traveling eastbound, the trail leaves Black Mountain Campground on the South Toe River and climbs gradually to the Blue Ridge Parkway (BRP),

at the Continental Divide to the Tennessee Valley. It travels through mostly mature forest in the Pisgah National Forest or along the BRP.

The trail then descends to the North Fork of the Catawba River and climbs Bald and Dobson Knobs, among the most challenging ascents on the entire MST. From these heights, hikers see some of the most spectacular views of the region, from Lake James to Little Switzerland.

The next part of the trail offers views of the impressive Linville Gorge, as it descends to the Linville River on the west side then climbs to the eastern lip of the gorge at Shortoff Mountain and follows its eastern edge. Because this popular part of the trail has had frequent forest fires, there are stretches with little water or shade from the Linville River until descending again at Table Rock.

The trail then dips into remote wild-trout waters located in areas nominated for wilderness status. It follows tributaries in the western Wilson Creek basin to the confluence of Harper and Raider Camp Creeks and then climbs along Harper Creek before hopping over a ridge to Lost Cove Creek and Gragg Prong. The trail follows these streams until it nears the BRP at Grandmother Mountain and Beacon Heights. Much of this part of the trail travels alongside crashing wild streams and rocky outcrops, which also offer picturesque cascades and waterfalls. This area was heavily timbered in the early 20th century and the trail often follows the old roads and railroad beds. One may look for traces of once vigorous human activity among the resurgent timber, in the sagging banks of these passages, and in the hints of washed-out and vanished bridges and settlements and wonder how nature has reclaimed these valleys and coves.

If you are interested in an overnight backpacking trip, this segment may be divided into 4 sections of roughly similar lengths. The first 19.6-mile section is between Black Mountain Campground and US 221 at the Forest Service Work Center at Woodlawn. The second 13.6-mile section is between US 221 at Woodlawn Work Center and Old NC 105. The third 19.5-mile section is between Old NC 105 and NC 181. The fourth 22.5-mile section is between NC 181 and Beacon Heights on the BRP.

HIGHLIGHTS INCLUDE

- Spectacular views of Linville Gorge, which drops 2,000 feet into the valleys below the ridges, as well as surrounding areas with views of Lake Tahoma, Lake James, and Pisgah National Forest

- Impressive promontories such as Dobson and Bald Knobs, the Pinnacle, the Chimneys, Shortoff Mountain, Table Rock, and Hawksbill

- Several waterfalls including Steels Creek, South Harper Creek, Harper Creek, Hunt Fish, and Gragg Prong Falls

South Harper Creek Falls on a cold January day, when the falls are partially frozen
Photo by Robert Trawick

Total Distance: 75.2 miles (73 miles are on trails or abandoned logging roads and less than 3 miles are on gravel roads)
Difficulty: Moderate to very difficult—the section hiking down and out of Linville Gorge from the Linville River is strenuous.

Trail Updates

When planning your trip using this guide, take a moment to see whether Friends of the Mountains-to-Sea Trail (Friends) has posted any updates about the trail route by visiting Friends' "Trail Updates" page at www. MountainstoSeaTrail.org/updates.

Shuttle and Guide Services

Danny Bernstein maintains a list of people who provide shuttle services between Heintooga Rd. (Segment 1A) and Black Mtn. Campground (the western end of Segment 4). The list is at www.hikertohiker.net/hiking/mountains-sea-trail-heintooga-road-black-mountain-campground.

EB Miles 52.7-75.2; WB Miles 0.0-22.5
HikeMore Adventures, 9041 NC 181, Jonas Ridge, 28641, 828-595-HIKE or 828-733-2303 (after hours), info@hikemoreadventures.com; www.hikemoreadventures.com. HikeMore Adventures provides shuttles between the Woodlawn Work Center on US 221 (Segment 4 WB Mile 19.7; WB Mile 55.5) and Aho Gap (Segment 5 EB Mile 30.2; WB Mile 60.1), as well as guide services in the Linville Gorge and Harpers Creek wildernesses. Their Base Camp, about 5 miles north of the MST on NC 181 (Segment 4 EB Mile 52.7; WB Mile 22.5), also has a store with hiking supplies.

Camping on the Trail

With certain restrictions, camping is readily available on this trail segment, which falls almost entirely within the Pisgah National Forest. The only campground directly on the trail is listed below, followed by information about backpack camping along the trail.

Eastbound (EB) Mile 0.0; Westbound (WB) Mile 75.2
Black Mtn. Campground, 50 Black Mtn. Campground Rd., Burnsville, 28714, 828-675-5616. Open April-October, primitive sites, with water, restrooms, and showers. Camping is $22/night, first come, first serve. Cash or check only.

Except in the Linville Gorge Wilderness, Wilson Creek, and Lost Cove Creek areas, primitive camping is allowed anywhere in the Pisgah National Forest. A number of the most obvious backcountry sites are noted in the hiking directions below, but there has been no attempt to completely catalog all suitable sites.

In Linville Gorge Wilderness, Wilson Creek, and Lost Cove Creek areas, free camping permits are required on weekends and holidays from May 1-Oct. 31. Permits are not required Nov. 1-April 30 or for visitors who do not stay overnight. Reservations are taken on a first-come, first-serve basis, beginning the first working day of each previous month. For example, reservations for wilderness camping permits for June are accepted starting the first working day of May. Each visitor or group may get one weekend permit per month and may stay for up to three consecutive days and two nights.

Permits for campsites in Linville Gorge Wilderness, Wilson Creek, and Lost Cove Creek areas can be obtained from Grandfather Ranger District, 109 Lawing Drive, Nebo, 28761, 828-652-2144; grandfatherrd@fs.fed. us. Permits are issued by the district ranger office by mail or in person.

Regulations regarding camping near Linville Gorge Wilderness are at www.fs.usda.gov/generalinfo/nfsnc/recreation/camping-cabins/general info/?groupid=62891&recid=48974.

Camping is prohibited on all BRP property, which encompasses roughly EB Miles 5.3-8.1 and 74.8-75.2; WB Miles 0.0-0.4 and 67.1-69.9.

Before setting up a backcountry camp, please confirm that you are in a legal camping area.

Other Lodging and Campgrounds

Additional lodging within driving distance of the trail is available in Morganton and Marion and at other sites listed below. See the "Additional Information" section of this trail guide for tourism websites.

Near EB Mile 19.7; WB Mile 55.5 (4.0 miles south on US 221 to Marion; a few are listed here)
Sportsman Inn, 40 US 221, Marion, 28752, 828-659-7525.
Comfort Inn, 178 US 70W/221 Bypass/US 70 intersection, Marion, 28752, 828-652-4888.

Near EB Mile 19.7; WB Mile 55.5 or EB Mile 52.7; WB Mile 22.5 Blue Ridge View Farm. Aram and Linda Attarian make a loft apartment on their farm near Morganton available to MST hikers/backpackers. The loft has heat/AC, full bath, and an efficiency kitchen (no stove, has microwave, small refrigerator), and sleeps 4. They will provide shuttles. The cost is $80/night, and reservations can be made through Airbnb (look for Blue Ridge View Farm on the Airbnb website) or contact Aram Attarian directly at 919-815-8869. Be sure to mention that you are an MST hiker, and they will donate 10% of nightly fees to Friends.

Near EB Mile 52.7; WB Mile 22.5
10 miles from parking area at MP 21 on NC 181: Steele Creek Campground, 7081 NC 181, Morganton, 28655, 828-433-5660; www.steelecreekpark.com. $25; waterslide, swimming pool. Cash or check only. *Note*: the campground is spelled differently than the creek.

Near EB Mile 52.7; WB Mile 22.5
9 miles from parking area at MP 21 on NC 181: Daniel Boone Family Campground, 7360 NC 181, Morganton, 28655, 828-433-1200. No website and no cell service at campground but plenty of other amenities.

Near EB Mile 66.6; WB Mile 8.9
3 miles from Hunt Fish Falls parking area: US Forest Service Mortimer Campground www.fs.usda.gov/recarea/nfsnc/recreation/camping-cabins/recarea/?recid=49006&act; $10 nightly fee; flush toilets & showers; open April 1 to October 31.

Near EB Mile 75.2; WB Mile 0.0
3 miles south on US 221: Town of Linville.
8 miles east on the MST: campground at Grandfather Mtn. State Park, 9872 NC 105 S., Banner Elk, 28604, 828-963-9522. Primitive tent campsites have drinking water and fire rings. The park asks that you make a reservation by phone number above or online at www.ncparks.gov/Visit/parks/grmo/main.php

Food/Supplies/Services/Post Office
There are no amenities directly on the trail. The nearest towns are Linville, Marion, and Morganton.

▲ Camping　🛏 Lodging　Ⓟ Parking　🍴 Food　🚻 Restrooms　🏬 Supplies　💧 Water　🪑 Picnic

EB Mile 19.7; WB Mile 55.5 (2.1 miles south on US 221)	KG's Quik Stop, 4613 US 221, Marion, 28753, 828-756-4975
Near EB Mile 52.7; WB Mile 22.5 (5.0 miles to Jonas Ridge)	Mountain Crossing Mercantile, 9041 NC 181, Jonas Ridge, 28641, 828-733-1488
	Jonas Ridge post office, 9042 NC 18, 28641, 828-733-4711; weekdays 12:30 to 4:30; Saturday, 8:30 to 11:30
Near EB Mile 75.2; WB Mile 0.0	Town of Linville is 3 miles south of BRP from Beacon Heights on US 221.
	Linville post office, 4235 Mitchell Ave., 28646, 828-733-5745; weekdays 8:00 to noon & 1:00 to 4:00; Saturday, 8:00 to 11:30

Water/Restrooms

Water is generally abundant in this segment except between EB Mile 4.0 and EB Mile 16.7 (WB Mile 57.7 and WB Mile 71.2) where the trail follows a ridgeline. The hiking directions below do not attempt to catalog every potential source, keeping in mind that a decent-sized stream in wet weather may stop flowing completely in dry periods. Only larger, named creeks; those useful for wayfinding; and water sources in areas where they are more widely scattered are listed here. All surface water should be treated before drinking.

In addition to surface water on the trail, water and/or restrooms are available at the following sites.

EB Mile 0.0; WB Mile 75.2	Black Mtn. Campground
EB Mile 19.7; WB Mile 55.5	Woodlawn Work Center
EB Mile 44.3; WB Mile 30.9	Table Rock Picnic Area

Camping Lodging Parking Food Restrooms Supplies Water Picnic

Hunting

Hunting is allowed throughout the Pisgah National Forest during hunting season and is prohibited on BRP property. Linville Gorge Wilderness Area is very popular as a hunting destination. See www.ncwildlife.org/hunting.aspx for information about seasons and licenses. During hunting season, hikers and any dogs accompanying them should wear blaze orange.

Signs/Blazing

Much of this segment travels through wilderness areas, so even MST blazing may be sparse. There is some signage along forest service roads in the vicinity of the Linville Gorge Wilderness Area. There are some blazed trails in the Harper Creek and Lost Cove Creek areas.

Special Considerations

The Linville River is approximately 60 yards wide at the crossing point. The water is usually at least knee deep, but it can be much higher and dangerous after rains and in cold weather. The hiking directions in this guide offer an alternate route to cross the river via a bridge if you reach the river when it is at dangerous levels.

There have been several major forest fires in this segment in recent years. As a result, there are sections where there are no large trees offering shade and some areas may appear rather desolate after the fires.

- All hikers should be able to identify and closely watch for two poisonous snakes—the copperhead and timber rattler.

- Fire can be a problem during dry periods. Please use fire rings and extinguish fires completely before leaving.

- Lock your car and carry valuables with you. Thieves can easily gain access to your car and its trunk.

- Carry a map and compass and let someone know where you plan to be and when you will return.

- Dogs are permitted on this segment, but should be leashed at all times.

ADDITIONAL INFORMATION

Friends office: 919-825-0297 or info@MountainstoSeaTrail.org

Pisgah National Forest:
www.fs.usda.gov/recarea/nfsnc/recarea/?recid=48114

Grandfather Ranger District, 109 Lawing Dr., Nebo, 28761, 828-652-2144

Appalachian Ranger District, 632 Manor Rd., Mars Hill, 28754, 828-698-9694

Linville Gorge: www.lgmaps.org

Yancey County: yanceychamber.com

McDowell County and Marion: www.mcdowellchamber.com

Burke County and Morganton: www.discoverburkecounty.com

Avery County and Linville: www.averycounty.com

Caldwell County and Lenoir: www.explorecaldwell.com

Trail Maps

Google map of entire MST: www.MountainstoSeaTrail.org/map

Linville Gorge and Mount Mitchell (National Geographic Map #779): www.natgeomaps.com/
linville-gorge-mount-mitchell-pisgah-national-forest

South Toe River, Mount Mitchell and Big Ivy (US Forest Service): www.theforeststore.com/product/
south-toe-river-mount-mitchell-big-ivy-trail-maps

Linville Gorge Wilderness (US Forest Service): www.theforeststore.com/
product/linville-gorge-wildnerness

Wilson Creek/Harper Creek/Lost Cove Areas: Wilson Creek Visitor Center, 7805 Brown Mtn. Beach Rd., Collettsville, 28611, 828-759-0005; available at www.nationalforestmapstore.com/product-p/nc-16.htm

Other Valuable Links

Wilson Creek Visitor Center:
www.explorecaldwell.com/wilson-creek-visitor-center

Cradle of Forestry Interpretive Association: www.cfaia.org

Overmountain Victory Trail Association: www.nps.gov/ovvi

Ray's Weather: www.raysweather.com

Avery County: www.averyweather.com

McDowell County: www.mcdowellweather.com

PRIMARY PARKING LOCATIONS

Black Mtn. Campground on Forest Service Rd. (FS) 472 (South Toe River Rd.)
EB Mile 0.0; WB Mile 75.2
Ⓟ 🔺 💧 🚻
N35.751262, W82.220684

Singecat Ridge Overlook (BRP Milepost [MP] 345.3)
EB Mile 6.2; WB Mile 69.0
Ⓟ
N35.756419, W82.176647

BRP Intersection with NC 80 at Buck Creek Gap (MP 344)
EB Mile 7.8; WB Mile 67.4
Ⓟ
N35.770427, W82.164191

Green Mtn. Rd. Opposite the Forest Service's Woodlawn Work Center
EB Mile 19.7; WB Mile 55.5
Ⓟ 🏕 🚻
N35.767766, W82.042125

Bald Mtn. Trail Rd.
EB Mile 20.0; WB Mile 55.2
Ⓟ
N35.766256, W82.040740
Four-wheel drive to parking is advised. The gate for this road may be locked. Check with the ranger station at 828-652-2144 if you are hoping to park there.

FS 106 (Dobson Knob Rd.)
EB Mile 30.4; WB Mile 44.8
Ⓟ
N35.8200, W81.95942

Old NC 105/Kistler Memorial Hwy.
EB Mile 33.2; WB Mile 42.0
Ⓟ
N35.81415, W81.93758

Improved Parking Area Heading into Linville Gorge at the Pinnacle
EB Mile 34.0; WB Mile 41.2
Ⓟ
N35.82229, W81.93120

NC 126, Entrance to NC Wildlife Game Lands
EB Mile 37.1; WB Mile 38.1
Ⓟ
N35.80018, W81.88173

End of Wolf Pit Rd.
EB Mile 38.3; WB Mile 36.9
Ⓟ
N35.824155, W81.889419

Table Rock Parking Lot
EB Mile 44.3; WB Mile 30.9
Ⓟ 🏕 🚻
N35.886467, W81.884597

Coordinates can be entered in your mapping software just like a street address.

 Camping Lodging Parking Food Restrooms  Supplies Water Picnic

PRIMARY PARKING LOCATIONS (Page 2)

FS 496 Just Before the Intersection with FS 210
EB Mile 46.3; WB Mile 28.9
℗
N35.896625, W81.869542

FS 496, 1.2 Miles from NC 181 at Ripshin Ridge
EB Mile 51.5; WB Mile 23.7
℗
N35.942106, W81.858103

NC 181 near FS 496 (MP 21)
EB Mile 52.7; WB Mile 22.5
℗
N35.952332, W81.846379

Brown Mtn. Beach Rd. (MP 7.0)
1.3 miles east of EB Mile 60.8;
WB Mile 14.4
℗
N35.977643, W81.766574

FS 464 (Pineola Rd.)
EB Mile 65.1; WB Mile 10.1
℗
N36.005759, W81.808519

FS 464 at Forest Service Trail (FST) 263 Parking Lot (Hunt Fish Falls)
EB Mile 65.6; WB Mile 9.6
℗
N36.0075, W81.801034

Roseborough Rd. Parking Area near FS 981
EB Mile 69.2; WB Mile 6.0
℗
N36.031273, W81.803718

Beacon Heights Parking Area (MP 305.2)
EB Mile 75.2; WB Mile 0.0
℗
N36.08396, W81.83006

Coordinates can be entered in your mapping software just like a street address.

Camping Lodging Parking Food Restrooms Supplies Water Picnic

Bridge on North Fork of Catawba River
Photo by Allen de Hart

Hiking Directions, Eastbound

0.0 From the parking area on FS 472 (South Toe River Rd.), take the trail past a kiosk, south up the slope, to begin Segment 4. The MST, Green Knob, and River Loop Trails are together at this point. *Note*: To reach the parking area by car from the BRP, take NC 80 (at MP 344) toward Burnsville. After the small community of Busick, turn left onto South Toe River Rd. This road will eventually turn to gravel and follow the river. At the gravel road intersection, make a slight turn on the first right. The parking area is on your left just before a bridge and the entrance to the Black Mtn. Campground on the right. See the "Camping on the Trail" section for this segment for information about camping at the Black Mtn. Campground. Ⓟ 🔺 💧 🚻

Segment 4 Eastbound

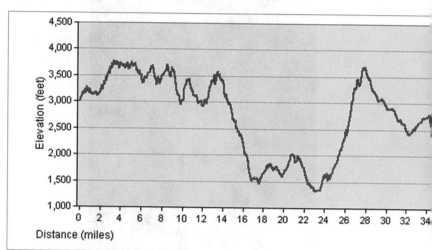

0.3 Green Knob Trail (FST 182) and River Loop Trail (FST 200) go right and south, MST continues east.

0.5 MST joins an old logging road.

1.0 The logging road splits and MST goes right.

1.2 Wildlife field is on the left.

1.3 MST goes right, leaving the logging road, which continues to FS 472.

1.4 Cross Lost Cove Creek. 🌢

1.5 Cross a rocky wet-weather streambed and then pass a wildlife field and old apple trees on the left.

1.6 Join an old logging road.

1.8 Arrive at a gate. The trail will join a logging road before crossing bridge over Neal's Creek. 🌢

2.0 Cross FS 2074 and pass through a gate onto an old logging road.

2.1 Trail climbs and offers a view of the Neal's Creek bowl.

2.2 MST leaves the old road, going right up the spine of the ridge, while an old road continues straight.

2.3 To the north-northwest, across the Toe River valley, there is a view of Maple Camp Bald and beyond it, 6,000-foot Cattail Peak. MST leaves the spine of the ridge going left, bending north with the contour.

Elevation Profile

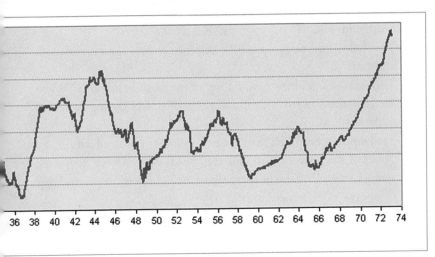

2.5   Trail follows an old road, which disappears when the trail narrows as the slope steepens. On the ridge, there is another view of the bowl, with the sound of the South Toe River in the background. You gradually climb this ridge through several wide switchbacks, which travel back and forth across its spine.

3.0   Cross over the ridge and leave the Neal's Creek basin.

3.1   To the northwest, across the valley, there is a view of the ridge with Balsam, Cattail Peak, Potato Hill, and Winterstar (L-R), all over 5,000 feet.

3.3   Trail goes through the gap between Big Laurel and Big Ridge, crossing into the Roaring Fork basin.

4.0   Cross a Roaring Fork tributary where there is camping downstream to the left. A 4,160-foot rocky peak looms to the south. ▲ 💧

4.3   On a steep slope, the trail goes between boulders and over slick rocks.

4.4   Cross the remnants of an old logging road.

5.0   Trail goes parallel to a distinctive flat ridge to the south, which is the BRP.

5.3   After a gradual climb, reach a gap and then descend to BRP.

5.7   Cross the BRP. There is no parking access here.

6.1   MST follows a ridge south of BRP, heading east.

▲ Camping   🛏 Lodging   Ⓟ Parking   🍴 Food   🚻 Restrooms   🏪 Supplies   💧 Water   ⛺ Picnic

6.2 Descend the ridge into the Singecat Overlook parking area (MP 345.3), where there is daytime access, and cross BRP again to the north and west. (P)

6.6 Trail follows the ridge along BRP and then crosses again to the south and east.

7.6 Trail makes a gradual climb on top of the ridge beside BRP. When the trail turns north with the ridge, BRP passes through a tunnel underneath MST.

7.8 Trail empties onto BRP just west of a viaduct under which NC 80 passes at Buck Creek Gap. The trail heads east on BRP across the viaduct and exits, past the overpass, to the right onto an old road that climbs the ridge, parallel to BRP. (P)

8.1 MST gains the top of the ridge in rhododendrons and swings away from BRP.

8.4 Reach a white gate just before a gap with views south. MST leaves an old road and goes right.

8.6 Trail makes an easy-to-moderate descent to a saddle where MST goes left, following the contours around the south and east side of the knob.

8.7 Reach Horse Gap where Armstrong Creek Trail (FST 223) goes north.

8.8 MST reaches the top of a knob with views back west to Buck Creek Gap before making a brief descent to a ridge across to the next knob.

9.0 Round the next knob and then make a moderate descent.

9.5 Reach a rounded knob and then descend to a saddle, continuing on the rounded ridge.

9.8 Make a moderate descent to the south side of a knob and then out onto a narrow ridge.

9.9 Reach a saddle with crossing trail, then continue, going up and skirting a knob on the right (south).

10.0 Trail is on a narrow ridgeback where it is level before making a moderate ascent of the next knob on left (north) side.

10.2 Trail takes switchbacks to climb the next knob, and then within 0.2 mile makes a moderate ascent to the top of another knob.

10.5 Trail levels out on top of the ridge, in rhododendrons going north. It then descends, switching back on the east side.

Bald Knob looking toward Woodlawn
Photo by Bill Hodge

11.0 Trail is on top of the ridge and descends with the ridge to a gap in 0.2 mile, where there is a fire ring, before climbing the next knob on the left.

11.6 Trail is on top of a narrow ridge with views of Lake Tahoma before going left off the ridge.

12.5 Begin an ascent of Woods Mtn. along the ridge. Starting moderate, the climb will become strenuous with switchbacks and in 0.4 mile reaches the top where there is a fire ring and good views to the north.

13.1 Trail stays level on the ridge and then climbs some more. It will then descend around the peak and cross on a narrow ridge.

13.3 After a sharp ascent on the ridgeback, the trail goes left (north) around the knob, then turns hard right (south) on the east side.

13.4 A trail to the left leads to the site of the Woods Mtn. Lookout Tower. The only vestiges of the tower are the four concrete corner footings.

13.6 Make a moderate descent before the trail becomes wide with easy descent on rounded ridge.

13.9 Make a gradual descent on the left (east) side of the ridge. When the leaves are down there are good views to the east and southeast.

14.0 Trail wraps around the south end of the ridge and then descends moderately south and back east.

Camping Lodging Parking Food Restrooms Supplies Water Picnic

Blazing Star over Linville Gorge
Photo by Adam Warwich

14.2   In a gap, where there is a fire ring, the trail goes right off the ridge. It begins a gradual-to-moderate descent on an old road.

14.4   MST is gradual to level, following the contour. Lake Tahoma is visible to the south.

14.9   Continue a gradual descent on an old road. Pass through scrubby burned-over pines.

15.3   Trail is still on an old road, passing through nice hardwoods. Another old road joins, coming up from left. MST continues a gradual descent on the contour.

15.5   The old road goes left while MST goes straight on the ridge. In 0.1 mile, a road comes in from the right and they both turn sharply left (east) and descend separately through an open hardwood forest.

16.0   In a gap, past interesting rock outcrops, MST goes left leaving the ridge. On the north side of the ridge, it enters rhododendron.

16.2   Return to the ridgeback and rejoin the road on a very wide corridor.

16.3   Leave the road and go left, following the ridge down in a moderate descent.

▲Camping 🛏Lodging Ⓟ Parking 🍴Food 🚻Restrooms 🛒Supplies 💧Water 🛆Picnic

16.7 Make switchbacks, still descending, ending at a level and well-traveled road at South Fork of Tom's Creek. Go left. In a few hundred yards, cross a designated wild-trout stream, flowing left to right on a concrete ford. Continue on the road for 0.8 mile as it stays in the creek bottom, going upstream. ◍

17.5 MST leaves the road, going right, and crosses a small creek, then the larger Tom's Creek. It briefly joins a wide trail going downstream before leaving the floodplain to go left up the hill, making a gradual climb up the western side of Grassy Knob. ◍

17.7 Reach an old road and go left.

18.4 Round the end of the ridge.

18.6 Join a well-traveled road coming from the right. Continue on this road for 1.0 mile.

19.6 MST is now close to US 221 at Woodlawn Park. Pass through stanchions into the park at the edge of a field. Trail goes right and switches back to descend to parking area at US 221 and the USFS Work Center at the community of Woodlawn.

19.7 Pass through the parking lot on Green Mtn. Rd. opposite the Woodlawn Work Center and go east to cross US 221. To the right (south) it is 2.0 miles to a convenience store on US 221; it is 4.0 miles to motels, restaurants, grocery store. Ⓟ 🚻 🏬 🛏 🍴

20.0 From US 221, the trail follows a rough, but traveled road, until it ends at a possible parking spot. Four-wheel drive is advised. The trail leaves the road on the right, going into rhododendrons. *Note:* The gate for this road may be locked. Check with the ranger station at 828-652-2144 if you are hoping to park there. Ⓟ

20.2 Other trails follow a dry streambed here, but MST takes a right across the stream and then makes a short climb to a wildlife field, which it skirts on the left (north and east). ◍

20.6 Past the field, the trail switches back and begins a climb, going into a pine forest.

20.9 Reach FS 149, where MST goes right on the road.

21.2 FS 149 reaches a T-intersection with FS 150. MST goes left on the road, up the hill.

21.4 Reach the rounded grassy summit where several roads intersect. Go left following one of the roads. Good camping. ⛺

21.5 Arrive at the end of the road, which circles around the knob. MST goes left to descend to the North Fork of the Catawba River.

22.3 After a moderate descent, reach a good road coming down the hill from the right. MST goes left on the road, an easy descent along the contour.

22.6 Reach a creek and enter a floodplain, on the road.

22.9 Reach a gate at the edge of a field and a power-line corridor. In 100 yards, MST goes under the power lines and crosses a gravel maintenance road. *Note*: The gate may be open or removed.

23.2 Trail bends left into the North Fork Catawba River floodplain, going upstream along an old road. 💧

23.5 Reach an entry to a nice 200-foot pedestrian bridge crossing the river. Leave the road to the right. The former crossing point for waders is 0.1 mile downstream.

23.6 Past the river, the trail crosses the railroad and begins a moderate climb.

23.8 Reach an old road, following the contour. Go left.

24.2 The road makes a gradual ascent, following the contours of the base of Bald Knob. As it makes turns around the mountain, there are occasional views of the valley, which the trail just crossed.

24.6 Leave the old road, going right into a hollow along an older road that follows a creek. 💧

24.7 There is a short path on right that leads to a piped spring. 💧

24.9 After an easy climb through open forest, the trail reaches the back of a ridge. It follows the ridge up, going left. In this area, there are several good camping spots. 🏕️

25.2 The ridge becomes narrower and rock-strewn, but the climb has been easy to moderate.

25.4 Trail leaves the ridgetop to the left and crosses a rocky intermittent streambed.

25.6 Still climbing easy to moderate, reach a spot with a view to the west across the valley up to the Blue Ridge.

25.7 Pass a strange sinkhole on the left (uphill) side of the trail.

25.9 The climb has become moderate as the trail narrows on the steep slope.

🏕️ Camping 🛏️ Lodging Ⓟ Parking 🍴 Food 🚻 Restrooms 🏪 Supplies 💧 Water 🏕️ Picnic

Linville Gorge
Photo by Donnie Williams

26.2 Reach a rock outcrop with a spectacular view to the north and west. Looking uphill (east and north) you can see Bald Knob above and beyond (northeast) to Dobson Knob.

26.3 Very shortly, the trail reaches the top of a ridge with an overlook to the right with dramatic views to the south. The trail stays on top of the ridge and climbs moderately before beginning a series of rapid switchbacks.

26.5 Continuing switchbacks, the trail affords nice views to the north.

26.8 Trail reaches a very rugged fire road on the southwest-northeast spine and provides the first views of Lake James and the east. Go left on the spine, ascending.

26.9 Reaching the top of the knob, the trail continues to follow the sharp spine with only gradual changes in elevation.

27.1 Begin a series of dramatic rock outcrops with views to the west.

27.2 Begin a moderate descent of the northern end of Bald Knob, going into rhododendrons.

Camping Lodging Parking Food Restrooms Supplies Water Picnic

27.4 Trail sags to the east below the gap between the knobs, traveling in open forest.

27.5 Trail makes a short, strenuous climb back to the top of the ridge.

27.6 Trail reaches the top of the ridge.

27.7 Trail reaches the top of the knob, where there is a fire ring and a one-tent campsite. ▲

28.2 Trail makes a gradual descent on moss and then goes along a stream-bed. ◆

28.3 Trail becomes an old, fairly level road.

28.4 A trail joins from the left.

28.5 The descent is steady, easy to moderate.

28.7 Still on the old road, the trail levels out into rhododendrons, then passes a wildlife field on the left. At an intersection of rutted roads, the trail goes straight, then left, following a road. There are campsites here. ▲

29.2 Pass a wildlife field on the left.

29.8 Trail continues on the road, which is badly rutted.

29.9 Campsite is on left at a bend in the road. ▲

30.4 Pass through a gate onto FS 106 (Dobson Knob Rd.) and reach a parking area. Ⓟ

30.5 Reach two communication towers, then shortly a third.

31.5 Continue to follow FS 106. Pass a gated wildlife field on left with vehicle parking.

31.8 The Overmountain Victory Trail comes through a gate from the left and crosses FS 106, joining MST as it leaves FS 106 to the right onto an old road.

32.0 Trail leaves the old road to the left, where there is a nice campsite. ▲

32.2 After descending on a deeply rutted old road, cross a stream just below the juncture of two small streams. The trail makes a gradual climb to the ridge on the western edge of Linville Gorge. ◆

32.9 Reach 2 small creeks. MST stays east of them. ◆

33.2 Turn left off the old road into parking and access on Old NC 105 (SR 1238, also called Kistler Memorial Hwy.). MST leaves small parking area and goes left (north) on Old NC 105. Ⓟ

34.0 After level-to-slight climb along the road, MST turns right at an improved parking area, heading toward the Linville Gorge. Ⓟ

▲ Camping   🛏 Lodging   Ⓟ Parking   🍴 Food   🚻 Restrooms   🏪 Supplies   ◆ Water   ⛱ Picnic

34.3 Reach the Pinnacle, where a short trail goes right to an observation platform and rock outcrop with spectacular views to the east, south, and west. MST skirts the Pinnacle to the left (north) and begins a descent into the gorge on a ridge. Slope is burned over with little shade.

34.7 After a moderate-to-strenuous descent on the ridge, the trail's descent becomes gentler.

34.9 Before another sharp descent, the trail affords good views of Lake James and Shortoff Mtn.

35.1 Trail reaches a saddle and leaves the ridge going right, while another trail continues on the ridge up the other side of the saddle. The trail goes through open forest.

35.2 After a sharp descent from the saddle, reach a creek, which the trail will follow for 0.3 mile.

35.4 Shortly, another creek flows in from the right.

35.5 Trail goes left to cross the creek and to head up the slope toward the gorge.

35.7 Begin a climb up a knob separating the trail from the river.

35.9 After a moderate-to-strenuous climb with dramatic views of Shortoff Mtn., reach the top of the knob in thick young pines and begin the final descent to the river.

36.6 After a gentle-to-moderate descent, reach the river floodplain, where a trail joins from the right. Shortly, the trail reaches a road running along the river. MST goes right (south) on the road. Within a few hundred yards, MST turns left off the road, heading toward the river. *Note:* If the river is too high to cross, use the following route to reach a bridge to safely cross. Rather than take the MST, continue on the road 0.9 mile across private land to Parks Drive, which comes out on NC 126 at the Linville River bridge in another 0.3 mile. Going left (east) on NC 126, it is 0.7 mile to a NC Wildlife Game Lands entrance on the left, where the blue-dot Linville River Connector Trail goes 2.5 miles to join the MST at EB Mile 41.1 on the slopes of Shortoff Mtn.

36.7 Reach the "Boy Scout" campsite beside the river where the trail goes left upstream.

36.8 Reach the west bank of the Linville River. The river is about 60 yards wide here and typically no more than knee high.

Camping Lodging Ⓟ Parking Food Restrooms Supplies Water Picnic

36.8 Arrive on east bank of Linville River and begin hiking left, upstream through heavily used campsites and fire rings. ▲ 💧

36.9 Trail turns right and heads northeast away from the river. It begins a steady climb up the ridge that becomes Shortoff Mtn.

37.1 MST intersects with a blue-dot trail (Linville River Connector Trail), heading east (right) while MST goes straight up the ridge. On the connector trail, it is 2.5 miles to NC 126, a possible access point. At the NC 126 access location, there is a locked gate and limited parking at the entrance to NC Wildlife Game Lands. This trail forms an alternative route to avoid fording the Linville River by using NC 126 and Parks Drive. Ⓟ

37.4 You see the face of Shortoff Mtn. on the gorge side, and as the ridge narrows, you can also see Lake James.

38.2 Trail settles on the right (east) side of the ridge spine.

38.3 MST reaches a T-intersection with a trail from the right, which is accessible on Wolf Pit Rd. (about 1 mile away) from NC 126. MST goes left toward the gorge and spectacular views. An alternate trail around the east side of Shortoff Mtn. goes straight, which reconnects with MST in 0.8 mile. Ⓟ

38.5 Trail swings west, giving a view of the gorge and peaks of the Black Mtns. to the west.

38.6 Trail levels out on the plateau, having climbed over 1,700 feet from the river. It now follows the lip of the gorge. It will not descend or ascend significantly for another 2.3 miles.

38.7 Trail follows a narrow passage, across a crevice and past a seep that is a possible, but not abundant, water source. 💧

39.0 Traversing the rounded summit, the trail heads back east where there are many campsites. ▲

39.1 Lake James comes into view and the trail rejoins the alternate and goes left (north) along the ridge. MST goes through some rhododendron and some large living oaks. This area is level with camping spots. ▲

39.2 As the ridge narrows, the trail follows the rim where one can see down into the gorge with views of the Linville River and mountain ranges to the west.

39.3 Pass an unusual pond on top of the mountain; it is often dry.

▲ Camping 🏠 Lodging Ⓟ Parking 🍴 Food 🚻 Restrooms 🏪 Supplies 💧 Water 🏕 Picnic

Wolf Pit and Shortoff Mtn.
Photo by Christine White

39.5 Trail passes through a desolate burned-over area with lots of downed wood and charred trunks where mountain laurel is the only live vegetation of any size.

40.8 There are views north of the Chimneys and Table Rock. The trail turns to right (east) and climbs to top of the ridge.

41.0 Begin the first descent since leaving the Linville River.

41.6 Trail follows a ridge, turning back west, with dramatic views to the north.

41.7 Reach the top of small knob.

41.9 Pass a fire ring on the ridge; the trees here have not been burned.

42.0 Sometimes easy to miss, MST turns sharp right to descend to Chimney Gap while Cambric Trail (FST 234), which is not maintained, follows the ridge west into the gorge.

42.1 Steady moderate descent.

42.3 Reach a saddle where there are campsites.

42.5 Pass through an area of severely burned pine, where all big trees are dead.

42.6 Reach an extensive campsite in the gap without a reliable water source.

42.7 Trail begins a steady climb to the Chimneys.

42.8 The climb is strenuous, but quickly reaches a small saddle.

Camping Lodging ⓟ Parking Food Restrooms Supplies ◆Water Picnic

43.1 Dramatic overlook with a view of the east side of the ridge up to Table Rock.

43.6 Trail turns right to the north, following the west side of the ridge with views of the gorge and river, looking along the gorge side of the Chimneys and to Table Rock ahead.

43.9 Trail follows the west side of the ridge into the Chimneys, passing around and among remarkable shapes and stacks of rock.

44.0 Trail goes on top of the ridge past the Chimneys.

44.1 Descend to an extensive and heavily used camping area. 🔺

44.3 Reach the south side of the Table Rock parking lot where there are trash receptacles, vault toilets, and picnic tables, but no water. On FS 210, it is 13 miles to NC 181. MST continues from the north side of the parking lot and combines with a trail to climb Table Rock. Ⓟ 🚻 🏚

44.7 MST and Table Rock Trail turn right to follow a ridge up, while Little Table Rock Trail (FST 236) goes left and follows the ridge down. At this junction, there is a spring directly ahead and down the mountainside. In less than 100 yards, MST will go left to continue around the mountain while the Table Rock Trail goes right to continue its ascent. 💧

45.4 MST descends gradually and at this point begins a moderate descent through open mature forest with a view of Hawksbill straight ahead.

45.6 Reach a series of wooden steps and enter a campsite where an old road goes left to Spence Ridge Trail (FST 233) and FS 210. MST goes right and joins a small stream. 🔺 💧

45.8 Reach FS 210, where MST goes right along the road about 200 feet before turning left to continue its descent along a tributary of Buck Creek. 💧

46.2 Reach FS 496 and go right.

46.3 Trail leaves FS 496 just before the intersection with FS 210. MST goes left. Ⓟ

46.7 Trail climbs a small knob and you can hear Buck Creek to the left.

46.9 Trail rounds a ridge and levels out.

47.0 Reenter rhododendron and descend sharply before leveling out into a cove.

47.3 Trail tees into another trail, which is often overgrown. Go left.

47.5 Trail enters an opening in the forest with a fire pit on the left, a possible camping spot.

47.6 Trail is squeezed beside rock faces on the right and a steep rhododendron slope to the left.

47.9 Small streams and springs cross the trail during the wet season.

48.3 After hugging the north side of a ridge, the trail rises and stays on top for 0.1 mile, then cuts left, descending the slope, then switches back.

48.4 After following the ridge, the trail cuts back left (west) so that the slope is from left to right, and you can hear the creek.

48.5 Another trail joins from left and crosses MST. It will re-cross in a few 100 yards. This old road will descend on top of the ridge while MST stays on south side. Follow blazes.

48.7 After a moderate descent, reach a floodplain where there is good camping to the right. Follow the trail left through open forest where there is more camping.

48.8 Cross Buck Creek, flowing left to right just before it joins Steels Creek. There are many fishing trails to the right going downstream. MST does not cross Steels Creek here, but follows it upstream on the west side, climbing the slope where possible to stay out of the flood zone.

48.9 Trail comes close to Steels Creek. Look for blazes that show where the trail climbs the slope to the left; they may be difficult to find.

49.1 Trail stays above and away from creek, but here they are forced together through a narrows and then climb rapidly.

49.4 Trail arrives at a floodplain with good camping spots. The trail then leaves the creek and camping area, switching back to climb the slope. Steels Creek Falls is 100 yards upstream from the camping area and worth the side trip, which requires climbing over a few boulders.

49.7 Trail goes through open forest of maples and poplars with lush fern ground cover.

50.2 Trail follows an old road and passes a wildlife field with apple trees to the left.

50.3 Trail reaches Steels Creek tributary, Gingercake Creek, where there is good camping. Very shortly, you cross Steels Creek.

50.4 Trail merges with another road coming in from the right.

50.6 Re-cross Steels Creek, where there are good campsites.

51.0 Trail leaves the creek and goes into a pine, magnolia, and oak forest where it begins to climb a ridge dividing Steels Creek and Gingercake Creek.

51.3 Trail continues a moderate climb and reaches the end of the ridge.

51.4 You reach the end of a road spur from FS 496. Head through a notch to the right. Once through the notch, stay left. An old trail goes right.

51.5 Pass through locked gate onto FS 496, where parking is possible. To the right on FS 496 it is 1.2 miles to NC 181 at Ripshin Ridge. Ⓟ

51.9 Pass a fire ring and campsite where the old MST comes in from right. You can take this side trip to Steels Creek Falls. ⛺

52.7 FS 496 terminates at NC 181 and MST crosses the highway, over the guardrails and into the forest. There is a parking area on the east side of NC 181, just north of MP 21. It is 5.0 miles north on NC 181 to general store and post office; 10.0 miles to full-service private campgrounds. After leaving NC 181, the trail bears right through rhododendron and emerges into a wildlife field. ⛺ Ⓟ 🛒

52.8 Trail begins a descent on a 2-3-foot-deep, washed-out gully.

52.9 Trail, which has been following just north of a ridge, crosses at a saddle and turns right and begins a descent beside a small creek on the right. 💧

53.2 Trail crosses a small creek, flowing left to right into the main creek and levels out, entering open forest with good camping spots. ⛺

53.3 Trail descends with the creek along rock outcrops, which make nice picnic spots. The creek falls away quickly to the right.

53.6 Cross a small spring as the trail follows the south side of a slope.

53.8 Trail bottoms out and rejoins a much larger creek. There are many side trails to the creek. Upper Creek comes in from the left and the trail follows it upstream a short distance to a crossing point. Good camping area. This area is known as Greentown where there was once a post office during the logging days. ⛺ 💧

53.9 Trail turns right and crosses the creek. Rock-hopping is possible. The trail then turns right on the other side and follows it downstream, entering a rhododendron tunnel before moving away from the creek.

54.1 Trail levels out into open forest of poplars and maples.

54.4 Trail crosses one of many small creeks, some with culverts, some with timbers.

⛺ Camping 🛏 Lodging Ⓟ Parking 🍴 Food 🚻 Restrooms 🛒 Supplies 💧 Water ⛱ Picnic

Bridge over North Fork of Catawba River
Photo by Mark Moser

54.5 Trail follows the south and east slope with occasional views across the valley to Chestnut Mtn. The slope is steep to the right while the trail moves in and out of deciduous forest and rhododendron thickets.

56.3 Merge onto FS 198 coming from the right. Pass through a gate. This area, with good campsites, is known as Wilderness Camp. Although you will see improved parking here, vehicle travel on FS 198 is generally blocked at FS 982 to prevent travel on an extremely rough road. ▲

56.4 Merge into an old road and follow it left. You will see an improved parking area on the left and come to another gate. This road will widen and continue for about 0.5 mile. Blazes may be hard to find here due to overgrowth, but the trail follows a north-south corridor along the old roadbed.

57.1 The road ends and MST crosses another trail with blue vertical-rectangular blazes, which join the white dots of MST. The blue-blaze trail goes right to Chestnut Mtn. The MST goes straight, and

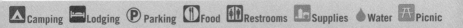

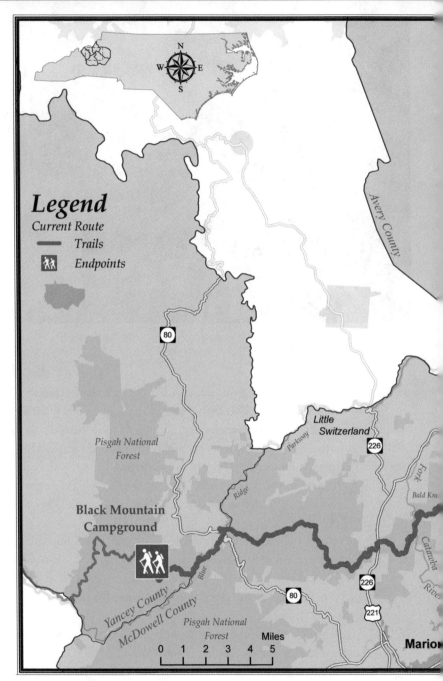

Map and elevation profile produced for Friends of the Mountains-to-Sea Trail by Curtis Belyea, 2016.

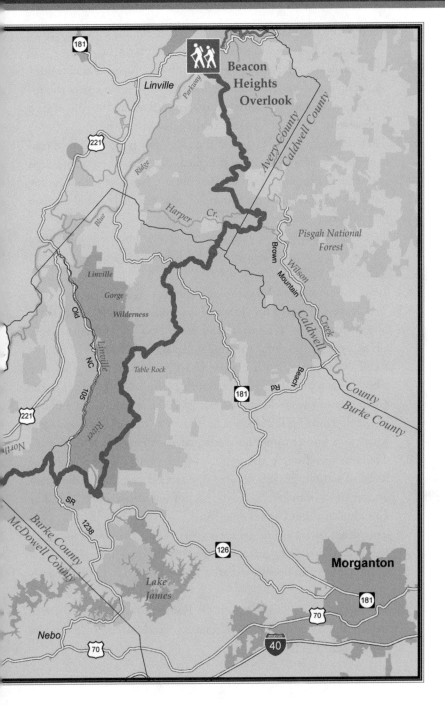

will dip into the Harper Creek basin before coming into the Raider Camp Creek basin on the other side of Chestnut Mtn.

58.1 MST turns right, following the contour while the other trail continues straight and upward through a notch. MST soon enters rhododendron and mountain laurel and wraps left around the slope on a narrow ledge while giving views to the northeast.

58.2 After descending, MST crosses the ridge and is rejoined by a trail from the left; MST continues straight and descends several hundred yards further to join a trail on the contour, which it follows, going right. It then follows a broad rounded ridge gently downhill through mature forest.

58.3 Trail, which has been in a deep narrow gully, now levels out onto a flat trail and reaches a T-intersection where MST goes right onto an old railroad bed.

58.4 Good camping spots. Magnificent large oaks. ▲

58.5 Trail leaves the top of the ridge and descends gradually, going north. Shortly it reaches a T-intersection with FST 277 (Raider Camp Creek Trail). MST joins this trail going right. Left, it is 0.2 mile to a cliff overlooking South Harper Creek with a dramatic view into a box canyon and the 250-foot South Harper Creek Falls. On the north side of the creek, approximately 200 feet below, is the Harper Creek Trail (FST 260), which is reachable from FS 58 going to Kawana (a former community designated on Forest Service maps).

58.6 Trail emerges from a mature forest into a burned-over recovering forest of scrubby growth. It turns east around a bend, affording panoramic views of mountains to the north from west-to-east, including Grandmother and Grandfather Mtns.

58.9 Trail ascends to a saddle, where it crosses a trail following the ridge. MST continues straight and begins to descend into the Raider Camp basin in an open forest of mature hardwoods, predominantly poplar.

59.8 The descent slows as the trail nears Raider Camp Creek. The trail follows the creek until it meets Harper Creek, dropping rapidly in places. ▲ ◊

▲ Camping ▭ Lodging Ⓟ Parking ⑪ Food ⊞ Restrooms ▦ Supplies ◊ Water ⩓ Picnic

Harper Creek Falls
Photo by Robert Trawick

60.3 Trail emerges onto a floodplain where there are plentiful campsites. It then passes through an open rhododendron valley with lush moss and dog hobble before reaching Harper Creek.  🔺 💧

60.8 Reach Harper Creek, which usually cannot be rock-hopped without getting wet. MST crosses the creek, going east into an extensive and heavily used camping area. Enter the clearing on the western edge of the campsite, go left and ascend on an old railroad bed. There is an access to this campground from a parking area at Mile 7 on Brown Mtn. Beach Rd. (SR 1328); the parking area is 1.3 miles east on red-blazed FST 260. Ⓟ 🔺 💧

61.0 Trail hugs a slope and rises over 30 yards above the creek as the gorge narrows. As it climbs the slope, a trail goes straight, following an old railroad bed. Within 100 yards, this trail ends at an overlook of Harper Creek Falls, a series of 15-foot falls.

61.3 The gorge widens and the trail levels out, coming closer to the creek. Good camping sites. 🔺 💧

61.4 Trail crosses a small stream, flowing right to left, and passes by a level camping spot as it follows a sunny overgrown margin of the creek. 🔺

61.5 Trail crosses the creek to the west side, where there is a campsite and fire ring; rock-hopping may be possible. Trail goes right upstream. You may see signs of a railroad including rails and a railbed.

61.8 Cross the creek again from west to east side.

62.1 Trail is in an open mature hardwood forest with level camping spots 30-40 feet from the creek. ▲ ⬦

62.6 Trail crosses the creek again at a shallow spot from east to west and goes right upstream and then soon crosses back to the east side and goes left upstream.

62.7 Reach a wide spot under mature hardwoods with fire rings and camping spots. ▲ ⬦

62.8 Trail crosses creek again from east to west.

63.0 Reach a level open area on west side of creek with camping area big enough for 1-2 tents, shortly before crossing back from west to east. ▲ ⬦

63.1 Cross the creek east-to-west and reach a wide extensive camping area under hollies. ▲ ⬦

63.5 Trail is 50 feet above the creek, where it flows as a white sheet of water over the rocks. For the next 0.1 mile the trail stays on a steep slope beside the creek as it crashes through the cascades and among large rock outcrops below. Picturesque picnic spot.

63.9 Cross the creek again from west to east.

64.0 Trail enters open mature forest with possible campsites. ▲ ⬦

64.1 MST turns right and away from creek; blue blazes are visible going straight, the continuation of North Harper Creek Trail (FST 266A). MST soon begins to climb a ridge to FS 464. Over the next mile, the trail climbs, winding in and out of steep coves among big oaks, maples, and pines.

64.6 Trail crosses a ridge and heads left on the north and east side.

65.1 Emerge into a clearing and go left to reach the road, then right on the road (FS 464 or Pineola Rd.). Ⓟ

65.6 Reach a pullout and improved parking with a sign for "Hunt Fish Falls" indicating the trail is also FST 263. Trail leaves road to left (north). For 0.7 mile the trail will descend through mostly rhododendron to Lost Cove Creek. Ⓟ

66.0 Trail begins to follow a small creek. ⬦

▲ Camping   🛏 Lodging   Ⓟ Parking   🍴 Food   🚻 Restrooms   Supplies   ⬦ Water   ⊞ Picnic

Hunt Fish Falls
Photo by Kenneth Johnson

66.3 Trail reaches Lost Cove Creek near the top of Hunt Fish Falls, where there are two small falls of 6-8 feet. The trail goes right, following the creek downstream. There are possible campsites. Within 100 yards, the trail crosses the base of Hunt Fish Falls, where the creek that the trail followed down the slope from Pineola Rd. flows over a series of falls 50 feet high. ▲ ⬤

66.7 Trail opens out into broad plain with lots of camping and fire rings. The trail continues, hugging the slope away from the creek. ▲ ⬤

66.9 Cross the creek and go right.

67.0 Timber Ridge Trail (FST 261) comes down the slope from Timber Ridge from the left and joins MST as it continues downstream. In a few 100 yards, leave Lost Cove Creek before it meets Gragg Prong and go left (north), climbing a bank, going up the west side of Gragg Prong.

67.2 Cross Gragg Prong west to east and go upstream on a narrow trail on the slope.

67.3 Pass a fire ring beside the creek.

67.8 Trail, which has been 20-40 yards above the creek on the slope, now descends to an area of good swimming, wading, sunning at 35-foot Gragg Prong Falls, a series of rocks and falls.

67.9 A nice rock juts out into the creek.

68.0 Campsite down at the creek at the foot of another falls series with rock outcrops and pools. ▲ ◊

68.1 Cross Gragg Prong from east to west.

68.2 Cross again, rock-hopping, west to east.

68.3 Pass by an overlook a few yards from the trail. Here you can see Gragg Prong flow rapidly through a narrow rock sluice 20 yards below.

68.6 Pass a fire ring and campsite beside the creek. ▲ ◊

68.7 Another nice side trail to rocks and rapids where there is a 3-foot cataract and several pools.

68.8 Cross Gragg Prong from east to west.

68.9 Trail clings to the slope above the creek in places, where across the creek there are heavily used car camping areas on FS 981/SR 1511. ▲ ◊

69.2 Reach the parking area near Roseborough. Follow the drive out of parking lot to road (FS 981), then right across bridge over Gragg Prong and left up washed-out FS 192 on the east side of Gragg Prong. Ⓟ ◊

70.0 Road is relatively straight and wide and climbs steadily. It reaches a knoll where 25 yards to the left there is a campsite and fire ring. The road then descends slightly or stays level for a short distance. ▲

70.2 Road comes back within earshot of Gragg Prong, still to the west. There is a campsite and water source, where a tributary of Gragg Prong crosses the road. ▲ ◊

70.4 Pass private posted land with a gate on the left.

70.6 Trail steadily climbs on the road.

70.8 You can hear Gragg Prong far below.

71.5 Trail is within 50 yards of Gragg Prong.

71.6 A road on the left goes 200 yards to a campsite beside the creek. ▲ ◊

Gragg Prong Falls
Photo by John Mitchell

71.8 Road comes within 10 yards beside and 15 yards above Gragg Prong. The road will leave Gragg Prong as it climbs to Old House Gap.

72.1 The road forks, with MST going to the right and another road continuing left to a gate. Stay right.

72.3 A spur goes left to a campsite.

72.4 Reach a crossroads at Old House Gap. MST goes left on FST 4053, which passes through a white gate, climbing on the ridge and crossing to the north side on an old road.

72.5 On the north side of the ridge, there are views across the valley to BRP and Grandfather Mtn. beyond.

Camping Lodging ⓟ Parking Food Restrooms Supplies ◆ Water Picnic

72.8 On the old overgrown road, trail is level at first, then with a moderate steady climb in a washed-out center of the road.

73.0 MST leaves the old road and goes right around the north and east side of ridge while road continues straight on the south side. As it curves around to the north side, the trail enters rhododendrons.

73.5 Trail descends into the cove and crosses one of the many small tributaries of Andrews Creek. ◊

73.7 Another small stream crossing.

73.8 Reach another stream, which the trail follows in an eroded gully before crossing it and beginning to climb out on north side of the cove.

74.1 Up and over a finger of the ridge into the next cove.

74.3 Cross a small stream. ◊

74.4 Cross the stream again, climbing out of the cove.

74.6 The climb becomes strenuous in stretches.

74.8 Fabulous overlook to the south and east.

75.0 Join rocky road from Grandmother Mtn. Rd., coming in from the left.

75.1 Beacon Heights Trail goes right to Beacon Heights. Be sure to take this short detour because the views from the rock outcroppings encompass Grandfather Mtn. and a large portion of Pisgah National Forest.

75.2 Tanawha Trail begins to run conjunctively with MST; the eastern end of Segment 4 is 130 yards to the left at Beacon Heights parking area (BRP MP 305.2). *Note:* The parking area is 4 miles east of Linville. From Linville, take US 221 toward the BRP. You pass Grandfather Mtn. entrance after 2 miles; 2 more miles at intersection with BRP, turn south and go 0.2 mile to parking area on left. Ⓟ

Falls along Gragg Prong
Photo by Robert Trawick

Hiking Directions, Westbound

0.0 Segment 4 starts at the Beacon Heights parking area (BRP MP
305.2), where the MST begins running eastward conjunctively
with the Tanawha Trail. From the parking area, cross gravel road
and follow signs to Beacon Heights. When the trail intersects with
Tanawha Trail, turn right. *Note*: The parking area is 4 miles east of
Linville. Take US 221 toward the BRP. You pass Grandfather Mtn.

Camping Lodging Parking Food Restrooms Supplies Water Picnic

entrance after 2 miles; 2 more miles at intersection with BRP, turn south and go 0.2 mile to parking area on left. Ⓟ

0.1	Beacon Heights Trail goes left to spectacular views from bald rock outcrops to the southeast.
0.2	MST goes left, descending, as the rocky road continues to Grandmother Mtn. Rd. (SR 1513).
0.4	Fabulous overlook to the south and east as the descent continues.
0.6	Drop is rapid in stretches.
0.8	Cross a very small stream. 💧
0.9	Encounter the stream again.
1.1	Travel over a ridge into the next cove.
1.4	Cross another stream and follow it in an eroded gully.
1.5	Come to another small stream crossing. These are tributaries of Andrews Creek.
1.7	Leave a small creek and begin a moderate climb out of the cove. 💧
2.2	Coming out of rhododendrons on the north side of a ridge, and rounding its east end, MST joins an old impassable road (FS 4053) coming from the right on the south side of the ridge.
2.4	Make a moderate descent on the old overgrown road, which is washed out in the center.
2.7	Views back to the left (north) across the valley to BRP and Grandfather Mtn. and beyond.
2.8	Mount the ridge and descend on its crest until passing through a white gate to reach a crossroads at Old House Gap. MST goes right on FS 192 and descends for 3.0 miles. This road is passable and sometimes traveled, but very rugged.
2.9	A spur road goes right to a campsite.
3.1	Another road goes back sharply to the right, continuing to a gate. Continue straight.
3.4	The road comes within 10 yards beside and 15 yards above Gragg Prong. The trail will stay within a few hundred yards of Gragg Prong for the next 5 miles.
3.6	A road goes right 200 yards to a campsite beside the creek. ⛺ 💧
3.7	Near Gragg Prong again.
4.4	You can hear Gragg Prong far below.
4.6	The trail steadily descends on the road.

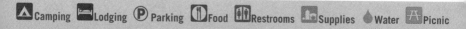

Hunt Fish Falls
Photo by Donnie Williams

4.8 Private posted land with a gate is on the right.

5.0 The road comes back within earshot of Gragg Prong, which is still to the west. There is a campsite and water source where a tributary of Gragg Prong crosses the road. △ ●

5.2 Brief climb to a knoll; on right is a campsite and fire ring. The road becomes relatively straight and wide. △

6.0 Reach relatively well-travelled FS 981 near Roseborough. There is a heavily used parking and camping area along creek straight ahead. Go right and cross the bridge over Gragg Prong. MST then goes left and reaches a parking area. MST then hugs the west and south side of Gragg Prong. △ Ⓟ ●

6.3 The trail clings to the slope across from the camping area.

6.4 Cross Gragg Prong from west to east.

6.5 There is a nice side trail to rocks and rapids where there is a 3-foot cataract and several pools.

6.6 A fire ring and campsite are located beside the creek. △ ●

6.9   Pass by an overlook a few yards from the trail. Twenty yards below, Gragg Prong flows rapidly through a narrow rock sluice.

7.0   Cross Gragg Prong, rock-hopping, east to west.

7.1   Cross west to east, rock-hopping.

7.2   Campsite down at the creek at the foot of another falls series with rock outcrops and pools. 🔺 💧

7.3   A nice rock juts out into the creek.

7.4   The trail reaches an area of good swimming, wading, sunning at 35-foot Gragg Prong Falls, a series of rocks and falls, then ascends to stay 20-40 yards above the creek.

7.9   There is a fire ring beside the creek.

8.0   From a narrow trail on the slope, descend to the creek and cross it east to west.

8.2   Descend a bank to the confluence with Lost Cove Creek and go right, upstream along the north side of Lost Cove, where within 100 yards Timber Ridge Trail (FST 261) departs going right uphill. MST continues upstream along Lost Cove.

8.3   Cross to the south side of Lost Cove Creek, rock-hopping.

8.5   Enter a level plain beside the creek with lots of campsites and fire rings. 🔺 💧

8.9   A small tributary of Lost Cove Creek falls 50 feet from the slope to the left. In 100 yards, reach Hunt Fish Falls, two small falls of 6-8 feet. There are possible campsites here. Near the top of the falls, MST goes left up the slope. It climbs moderately 0.7 mile to Pineola Rd. 🔺 💧

9.2   Leave the small tributary. 💧

9.6   Reach moderately well-traveled Pineola Rd. (FS 464) at an improved parking area. MST goes right on FS 464 for 0.5 mile. Ⓟ

10.1 Leave FS 464 to the left in a clearing. For the next mile, MST winds in and out of steep coves among big oaks, maples, and pines. Ⓟ

10.6 Cross a ridge.

11.1 Reach Harper Creek in a flat floodplain. Blue blazes of FST 266A go right upstream, and MST goes left downstream on the north side of the creek. MST will be beside Harper Creek for 3.3 miles. 💧

11.2 Trail enters open mature forest with possible campsites. 🔺 💧

11.3 Cross the creek from east (north) to west (south), rock-hopping.

11.7 Picturesque picnic spot. For the next 0.1 mile, the trail stays on a steep slope beside the creek as it crashes through the cascades and among large rock outcrops below. The trail is 50 feet above the creek; here it flows as a white sheet of water over the rocks.

12.1 Enter an extensive camping area under hollies before crossing the creek from west to east.

12.2 Cross back from east to west and reach a level open area on the west side with a campsite big enough for 1 or 2 tents.

12.4 Cross creek again, from west to east.

12.5 Reach a wide spot under mature hardwoods with fire rings and camping spots.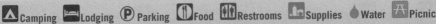

12.6 Cross the creek from east (north) to west (south), rock-hopping and then cross back to the east side in a shallow spot, going right, downstream.

13.1 Enter an open mature hardwood forest with level camping spots 30-50 feet from the creek.

13.4 Cross the creek from east to west.

13.7 You may see signs of a railroad including rails and a railbed. Reach a camping spot and fire ring and then cross the creek to the east side.

13.8 Trail crosses small stream flowing left to right and passes by a level camping spot as it follows a sunny overgrown margin of the creek. ▲

13.9 Pass good campsites before the gorge narrows and the trail descends, separating some from the creek. ▲ ◆

14.2 Trail is 30 yards or more above the creek on an old railroad bed. Below is Harper Creek Falls, a series of 15-foot falls that may be reached in 100 yards by a trail to the right.

14.4 Descend into an extensive floodplain and heavily used campsite area. Go right around the western edge of the clearing to cross Harper Creek. Staying left, on the north side of this camping area is the Harper Creek Trail (FST 260), which leads 1.3 miles to parking on Brown Mtn. Beach Rd. (SR 1328), which parallels Wilson Creek. Harper Creek here is not deep, but it is difficult to rock-hop without getting wet. Continue across to the west side. This is just above the confluence with Raider Camp Creek. You will go upstream on the north side of Raider Camp Creek. ▲ ◆ Ⓟ

Harper Creek Trail
Photo by Eileen Kelly

14.9 Enter an open rhododendron valley with lush moss and dog hobble before passing through a floodplain where campsites are plentiful. ▲ ◆

15.4 Continue following the creek upstream, climbing rapidly in places. Reach a floodplain where there is a fire pit and campsite; the trail leaves the creek. ▲ ◆

16.3 Ascend through an open forest of mature hardwoods, predominately poplar, to a saddle where MST crosses a trail following the ridge. Leave the Raider Camp Creek basin to enter the Harper Creek basin. The MST runs conjunctively with blue-blazed Raider Camp Creek Trail (FST 277).

16.6 Round a ridge on the north and east side in a burned-over area of scrubby growth, affording panoramic views of mountains to the north from west to east, including Grandmother and Grandfather Mtns., before entering a mature forest.

16.7 MST goes left and FST 277 (Raider Camp Creek Trail, a blue-blazed connector trail) continues straight, leading 0.2 mile to a cliff overlooking South Harper Creek with a dramatic view into a box canyon and the 250-foot South Harper Creek Falls. On the north side of the creek, approximately 200 feet below is FST 260, which is reachable from FS 58 going to Kawana (a former community designated on Forest Service maps).

16.8 Come to some magnificent large oaks. Good camping spots.

16.9 Past the intersection with the connector trail, MST turns left, leaving an old railroad bed and ascending in a deep narrow gully.

17.0 MST is joined by a trail from the left and follows a broad rounded ridge, ascending gently uphill through mature forest.

17.1 MST passes through rhododendron and mountain laurel as it wraps right across a slope on a narrow ledge, giving views to the northeast before entering open forest, where a trail joins from the right.

18.1 A blue rectangle-blazed trail crosses MST and goes left to Chestnut Mtn. MST emerges onto an old road, which will widen and continue for 0.5 mile.

18.8 Trail reaches an improved parking area and passes through a gate. Blazes may be hard to find here due to overgrowth, but the trail follows a north-south corridor along the old roadbed.

18.9 FS 198 forks to the left. Go right and pass through a gate. This area, with good campsites, is known as Wilderness Camp. Although you will see improved parking here, vehicle travel on FS 198 is generally blocked at FS 982 to prevent travel on an extremely rough road.

20.7 Trail is following the south and east slope with occasional views across the valley to Chestnut Mtn. The slope is steep to the left while the trail moves in and out of deciduous forest and rhododendron thickets.

20.8 Trail crosses one of many small creeks, some with culverts, some with timbers.

21.1 Trail levels out into open forest of poplars and maples.

21.3 After passing through a rhododendron tunnel, the trail reaches Upper Creek. It goes upstream a short way before crossing, where rock-hopping is possible. The trail then goes left downstream.

21.4 Come to an area with many good campsites, which is known as Greentown from the post office that existed here during logging days. There are many side trails. The trail goes away from Upper Creek along a small tributary. It ascends with this creek for the next 0.5 mile. 🔺 💧

21.6 Trail follows the south side of a slope and crosses a small spring.

21.9 Trail ascends with the creek along rock outcrops that make nice picnic spots.

22.0 After passing through level open forest with good camping spots, the trail crosses a small creek flowing right to left into the main creek and begins to climb.

22.3 Climb beside a small creek on the left before turning left and crossing a saddle. The trail will follow the north side of the ridge. 💧

22.4 Ascend in a 2-3-foot-deep washed-out gully and emerge into a wildlife field.

22.5 Past the wildlife field, MST passes through rhododendron before reaching NC 181 where there is parking on the east side. This is just north of MP 21. The trail continues over the guardrails to the other side, where it follows FS 496, which is usually open to vehicle travel. The trail will be on the gravel road the next 1.2 miles. It is 5.0 miles north on NC 181 to general store and post office; 10.0 miles to full-service private campgrounds. 🔺 Ⓟ 🏪

23.3 Pass a fire ring and campsite on the left where the old MST comes in. You can take this side trip to Steels Creek Falls. 🔺

23.7 Leave FS 496, going left to pass through a locked gate. Parking is possible. Ⓟ

23.8 An old trail goes left. Stay right, pass through a notch, and reach the end of the road spur from FS 496.

23.9 Trail makes a moderate descent out on a ridge.

24.2 Descend the ridge dividing Steels Creek and Gingercake Creek to a pine, magnolia, and oak forest where the trail reaches good camping sites and Steels Creek. 🔺 💧

24.6 Re-cross Steels Creek. 💧

24.8 MST, on an old road, goes right when the road forks.

24.9 Cross Steels Creek and reach tributary Gingercake Creek, where there is good camping. 🔺 💧

🔺Camping 🛏Lodging ⓅParking 🍴Food 🚻Restrooms 🏪Supplies 💧Water ⛩Picnic

25.0 On the old road, MST passes a wildlife field with apple trees on the right.

25.5 Trail goes through open forest of maples and poplars with lush fern ground cover.

25.8 Descend on switchbacks, to a floodplain on Steels Creek with good camping spots. Steels Creek Falls is 100 yards upstream from the camping area and worth the side trip. It will require climbing over boulders. ▲ ⬥

26.1 Trail stays up and away from the creek on the west side, descending with it as it falls, sometimes rapidly. The trail and creek are forced together in a narrows. Signage here may not be visible; follow along the creek—do not cross it.

26.3 Trail leaves Steels Creek just before Buck Creek joins it from the right. Go upstream beside Buck Creek a short distance. Many fishing trails lead downstream.

26.4 Cross Buck Creek. The trail remains in a floodplain where there is good camping. ▲ ⬥

26.5 Begin an ascent from the floodplain.

26.7 Another trail on an old road crosses MST. Follow the blazes. MST stays on the south side of the ridge.

26.8 Trail cuts back right (south) to follow the ridge, leaving the sound of the creek. It will stay on top of the ridge for 0.1 mile.

26.9 Trail is on the north side of the ridge.

27.3 Small streams and springs cross the trail during wet season. ⬥

27.6 Trail is squeezed beside rock faces on the left and a steep rhododendron slope to the right.

27.7 Trail enters an opening in the forest with a fire pit on the right, a possible camping spot. ▲

27.9 MST goes right. Straight is FS 210C, which may be overgrown and impassable.

28.2 Leave a cove and ascend sharply into rhododendron before reaching a level section.

28.3 Round a ridge and begin climbing again.

28.5 Reach a knob where you can hear Buck Creek to the right.

28.9 MST arrives at FS 496 close to its intersection with FS 210 on the left. Go right onto FS 496. Ⓟ

▲ Camping   🛏 Lodging   Ⓟ Parking   🍴 Food   🚻 Restrooms   🛒 Supplies   ⬥ Water   ⛱ Picnic

29.0 Leave FS 496 and go left ascending along a tributary of Buck Creek.

29.4 Reach FS 210. Go right on it about 200 feet before turning left.

29.6 MST leaves the creek and passes through a campsite where an old road goes right to Spence Ridge Trail (FST 233) and FS 210. Begin a moderate ascent to Table Rock on a series of wooden steps in open mature forest.

29.8 The ascent slows somewhat. Looking back you may get a view of Hawksbill.

30.5 MST joins Table Rock Trail, which goes left to the summit of Table Rock. Go right and in less than 100 yards, MST and Table Rock Trail turn left. Straight is Little Table Rock Trail (FST 236), which follows the ridge down. Right, a trail goes down the mountainside to a spring, which may be last water source before Linville River.

30.9 Reach the south side of the Table Rock parking lot where there are trash receptacles, vault toilets, and picnic tables, but no water. On FS 210, it is 13 miles to NC 181. MST continues on the south side of the parking lot.

31.1 Ascend into an extensive and heavily used camping area.

31.2 On top of the ridge, begin passing among the Chimneys, remarkable shapes and stacks of rock. Dramatic views in all directions.

31.3 Trail is on the west side of the ridge with views into gorge.

31.6 Trail turns left (east) and begins to descend.

32.1 Dramatic overlook with a view of the east side of the ridge up to Table Rock.

32.4 Leave a small saddle and descend rapidly.

32.5 Reach an extensive campsite in the gap without a reliable water source.

32.6 Leave the camping area.

32.7 Pass through an area of severely burned pine, where all big trees are dead.

32.9 Reach a saddle where there are campsites.

33.1 Steady moderate climb.

33.2 Reach the ridge top and junction with Cambric Trail (FST 234), which is not always maintained. That trail goes right on the ridge (west) into the gorge. Go left.

Lake James
Photo by Christine White

33.3 Pass a fire ring on the ridge.

33.5 Reach the top of small knob.

33.6 Trail follows a ridge with dramatic views to the north.

34.2 Trail's ascent ends. It will not climb again until past the Linville River in about 4.5 miles.

34.4 Here there are views north of the Chimneys and Table Rock. Make a slight descent from the ridge and stay level for the next 2.2 miles.

35.7 Trail passes through a desolate burned-over area with lots of downed wood and charred trunks, where mountain laurel is the only live vegetation of any size.

35.9 Pass an unusual pond, which is often dry, on top of the mountain.

36.0 As the ridge narrows, trail follows the rim where one can see down into the gorge with views of the Linville River and mountain ranges to the west.

36.1 MST goes through some rhododendron and some large living oaks. Area is level with camping spots. Lake James is in view. Reach a

Camping Lodging Parking Food Restrooms Supplies Water Picnic

junction where MST goes right to the west side of the ridge; there are extraordinary views from Shortoff Mtn. An alternate trail goes straight. It rejoins MST beyond Shortoff Mtn. in 0.8 mile.

36.2 Leave the campsites and traverse the rounded summit, heading west and then south to the lip of the gorge where there are breathtaking views into the gorge and across the river to the Black Mtns. in the west.

36.5 Trail follows a narrow passage, across a crevice and past a seep that is a possible but not abundant water source. 💧

36.6 Leave the gorge and begin a descent of 1,700 feet in the next 1.7 miles to the Linville River. The trail turns back east.

36.7 Trail goes east away from the gorge.

36.9 MST turns right. Left is the alternate trail that traverses the east side of Shortoff Mtn. Straight is a trail that leads to a parking area on Wolf Pit Rd. coming off NC 126 in about 1.0 mile. Go right on MST and descend toward the Linville River. ⓟ

37.0 Trail descends on the left (east) side of the ridge spine.

37.8 Looking back right, you can see the face of Shortoff Mtn.

38.1 A blue-dot trail (Linville River Connector Trail) joins from the left (east). *Note:* This connector trail forms an alternate route to avoid fording the Linville River if it is too high to cross safely. On the connector trail, it is 2.5 miles to NC 126, a possible access point. The NC 126 access location is at a locked gate at the entrance to NC Wildlife Game Lands. There is limited parking here. After the 2.5-mile walk to NC 126, it is 0.7 mile to the right on NC 126 to Parks Drive, which is across the Linville River Bridge, then right on Parks Drive for 0.3 mile to where the road is gated and crosses private land for 0.9 mile before joining MST at WB Mile 38.6. ⓟ

38.3 Reach the east side of the Linville River after a steady descent. MST goes left downstream. 💧

38.4 Pass through heavily used campsites and beside fire rings to reach a river crossing. The river is about 60 yards wide here and typically no more than knee high. 💧

38.4 Reach the west bank of the Linville River. Go left downstream.

38.5 Reach the "Boy Scout" campsite beside the river. MST goes right, away from the river. 💧

38.6 Reach a private road running along the river. Left, in 0.9 mile is Parks Drive and 0.3 mile further, NC 126. There is no public access here. MST goes right (north) on the road and then left in a few hundred yards, out of the river floodplain to begin ascending the western side of Linville Gorge.

39.3 After a gentle-to-moderate climb, reach the top of a knob in thick young pines with dramatic views of Shortoff Mtn. across the river.

39.5 Descend the knob to a tributary of the Linville River.

39.7 Cross the creek, going left.

39.8 Continue upstream. Another creek will join from the left, and then a trail comes in from the left.

40.0 Leave the creek and begin a strenuous climb to a saddle in open forest. ◊

40.1 Reach a saddle and go left on MST up the ridge. Another trail goes right on the ridge.

40.3 Make a strenuous climb to views of Lake James and Shortoff Mtn. back to the east.

40.5 After a gentle ascent on the ridge, begin a moderate-to-strenuous climb up a burned-over slope with little shade.

40.9 Reach the Pinnacle. MST skirts it to the north, but just past it, a trail goes left a short way to an observation platform and rock outcrop with spectacular views to the east, south, and west. Continue west on a heavily used trail to Old NC 105 (SR 1328, also called Kistler Memorial Hwy.).

41.2 Reach Old NC 105 and a small parking area. MST goes left, down the road, for 0.8 mile. Ⓟ

42.0 MST goes right, off the road, at a small parking area. Ⓟ

42.0 MST joins an old road and makes a gradual descent.

42.3 Reach 2 small creeks. MST on the old road stays east of them and will continue to descend with the creek. ◊

43.0 Cross a stream just below the juncture of two small streams and ascend on a deeply rutted old road. ◊

43.2 Reach a nice campsite and go right on a larger old road that is the Overmountain Victory Trail. ◭

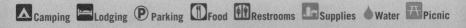

▲ Camping 🛏 Lodging Ⓟ Parking 🍴 Food 🚻 Restrooms 🛒 Supplies ◊ Water 🏕 Picnic

Linville Gorge ledge
Photo by Chris Adkins

43.4 Reach FS 106 (Dobson Knob Rd.), where the MST goes left. The Overmountain Victory Trail goes straight across FS 106 and through a gate. Go left on FS 106.

43.7 Follow FS 106 and pass a gated wildlife field on the right with vehicle parking.

44.7 Reach a communication tower, then two more.

44.8 Reach a parking area providing access. Pass through a gate at the end of FS 106. Ⓟ

45.3 Campsite on right at a bend in the road.

45.4 Continue on the road, which is badly rutted.

46.0 Pass a wildlife field on the right.

46.5 Reach an intersection of rutted roads. There are campsites here. MST stays right, passes another wildlife field on the right, and enters rhododendrons.

46.7 Still on an old road, begin an easy-to-moderate climb.

46.8 A trail goes right. MST stays left.

46.9 Trail is fairly level here; the road peters out.

47.0 Make a gradual ascent on a streambed, then on moss. This is the last water until you are past Bald Knob.

47.5 Trail reaches the top of Dobson Knob, where there is a fire ring and a one-tent campsite. Trail continues on top of the ridge.

47.6 Leave the ridge to the left (east).

47.7 Make a rapidly descending sag east in open forest before climbing back to the next knob.

47.8 Regain the ridge after a moderate-to-strenuous climb.

48.0 On the ridge, make a moderate climb through rhododendrons up the north end of Bald Knob.

48.1 Reach a series of dramatic rock outcrops with views to the west. On top of the spine, the trail has only gradual changes in elevation.

48.3 Begin a descent on the ridge down the south side of Bald Knob. There are views of Lake James and the east.

48.4 Trail goes right, leaving a rugged fire road that runs up the spine.

48.7 Start a series of rapid switchbacks down to reach the top of a ridge.

48.9 Make a moderate descent on top of the ridge, and come to the end where an overlook to the left gives dramatic views to the south. Trail goes right, off the ridge onto another series of rapid switchbacks.

49.0 Reach a rock outcrop with a spectacular view to the north and west. Looking uphill (east and north) you see Bald Knob; above and beyond (northeast) is Dobson Knob.

49.3 Make a moderate descent, where the trail is narrow on a steep slope.

49.5 Pass a strange sinkhole on the right (uphill) side of the trail.

49.6 Reach a spot with a view to the west across the valley up to the Blue Ridge. The descent is easy to moderate.

49.8 Cross a rocky intermittent streambed and join a ridge top.

50.0 Ridge is narrow and rock-strewn in places with easy-to-moderate descent.

50.3 Trail leaves the back of the ridge, going right into open forest. In this area there are several good camping spots.

50.5 Short path on left to a piped spring.

50.6 On an old road following a creek, emerge from a hollow and arrive at a more recent, but still old, road and go left.

51.0 The road makes a gradual descent, following the contours of the base of Bald Knob. As it makes turns around the mountain, there are occasional views of the valley of the North Fork of the Catawba River, which the trail will cross.

51.4 MST leaves the old road, going right and begins a moderate descent.

51.6 Cross a railroad and approach the river.

51.7 Reach a nice 200-foot pedestrian bridge crossing the North Fork of the Catawba River and arrive at an old road along the river. The crossing point for waders before the bridge was built is 0.1 mile downstream. Go left on the road. 💧

52.0 Continue downstream on the road, which is in the floodplain.

52.3 Going right, away from the river, the trail crosses a gravel maintenance road and passes under power lines. It continues across a field to a gate at its edge. Pass through the gate on the road. *Note:* The gate may be open or removed.

52.6 Reach a creek and leave the floodplain. Continue on the road, ascending gradually for 0.3 mile.

52.9 MST leaves the road to the right and begins a moderate climb.

53.7 Reach the top of the knob, which is circled by an old road. Stay right and emerge onto a grassy area where there is good camping. 🔺

53.8 Several roads intersect in the grassy area. Continue across and take FS 150, the most obvious road.

54.0 Follow FS 150 down the hill, then take a right onto FS 149.

54.3 Take a left, leaving FS 149.

54.6 Descend through a pine forest, through a series of switchbacks.

55.0 Reach a wildlife field. After skirting it to the right (north and east), make a short descent into rhododendrons and cross a normally dry streambed.

55.2 Emerge from rhododendrons onto a possible parking area at the end of a rough (four-wheel drive advised) but traveled road that leads to US 221. *Note:* The gate for this road may be locked. Check with the ranger station at 828-652-2144 if you are hoping to park there. Ⓟ

55.5 Reach US 221. To the left (south) it is 2.0 miles to a general store; 4.0 miles to all amenities. To the right (north) it is 0.8 mile to a

🔺Camping 🛏Lodging Ⓟ Parking 🍴Food 🚻Restrooms 🏪Supplies 💧Water ⛱Picnic convenience store. Cross US 221 onto Green Mtn. Rd. next to the USFS Work Center at Woodlawn. To the left is a parking lot and restrooms. Ⓟ 🛉🛉 ⌐∎ 🛏 🍴

55.6 MST takes a few switchbacks from the parking lot to a field and then passes through stanchions on a road, leaving the park. Continue on this road for 1.0 mile.

56.6 Leave the road, going right.

56.8 Round the end of the ridge.

57.5 Leave the old road and go right.

57.7 Make a gradual descent on the west side of Grassy Knob before reaching a floodplain and joining a wide trail. Go upstream along Tom's Creek. Cross it, then cross a smaller tributary and arrive at a well-traveled road. Go left on the road for 0.8 mile in the Tom's Creek floodplain. 💧

58.5 100 yards after crossing a designated wild-trout stream, flowing right to left on a concrete ford, leave the road to the right and begin an ascent on switchbacks.

58.9 Make a moderate climb on the ridge. A road will join the trail from the left.

59.0 Trail has been on an old road on a wide corridor, which narrows as it returns to the ridgeback.

59.2 Leave rhododendron from the north side of the ridge, cross the ridge, and ascend through open forest past interesting rock outcrops.

59.7 Continue a gradual ascent through open hardwood forest to a sharp right turn in the trail onto the ridge going north. An old road departs to the left. MST continues straight on the ridge.

59.9 Continue the gradual ascent, passing through nice hardwoods on an old road.

60.3 Pass through scrubby burned-over pines.

60.8 Lake Tahoma is visible to the south as MST ascends gradually on the contour.

61.0 Trail ascends moderately, then gradually, on an old road to a ridge and a gap where there is a fire ring.

61.2 Trail ascends moderately north and west before wrapping around the south end of the ridge.

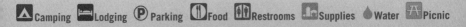

View from atop the Pinnacle
Photo by Otto Ofanador

61.3 Climb gradually on the right (east) side of the ridge. In winter, there are good views to the east and southeast.

61.6 Trail is wide, making a gradual ascent on the rounded ridge, before narrowing and becoming steeper.

61.8 A trail to the right leads to the site of the Woods Mtn. Lookout Tower. The only vestiges of the tower are the four concrete corner footings.

61.9 Trail goes north on the east side of the knob and then takes a sharp left to round the north side before making a rapid descent on the ridgeback.

62.1 Crossing on a narrow ridge, ascend around the peak of Woods Mtn., before staying level, then descending. In 0.2 mile around the top, there is a fire ring and good views to the north.

62.7 The descent on switchbacks is rapid, then trail becomes more gradual along a ridge.

63.6 Trail climbs to the top of a narrow ridge with views of Lake Tahoma.

△ Camping ⊞ Lodging ⓟ Parking ⏸ Food ⊞ Restrooms ⊞ Supplies ◆ Water ⏀ Picnic

64.2 Round a knob on the right, descend to a gap where there is a fire ring, then ascend on top of the ridge.

64.7 Trail descends, switching back on the east side, then levels out going south in rhododendrons.

65.0 Make a moderate descent from one knob to the next, then take switchbacks to climb the next knob.

65.2 Descend moderately from the knob on the north side before reaching a narrow ridge, staying level.

65.3 Skirt around the south side of a knob, then descend to a saddle where a trail crosses.

65.4 Continue on a narrow ridge, reach the south side of a knob, then make a moderate climb.

65.7 On a rounded ridge, reach a saddle, then make an ascent to a rounded knob.

66.2 Make a moderate ascent before rounding the next knob.

66.4 Make a brief ascent and reach the top of a knob with views west to Buck Creek Gap.

66.5 Reach Horse Gap where Armstrong Creek Trail (FST 223) goes north.

66.6 MST follows contours around the south and east side of the knob and makes an easy-to-moderate climb to a saddle.

66.8 Trail joins an old road that comes in from the right and reaches a gap with views south. Continue west through a white gate.

67.1 Leave the ridge and begin a descent to BRP on an old road parallel to BRP.

67.4 Reach BRP at Buck Creek Gap, where the trail goes left onto the parkway and crosses a viaduct that goes over NC 80. It exits past the overpass to the right. There is parking on NC 80 south of BRP. (P)

67.6 Trail follows a ridge, which turns south; BRP passes underneath through a tunnel. Make a gradual descent along the ridge, now on the south (east) side of the parkway.

68.6 Cross BRP again to the north (west) and follow a ridge along it.

69.0 Cross BRP to the south and east and emerge into Singecat Overlook parking area (MP 345.3), where there is daytime access. Leave the parking area on the south and west side and ascend the ridge going west. (P)

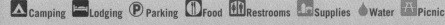
Camping Lodging (P) Parking Food Restrooms Supplies ◆ Water ⛺ Picnic

Table Rock becomes a shadow monster
Photo by Brandon Thrower

69.1 Continue on the ridge south of BRP, heading west.

69.5 Cross the BRP. No parking access.

69.9 Ascend from BRP to a gap, then make a gradual descent.

70.2 Parallel BRP, which appears as a distinctive flat ridge to the south.

70.8 Cross the remnants of an old logging road.

70.9 On a steep slope, the trail goes between boulders and over slick rocks.

71.2 Cross a Roaring Fork tributary, where there is camping downstream to the right. A 4,160-foot rocky peak looms to the south. 🛆 💧

71.9 Trail goes through the gap between Big Laurel and Big Ridge, leading into the Roaring Fork basin.

72.1 To the northwest, across the valley, a view of the ridge with Balsam, Cattail Peak, Potato Hill, and Winterstar (L-R), all over 5,000 feet.

72.2 Cross over the ridge and enter Neal's Creek basin. You will gradually descend with this ridge, making several wide switchbacks back and forth across its spine. On the ridge, you may hear the sound of the South Toe and have a view of the Neal's Creek bowl.

72.7 Trail widens as it follows an old road, crossing a more gradual slope.

72.9 MST joins the spine of the ridge, coming down from the left. To the north-northwest, across the South Toe River valley, there is a view of Maple Camp Bald and beyond it, 6,000-foot Cattail Peak.

73.0 MST joins an old road coming in from the right.

73.1 Trail continues its descent and offers a view of the Neal's Creek bowl.

73.2 Reach a gate, cross FS 2074 and pass through another gate onto an old logging road.

73.4 Cross bridge over Neal's Creek. Still on the logging road, pass through a gate.

73.6 MST leaves the old logging road.

73.7 Pass a wildlife field and old apple trees on the right, then cross a rocky wet-weather streambed.

73.8 Cross Lost Cove Creek.

73.9 MST merges with a logging road, coming from the right, which continues to FS 472.

74.0 Wildlife field on the right.

74.2 The old logging road merges with another old road coming from the right.

74.7 MST leaves the old logging road.

74.9 Green Knob Trail (FST 182) and River Loop Trail (FST 200) join from the left, and the combined trails continue west.

75.2 Arrive at a parking area on FS 472 (South Toe River Rd.) and the western end of Segment 4. *Note:* To reach the parking area by car from the BRP, take NC 80 (at MP 344) toward Burnsville. After the small community of Busick, turn left onto South Toe River Rd. This road will eventually turn to gravel and follow the river. At the gravel road intersection, make a slight turn on the first right. The parking area is on your left just before a bridge and the entrance to the Black Mtn. Campground on the right. See the "Camping on the Trail" section for this segment for information about camping at the Black Mtn. Campground. Ⓟ 🔺 💧 🛁

 Camping Lodging Ⓟ Parking Food Restrooms Supplies 💧 Water Picnic

View from Beacon Heights
Photo by Randy Johnson

The High Country—MST Segment 5

BEACON HEIGHTS NEAR GRANDFATHER MOUNTAIN TO DEVIL'S GARDEN OVERLOOK NEAR SPARTA

By Carolyn Sakowski

This section, covering almost 91 miles, offers the hiker some of the most astounding scenery in northwestern North Carolina. This part of the trail, which travels along the ridgeline where elevations range from 4,300 to 3,400 feet, offers views looking down the escarpment into the North Carolina Piedmont.

Most of this section runs parallel to the Blue Ridge Parkway (BRP) and often crosses the parkway as the trail goes back into the woods and away from the road. There are a few stretches that cross fields, which will sometimes share space with friendly cows. There are also a few patches where the trail travels along a backroad or the shoulder of the BRP, but most of this segment is on well-engineered footpaths that make the ascents and descents easy to hike. Although the BRP is always nearby, you often feel that you are deep in the woods, miles from civilization.

This section begins at Beacon Heights and follows the Tanawha Trail as it travels along the base of Grandfather Mountain, which is one of only 553 certified biosphere reserves in the world. It continues past the resort town of Blowing Rock, travels near West Jefferson, and ends near Sparta in the northwest corner of North Carolina near the Virginia border.

HIGHLIGHTS INCLUDE:

- The Linn Cove Viaduct, a 1,243-foot concrete engineering marvel that carries the BRP around the base of Grandfather Mountain

- Views of Grandfather Mountain, Table Rock, Hawksbill, and Pisgah National Forest that can encompass over 50 miles on a clear day

- Moses H. Cone Memorial Park, where the MST uses the park's former carriage trails and passes by Flat Top Manor, which now serves as the parkway's craft center

- E.B. Jeffress Park with the restored cabin of farmer Jesse Brown and Cool Springs Baptist Church as well as "The Cascades" waterfall, which slides over rocks for 250 feet

- Mount Jefferson Overlook, where you have a panoramic view of Grandfather, Sugar, and Beech Mountains to the south and Mount Jefferson looming over the town of Jefferson in front of you

- Doughton Park, whose 7,000 acres offer picnic areas, camping facilities, and hiking along ridges and through meadows with long-range views of the surrounding area

- Brinegar Cabin, built about 1885, which often offers hand-loom weaving and other mountain craft demonstrations during the summer

The nearby towns of Linville, Blowing Rock, Boone, West Jefferson, and Sparta offer all amenities. They also make it easy to break this segment into several day hikes.

Lunch hour at the Bull Thistle Café
Photo by Dave Fairall

Thanks to the following for their assistance: Dave Bauer, Allen de Hart, Nancy Dexter Wilson, Tom Dillon, Alton Franklin, Carmen Frankowski, Jim Hallsey, Randy Johnson, John Lanman, Doug Smith, and Jane Wallace.

Total Distance: 90.3 miles (8.3 miles on road or BRP shoulder; 82 miles on trail)
Difficulty: Easy to moderate with only a few strenuous parts

Trail Updates

When planning your trip using this guide, take a moment to see whether Friends of the Mountains-to-Sea Trail (Friends) has posted any updates about the trail route by visiting Friends' "Trail Updates" page at www. MountainstoSeaTrail.org/updates.

Trail Angels

Eastbound (EB) Mile 58.1; Westbound (WB) Mile 31.2

Terry Mohn has offered camping, water, electricity, and WiFi. He lives 0.4 mile from the intersection of the BRP and NC 16 at Horse Gap. His house is at the end of the gravel road where you pass around an iron gate on the southeast side of BRP. Please call ahead (336-813-2397) so Terry and his neighbors know you are coming.

EB Mile 66.2; WB Mile 23.0

Thomas & Theresa Haislip provide free camping with a picnic table, fire pit, water, and clothesline in a field next to their house. At MP 256, across from the driveway leading to Mountain View Lodge, follow Don Bare Rd. for 0.2 mile on west side of BRP, opposite of where MST goes. House can be seen from the road. Please call ahead (336-982-3082).

EB Mile 71.9; WB Mile 18.4

Marc Arnsdorff can provide camping and water. His farm is located on Peak Creek Church Rd., which is on the west side of the BRP, across from Darnell Woodie Rd. His is the 2nd white farmhouse on the right across from an old barn. It is approximately 500 yards off BRP. Please call ahead (336-982-4034).

Shuttle and Guide Services

EB Miles 0.0-30.2; WB Miles 60.1-90.3

HikeMore Adventures, 9041 NC 181, Jonas Ridge, 28641, 828-595-HIKE or 828-733-2303 (after hours), info@hikemoreadventures.com; www. hikemoreadventures.com. HikeMore Adventures provides shuttles between the Woodlawn Work Center on US 221 (Segment 4 EB Mile 19.7; WB Mile 55.5) and Aho Gap (Segment 5 EB Mile 30.2; WB Mile 60.1), as well as guide services in the Linville Gorge and Harpers Creek wildernesses. Their Base Camp, about 5 miles north of the MST on NC 181 (Segment 4 EB Mile 52.7; WB Mile 22.5), also has a store with hiking supplies.

Camping

Note: Camping on BRP/NPS land is limited to designated, approved areas. It is illegal to camp along the MST on these lands unless there is signage allowing camping or you have a proper permit on other approved land.

Friends is constructing 5 campsites along the parkway and expects they will open soon. Check the website at www.MountainstoSeaTrail.org/updates for additional information.

EB Mile 8.0; WB Mile 82.3
Grandfather Mountain State Park, www.ncparks.gov/Visit/parks/grmo/main.php (obtain free permit at sign-up box at the Grandfather Mtn. State Park sign at EB Mile 8.0; WB Mile 82.3.):
Streamside Campsite (fire ring) 0.7 mile from MST
Hermitage Campsite (no fire ring) 0.8 mile from MST
Storyteller's Rock Campsite (fire ring) 1.2 miles from MST
Refuge Campsite (fire ring) 1.4 miles from MST

EB Mile 13.0; WB Mile 77.3
Julian Price Memorial Park Campground, BRP MP 297, Blowing Rock, 28605, 828-963-5911; www.blueridgeparkway.org/v.php?pg=36. Half of these sites are available without reservations.

EB Mile 15.9; WB Mile 74.4
Backcountry site with bench & firepit with grate but no amenities; get permit from Price Park campground office. Maximum of 6 campers allowed.

EB Mile 62.6; WB Mile 24.7
Raccoon Holler Campground, 493 Raccoon Holler Rd., Jefferson, 28640, 336-982-2706; www.raccoonholler.com. Open mid-April through October.

EB Mile 75.6; WB Mile 14.6
Wild Woody's Campground, 14234 NC 18, Laurel Springs, 28644, 336-984-8088. 0.2 mile from MP 248, intersection of BRP and NC 18; also has eclectic antique store; open May-Oct.

EB Mile 76.0; WB Mile 14.1

Miller's Campground, 793 Miller Rd., Laurel Springs, 28644, 336-359-2828; www.millersc.com. Located 0.4 mile from intersection of BRP and NC 18, on the trail. Open April-Oct.; tent and RV camping sites. Ask about MST discounts.

EB Mile 84.6; WB Mile 5.1

Doughton Park (MP 239.2, located on the trail); reservations made on-line at RECREATION.gov or 336-372-8568. 110 campsites; 25 RV sites. Open April-Oct.

Food

EB Mile 0.0; WB Mile 90.3

Town of Linville is 3 miles south of BRP from Beacon Heights on US 221; www.averycounty.com.

EB Mile 25.1; WB Mile 65.1

Town of Blowing Rock is 1.0 mile from MST; www.blowingrock.com.

EB Mile 38.1; WB Mile 51.4

Blue Ridge Diner, 5176 Old Hwy. 421 South, Boone, 28607, 828-265-1999. Open 11-8 Monday through Friday.

EB Mile 51.9; WB Mile 37.9

Park Vista Restaurant, 1907 Park Vista Rd., West Jefferson, 28694, 336-877-5200; parkvistainn.com. Lunch and dinner daily.

EB Mile 58.1; WB Mile 30.2

Mountainaire Seafood and Steaks, 9930 NC 16, West Jefferson, 28694, 336-982-3060; www.mountainaireseafood.com. Located 1.0 mile from trail on NC 16. Closed Mondays. Open for lunch & dinner, Tues.-Sun. Winter hours vary. N36.315833, W81.369722.

EB Mile 61.9; WB Mile 27.3

Northwest Trading Post/Sally Mae's on the Parkway, 414 Trading Post Rd., Glendale Springs, 28629, 336-982-2543. Located at MP 259; sandwiches, sodas, fudge, gifts featuring Hand Made in the USA products. Closed during winter months.

EB Mile 75.6; WB Mile 14.6

Station's Inn Bar & Grille, 14355 NC 18 South, Laurel Springs, 28644, 336-359-2888; www.thestationsinn.com. 0.2 mile from MP 248, intersection BRP and NC 18; located on the trail.

EB Mile 75.6; WB Mile 14.6

Freeborne's Eatery & Lodge, 14300 NC 18, Laurel Springs, 28644, 336-359-8008; www.freebornes.com. 0.2 mile from MP 248, intersection BRP and NC 18; located across road from the trail; closed during winter.

Lodging/Supplies/Services/Post Office

EB Mile 0.0; WB Mile 90.3

Town of Linville is 3 miles south of Beacon Heights (MP 305.2) on US 221. Linville post office, 4235 Mitchell Ave., Linville, 28646, 828-733-5745; weekdays, 8:00 to noon & 1:00 to 4:00; Saturdays, 8:00 to 11:30. www.averycounty.com.

EB Mile 11.9; WB Mile 78.4

Foscoe Country Corner & Deli, 8937 NC 105 South, Foscoe, 28604, 828-963-9512. One mile east from Holloway Mtn. parking area.

EB Mile 11.9; WB Mile 78.4

Hidden Valley Motel, 8725 NC 105, Foscoe, 28604, 828-963-4372; www.hiddenvalleymotel.com. One mile east from Holloway Mtn. parking area, then go 0.3 mile north on NC 105.

EB Mile 25.1; WB Mile 65.1

Town of Blowing Rock is 1.0 mile or less from MST; www.blowingrock.com.

EB Mile 43.3; WB Mile 46.7

Dollar General Store, 146 Yuma Lane, Deep Gap, 28618, 828-355-4679. Located one mile west of BRP on US 421.

EB Mile 43.3; WB Mile 46.7

Jim's Produce, 7808 Old 421 South, Deep Gap, 28618, 828-264-5788. Located one mile west of BRP on US 421.

EB Mile 51.9; WB Mile 37.9

Park Vista Inn, 1907 Park Vista Rd., West Jefferson, 28694, 336-877-5200; www.parkvistainn.com. Parking is allowed at this motel if you let staff know. Resident manager's email is unclelewi@hotmail.com. MP 268; N36.27901777, W81.4153771.

EB Mile 58.1; WB Mile 30.2

Marathon Run-In (gas, convenience store, groceries & produce), 10703 NC 163, Glendale Springs, 28629, 336-982-4944; mymarathonstation.

com. Located one mile north of BRP at intersection of NC 16 & NC 163; N36.315833, W81.369722.

EB Mile 61.9; WB Mile 27.3
Northwest Trading Post/Sally Mae's on the Parkway, 414 Trading Post Rd., Glendale Springs, 28629, 336-982-2543. Located at MP 259; gift shop featuring crafts, food, and drinks.

EB Mile 62.0; WB Mile 28.5
New River Inn and Cottages, 264 Trading Post Rd., Glendale Springs, 28629, 336-982-8282; www.newriverinnnc.com. Located near the trail, 0.1 mile north of MP 259 & Northwest Trading Post.

EB Mile 66.2; WB Mile 23.0
Mountain View Lodge, 164 Mountain View Lodge Dr., Glendale Springs, 28629, 336-207-7677; www.mtnviewlodge.com. Pet-friendly cabins.

EB Mile 75.6; WB Mile 14.6
Station's Inn, 14355 NC 18 South, Laurel Springs, 28644, 336-359-2888; www.thestationsinn.com. 0.2 mile from MP 248, intersection of BRP and NC 18; located on the trail; has general store with sodas, snacks, beer/wine, light groceries.

EB Mile 75.6; WB Mile 14.6
Freeborne's Eatery & Lodge, 14300 NC 18, Laurel Springs, 28644, 336-359-8008; www.freebornes.com. 0.2 mile from MP 248, intersection BRP and NC 18; located across road from the trail; closed during winter.

Water/Restrooms
Note: Water sources from creeks are noted throughout this segment, but please exercise caution and treat water taken from creeks or springs before drinking.

EB Mile 1.6; WB Mile 88.7	Linn Cove visitor center at MP 304.4 (closed in winter) 🚻 💧
EB Mile 13.0; WB Mile 77.3	Julian Price Memorial Park picnic area and campground at MP 297.0 (closed in winter) 🚻 💧

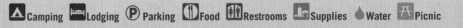
▲ Camping 🛏 Lodging Ⓟ Parking 🍴 Food 🚻 Restrooms 🛒 Supplies 💧 Water ⛺ Picnic

EB Mile 21.2; WB Mile 68.9   Moses H. Cone Memorial Park at MP 294.0

EB Mile 47.3; WB Mile 41.9   Cascades Recreation Area at MP 271.9

EB Mile 61.9; WB Mile 27.3   Northwest Trading Post/Sally Mae's on the Parkway at MP 259

EB Mile 82.8; WB Mile 7.1   Doughton Park at MP 239.2 (closed in winter)

Hunting

Hunting is not allowed on any of this segment.

Signs/Blazing

Where the MST runs conjunctively with the Tanawha Trail, the Tanawha Trail uses a white feather as signage. The MST uses a three-inch white dot on signs and trees. The section that follows carriage trails in Moses H. Cone Memorial Park has good signage but limited reference to MST. The Boone Fork Trail (BFT) near Price Park Campground uses an orange diamond. Bluff Mountain Trail (BMT) is maintained primarily by the National Park Service.

Special Considerations

There are several different locations using the name Boone Fork. Make sure you get the right location when looking for a specific site. Don't confuse Upper Boone Fork Trail along Tanawha Trail section with Boone Fork Trail in Price Park.

Some National Park Service facilities are closed from November to April, and many of the privately owned facilities are also seasonal. Consult the websites before planning your trip.

This section offers many opportunities for shorter day hikes, especially if you use shuttles between parking areas.

Dogs are allowed on this segment of the MST, but should be on leashes at all times.

Camping   Lodging   Ⓟ Parking   Food   Restrooms   Supplies   ⬧ Water   Ⓐ Picnic

ADDITIONAL INFORMATION

Friends office: 919-825-0297 or info@MountainstoSeaTrail.org

Carolyn Sakowski: sakowski@blairpub.com

Trail Maps

Google map of the entire MST: www.MountainstoSeaTrail.org/map

Grandfather Mountain trails:
www.grandfather.com/pdf/07trail_map.pdf

Price Park trails: www.nps.gov/blri/planyourvisit/julian-price-trails.htm

Moses H. Cone Memorial Park carriage trails:
www.nps.gov/blri/planyourvisit/moses-cone-trails.htm

Tanawha Trail: www.nps.gov/blri/planyourvisit/tanawha-trail.htm

Doughton Park Trails:
www.nps.gov/blri/planyourvisit/doughton-park-trails.htm

Park Websites

National Park Service Blue Ridge Parkway site:
www.nps.gov/blri/

Blue Ridge Parkway: www.blueridgeparkway.org

Grandfather Mtn. State Park:
www.ncparks.gov/grandfather-mountain-state-park

Tourism Sites

High Country Host: highcountryhost.com

Avery County Chamber of Commerce: www.averycounty.com

Visit Blowing Rock: www.blowingrock.com

Ashe County Chamber of Commerce: www.Ashechamber.com

Alleghany County Chamber of Commerce & Visitor Center:
www.visitalleghanync.com

PRIMARY PARKING LOCATIONS (Page 1)

Beacon Heights Parking Area
(MP 305.2)
EB Mile 0.0; WB Mile 90.3
Ⓟ
N36.083928, W81.830119

Stack Rock Parking Area
(MP 304.8)
EB Mile 0.9; WB Mile 89.4
Ⓟ
N36.088956, W81.822173

Linn Cove Visitor Center
(MP 304.4)
EB Mile 1.6; WB Mile 88.7
Ⓟ 🚻 ◍
N36.090133, W81.8146

Wilson Creek Overlook Parking Area
(MP 303.6)
EB Mile 2.9; WB Mile 87.4
Ⓟ
N36.100471, W81.808981

Rough Ridge Parking Area
(MP 302.8)
EB Mile 4.4; WB Mile 85.9
Ⓟ
N36.098269, W81.797310

Boulder Fields Overlook Parking Area
(MP 302.4)
EB Mile 5.1; WB Mile 85.2
Ⓟ
N36.098056, W81.7875

Boone Fork Parking Area
(MP 299.9)
EB Mile 8.1; WB Mile 82.2
Ⓟ
N36.1199, W81.78145

Cold Prong Pond Parking Area
(MP 299.0)
EB Mile 9.8; WB Mile 80.5
Ⓟ
N36.128964, W81.770168

Holloway Mountain Rd. Parking Lot
(MP 298.6)
EB Mile 11.9; WB Mile 78.4
Ⓟ
N36.139783, W81.7574

Julian Price Park Campground
(MP 297)
EB Mile 13.0; WB Mile 77.3
Ⓟ ⛺ 🚻 ◍
N36.13913, W81.73245

Trout Lake Parking Area
(Located off Shulls Mill Rd. from MP 296.4)
EB Mile 20.1; WB Mile 70.2
Ⓟ
N36.152613, W81.703562

Cone Manor House Parking Area
(MP 294.0)
EB Mile 21.2; WB Mile 68.9
Ⓟ 🚻 ◍
N36.14573, W81.69314

Coordinates can be entered in your mapping software just like a street address.

Camping Lodging Parking Food Restrooms Supplies Water Picnic

PRIMARY PARKING LOCATIONS (Page 2)

Thunder Hill Overlook
(MP 290.3)
EB Mile 27.1; WB Mile 62.4
Ⓟ
N36.136310, W81.643188

Raven Rock Overlook
(MP 289.5)
EB Mile 27.9; WB Mile 61.1
Ⓟ
N36.144508, W81.633430

Boone's Trace Overlook
(MP 285.1)
EB Mile 33.8; WB Mile 56.2
Ⓟ 🏕
N36.197903, W81.604227

Grandview Overlook
(MP 281.2)
EB Mile 37.4; WB Mile 52.2
Ⓟ
N36.227267, W81.567283

Osborne Mountain Overlook
(MP 278)
EB Mile 41.2; WB Mile 47.0
Ⓟ
N36.224783, W81.513033

Tomkins Knob Parking Area
(MP 272.5)
EB Mile 45.6; WB Mile 43.0
Ⓟ
N36.244275, W81.465830

Cascades Recreation Area
(MP 271.9)
EB Mile 47.3; WB Mile 41.9
Ⓟ 🚻 💧 🏕
N36.245648, W81.458453

Park Vista Inn
(MP 268)
EB Mile 51.9; WB Mile 37.9
🛏 🍴 Ⓟ ; ask staff for
permission
N36.289187, W81.415507

**Mount Jefferson Overlook Parking
Area**
(MP 267.0)
EB Mile 52.9; WB Mile 36.6
Ⓟ
N36.2948508, W81.4131549

**Jumpinoff Rock Overlook Parking
Area**
(MP 260.3)
EB Mile 59.1; WB Mile 28.4
Ⓟ 🏕
N36.324268, W81.368083

Northwest Trading Post
(MP 259)
EB Mile 61.9; WB Mile 27.3
Ⓟ 🚻 💧 🍴 🛏
N36.343949, W81.375461

Basin Cove Overlook
(MP 244.7)
EB Mile 78.8; WB Mile 10.9
Ⓟ
N36.3907529, W81.199762

Coordinates can be entered in your mapping software just like a street address.

Camping Lodging Ⓟ Parking Food Restrooms Supplies 💧Water 🏕Picnic

PRIMARY PARKING LOCATIONS (Page 3)

Bluff Mountain View Overlook
(MP 243.4)
EB Mile 80.4; WB Mile 9.3
Ⓟ
N36.40833, W81.19556

Alligator Rock Overlook Parking Area
(MP 242.3)
EB Mile 81.5; WB Mile 8.8
Ⓟ
N36.421121, W81.189732

Doughton Park
(MP 241.5)
EB Mile 83.2; WB Mile 6.9
Ⓟ 🚻 💧 ⛺ 🏕
N36.43384, W81.17726
GPS may not work in the park;
open April through Oct.

Brinegar Cabin Parking Area
(MP 238.5)
EB Mile 87.2; WB Mile 3.6
Ⓟ 💧 (seasonally)
N35.41866, W81.14648
GPS may not work in park

Devil's Garden Overlook Parking Area
(MP 235.7)
EB Mile 90.3; WB Mile 0.0
Ⓟ
N36.434037, W81.104296

Wildflower array
Photo by Jacqueline Brown

Coordinates can be entered in your mapping software just like a street address.

Camping Lodging Parking Food Restrooms Supplies Water Picnic

Hiking Directions, Eastbound

To help with directions, EB on BRP is going north; WB is going south. When going EB, west is on the left, east on the right. Going WB, west is on right, east on left.

0.0   The southern terminus of Segment 5 is Beacon Heights parking area on BRP (MP 305.2). The parking area is 4 miles east of Linville. Take US 221 toward the BRP. You pass Grandfather Mtn. entrance after 2 miles; 2 more miles at intersection with BRP, turn south and go 0.2 mile to parking area on left. To begin hike, cross paved road between parking area and woods and follow signs to Beacon Heights Trail, heading into the woods. (P) (II) (La) (bed)

0.1   At intersection with Tanawha Trail, which runs conjunctively with MST for next 13 miles of this segment, turn left (north).

0.4   Cross paved US 221.

0.5   Ascend to area with large boulders. Hike on boardwalk next to stone parkway retainer wall. Leave boulder field.

0.9   Ascend steps. Trail forks. MST goes right. Stack Rock parking area (MP 304.8) is 90 feet to left. (P)

1.1   Ascend and then descend on wooden stairway and boardwalk that goes around giant rock formation known as Stack Rock.

1.2   Cross bridge over Stack Rock Creek and pass waterfall. ●

1.3   Ascend wooden and stone steps. (This section is strenuous.)

1.5   Pass storage buildings on left.

1.6   Come to Linn Cove parking area and visitor center (MP 304.4). Follow paved path around outside of parking lot. (P) (restrooms) ●

1.7   Pass Linn Cove Viaduct sign.

1.9   Pass under viaduct and follow steps through large boulders to continue on MST/Tanawha Trail. ●

2.0   Cross bridge over Linn Cove Branch.

2.2   A side trail goes to right 60 feet to rock outcrop with good views of viaduct, Table Rock, Hawksbill, and Pisgah Forest.

2.5   Cross footbridge.

2.8   Balanced Rock is on right.

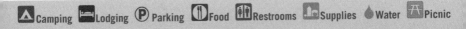

Segment 5 Eastbound

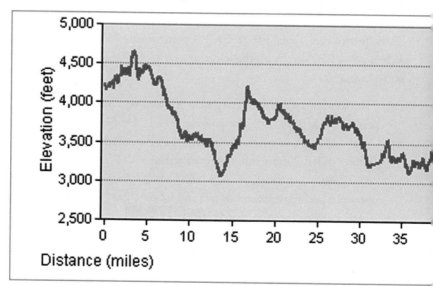

2.9 Trail to Wilson Creek Overlook (MP 303.6) is on right. Continue left and cross bridge over Wilson Creek. Next 1.23 miles ascend through large boulders. Ⓟ 💧

3.8 Side trail on right goes to rock outcrop with good views. Continue left on main trail.

4.2 Walk on Rough Ridge boardwalk.

4.4 Trail to Rough Ridge parking area (MP 302.8) goes right. Stay on main trail. Ⓟ

4.6 Cross Little Wilson Creek on arched footbridge. 💧

5.1 Side trail on right leads to Boulder Fields Overlook parking area (MP 302.4) but stay left. Ⓟ

6.6 Cross footbridge.

7.6 Daniel Boone Scout Trail goes left. Stay straight on main trail. Campsites are available 1.2 miles up the left-hand trail at Daniel Boone Campsite. 🔺

7.8 Nuwati Trail goes to left. The 4 campsites described in "Camping" are on the Nuwati Trail. Stay right for MST. 🔺

8.0 Asutsi Trail goes right for 0.4 mile to US 221 (winter parking when BRP is closed). Cross Upper Boone Fork bridge to stay on MST.

🔺 Camping   🛏 Lodging   Ⓟ Parking   🍴 Food   🚻 Restrooms   🏪 Supplies   💧 Water   🏕 Picnic

Elevation Profile

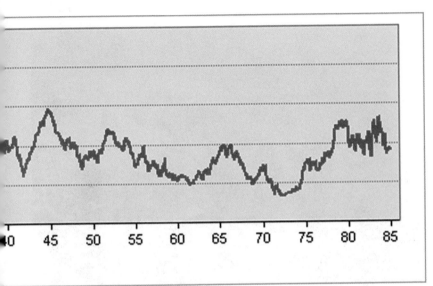

Upper Boone Fork Trail goes right 0.5 mile to Calloway Peak Overlook (MP 299.7). Continue left for MST. Just past Asutsi on the right, the Grandfather Mtn. State Park sign shows which campsites are in use and has permits to register for open sites located on Nuwati and Daniel Boone Scout Trails.

8.1 Boone Fork parking area (MP 299.9) is 400 feet to right. Go left to continue on MST. *Note:* Don't confuse this overlook with Boone Fork Trail in Price Park. Ⓟ

9.5 Cross bridge.

9.7 Cross another bridge.

9.8 Trail to Cold Prong Pond parking area (MP 299) is on right. Follow Tanawha Trail sign directing you toward Price Lake. You rock-hop 4 creeks in this segment. Ⓟ 💧

10.7 Pass through stile to enter meadow. Go 50 yards and follow Tanawha Trail signs to make right turn. Walk 50 yards to enter woods, following MST sign.

10.9 Leave woods and enter field. Follow Tanawha Trail markers as trail veers left.

🔺 Camping 🛏 Lodging Ⓟ Parking 🍴 Food 🚻 Restrooms 🏪 Supplies 💧 Water ⛺ Picnic

View from Rough Ridge
Photo by Randy Johnson

11.1 Go through wooded area to reach another meadow. Trail goes left (north) up the hill. On right, at bottom of hill, is graveled Holloway Mountain Rd. As you approach woods at top of hill, you'll see markers on the trees.

11.3 Trail goes in and out of wooded areas. Trail curves to left in field; gate at top of hill, but continue on trail.

11.4 Go through stile and enter meadow with good views of Grandfather Mtn. to right. At top of hill, there is tree-sheltered area. Signs for Tanawha Trail direct you to turn right here. You can follow that trail or head straight over the hill.

11.9 Descend downhill to Holloway Mtn. Rd. parking area. *Note:* BRP is 1.0 mile to the right from this parking area. The intersection with BRP is 6 miles west of Blowing Rock. To the left, it is 1.0 mile to the town of Foscoe and NC 105. Access MST through a stile across gravel road from the lot or go left for 30 yards to gated dirt road and follow that road. The two options merge later. Ⓟ 🍴 🏪 🛏

12.2 Follow Tanawha Trail signs to right; another trail goes left.

Camping Lodging Ⓟ Parking Food Restrooms Supplies 💧Water 🏛Picnic

12.3 Trail appears to fork. Leave old roadbed and go left onto single track.

12.4 Go through stile and join old roadbed. At fork, stay right for few yards, where you skirt and then walk through meadow.

12.8 Leave meadow and cross bridge.

12.9 Just after passing by stile on right is a second bridge.

13.0 Tanawha Trail intersects with Boone Fork Trail (BFT). It is 0.5 mile to right to Julian Price Park Campground. Continue left on BFT. Ⓟ 🔺 🚻 💧

13.3 Cross meadow. At top of meadow, there is a milepost sign for BFT (3.5 MP). Turn right at that sign and proceed downhill; this is the route laid out in 2014.

13.5 At large rock on left, trail goes right, following orange diamonds. You see closed trail to left. There are 3 creek crossings via rocks. The next 2 miles have numerous creeks where you can access water, but it should be treated. 💧

13.7 Cross bridge; a few yards later is BFT 3.0 milepost. Cross 2 creeks using rocks.

13.9 Cross second bridge, followed by 2 more quick creek crossings. After second creek crossing, trail goes uphill to the left. This is the route made in 2015.

14.0 In the next 0.2 mile, there are 3 more creek crossings.

14.2 Cross old log bridge and then metal bridge. About 100 yards later is BFT 2.5 milepost. It is 30 feet to first of 4 creek crossings, some of which may require getting your shoes wet. After the third creek crossing, you have to climb up large rocks. After the fourth creek crossing, it is 100 yards to a plank walkway.

14.5 Follow steps down to right to cross creek using large boulders. In the next 0.2 mile, you climb up and down hills, with a series of cascades in creek on left, followed by 3 sets of wooden steps.

14.7 Cross metal bridge, just past BFT milepost sign. Within a few yards, there are 2 easy creek crossings.

14.8 Trail goes right, following stone walkway uphill and around large rock formation. Go a few yards to wooden ladder leading down rocks, followed by BFT milepost sign.

15.3 Side trail to Hebron Falls is on left, but stay on main trail.

15.5 Old dam site is on left.

🔺 Camping   🛏 Lodging   Ⓟ Parking   🍴 Food   🚻 Restrooms   🏪 Supplies   💧 Water   🏕 Picnic

15.7 Leave BFT at large rock outcrop. Cross the Boone Fork bridge, then continue straight uphill. Climb over large boulders for 75 yards. At top of hill, stay right.

15.9 Backcountry campsite with bench and firepit with grate but no amenities. Permit required from Price Park campground office. Maximum of 6 campers allowed. ▲

16.3 Follow old roadbed. Side trail is on left. Keep on main trail.

16.4 Turn left as trail leaves old roadbed. Watch closely for trail sign on right, indicating left turn up the hill.

17.2 Pass gate to reach Shulls Mill Rd. Turn right and walk 75 yards on road's shoulder. On left, take wooden steps up the hillside, into the woods. The trail climbs 500 feet in elevation in next half-mile.

17.7 Climb over step stile to reach gravel road, which is part of Moses H. Cone Memorial Park's carriage trail system. Turn right onto that road. You are on Rich Mountain Trail.

18.3 At trail intersection in pasture, turn right.

18.4 Turn left onto trail leading to Trout Lake.

18.7 In next 0.3 mile, trail crosses over 3 culverted streams before reaching gate. ⧫

19.4 There is a short side trail to a stream on north near small dam. Continue on main trail. ⧫

20.1 Go left when trail forks to continue on MST. *Note:* To end the day-trip if you arranged for shuttle at Trout Lake, turn right and cross the bridge. The trail leads to the Trout Lake parking area. To continue on MST, cross over dam and continue to right on carriage trail along lake. Take left fork going to manor house. Cross road (Flannery Fork Rd.) to follow trail toward manor house. Ⓟ

21.2 At trail intersection, go right through tunnel under parkway. The trail passes in front of carriage house. Ⓟ 🚻 ⧫

21.4 Take trail to left before reaching manor house. It is an unsigned trail.

22.0 The carriage trail curves right. Continue straight, following signs to Watkin Rd.

24.1 Watkin Rd. intersects with Black Bottom Rd., which comes in from right. Follow signs to US 321.

24.8 There is lake on right.

▲ Camping 🛏 Lodging Ⓟ Parking 🍴 Food 🚻 Restrooms 🛍 Supplies ⧫ Water 🏕 Picnic

Ladder on Boone Fork Trail
Photo by Eileen Kelly

24.9 Cross creek by rock hopping. Go right on gravel Old Camp Catawba Rd. You are walking through an area with some residential traffic. 💧

25.1 Reach US 221/321. To the right is a nearby shopping center and the town of Blowing Rock. To the left, it is 7 miles to Boone. To continue on MST, turn left and walk 200 feet on shoulder of US 221/321. Turn left and walk up entrance ramp to BRP (MP 291.9). 🍴🛒🛏️

25.4 Reach BRP and turn right (north).

25.6 Walk on shoulder of BRP to where trail goes into woods on right, just after crossing bridge over US 221/321.

25.7 Follow trail along hillside to stile, after which trail bears left and follows barbed-wire fence to pasture.

25.8 Continue through pasture and enter woods near fence along BRP.

26.2 Emerging from woods, trail cuts right across pasture to point below a pine tree on far side of pasture. Trail then travels along side of hill, down to two bridges. After the second bridge, trail goes through section of clearing. Continue into woods to another stile.

26.6 Hike uphill and into rhododendron thicket before reaching another stile at top of ridge.

26.7 In pasture, trail bears left along BRP through short section of woods and out to pasture.

26.8 Cross pasture to angled treeline that borders dirt farm road, leading into trees again. Bear left at fork and go into another pasture.

26.9 Out of woods, angle right (away from BRP) to stile at Greenhill Rd. next to farm gate. Climb over stile and go left (west) 200 feet to the BRP (MP 290.7), then turn right (north) and walk 500 feet. Cross the BRP and go through stile. Follow trail uphill through meadow, then go right. Go to top of hill and then head downhill toward overlook.

27.1 Thunder Hill Overlook (MP 290.3) is across BRP at bottom of hill. Go through a stile at bottom of hill and turn left. Ⓟ

27.5 Walk along fence and then on west (left) shoulder to reach side road on left. Enter woods on north side of side road.

27.9 Walk 450 feet uphill. At top of hill, trail bears right, going steeply uphill then leveling off. Trail goes up and down hills. At one point, it goes sharply left and downhill away from BRP. At bottom of hill, take sharp right onto old forest road. Trail goes to right around large rock. After topping a hill, log bench is on left on way down. Trail continues downhill, curving back towards BRP before turning away. One final uphill section goes to Raven Rock parking area (MP 289.5). Ⓟ

28.8 From north side of overlook, continue north on BRP shoulder for 900 feet. At "Overlook Ahead" sign, trail goes left into woods. Trail veers right, meandering through woods for 800 feet before reaching stile. Climb over stile and go through pasture close to fence, which parallels BRP on right. Sometimes there are cows in this field, but they are no bother. A protective mule may be interested in your dog. From top of hill, you can see old cattle pens and Blackberry Rd. at

Autumn sunrise over Trout Lake
Photo by Victor Ellison

bottom of hill. Follow fence line to stile in right corner. Climb stile, continue few feet to bridge and go up steps to Blackberry Rd.

29.2 Cross Blackberry Rd. and climb stile into pasture. Walk uphill, staying near fence along BRP. Skirt to left of family cemetery near top of hill. At times, there are horses here; one horse may be aggressive to dogs. Continue 250 feet to stile.

29.6 Cross stile. Trail winds through woods and wetlands, crossing 3 bridges before coming out to BRP shoulder.

30.2 Turn left and walk on shoulder for 80 feet. Cross BRP to Sampson Rd. Walk on right shoulder of Sampson Rd. for 300 feet. Turn left onto George Hayes Rd. Walk along shoulder for 0.46 mile to set of wooden steps on left.

30.8 Go down steps through pasture, bearing right to boardwalk/bridge. Cross bridge and go uphill to left. Trail winds across ridgeline.

31.8 Trail goes under large fallen tree, immediately followed by creek crossing, which requires rock-hopping and may dampen your shoes. Ascend to follow old roadbed.

Camping Lodging Ⓟ Parking Food Restrooms Supplies Water Picnic

32.2 Cross impressive footbridge over cascading High Shoals Creek. *Note:* There are good photo opportunities from bridge.

32.3 A few yards past the bridge, a well-used trail leads uphill on left to a pull-out area on BRP, just south of Goshen Creek Viaduct. The pullout can accommodate several cars. Continue straight. ◢

32.4 Follow path along scenic creek bed. Cross stile under Goshen Creek Viaduct; BRP is overhead. Cross pasture under bridge. Cross over second stile to reach Bamboo Rd. ◢

32.6 Turn right and walk along shoulder of paved Bamboo Rd., which becomes gravel. After walking a short distance, you pass George Hayes Rd. For the next 0.7 mile, walk on road next to fields before reaching intersection of Bamboo and Little Laurel Rds. Continue straight past intersection along shoulder of Bamboo Rd. for 180 feet before trail goes right into pasture. In pasture, trail curves right into woods. Follow trail for a short distance to BRP.

33.5 From MP 285.5, turn left and walk shoulder of BRP beside meadow until trail enters woods on left.

33.8 Trail goes through woods and back to BRP. Turn left and walk shoulder about 100 feet north to Boone's Trace Overlook on east (right) side (MP 285.1). From the overlook, walk north about 900 feet to where trail goes right into woods. Ⓟ 🌲

34.1 Trail returns to BRP. Turn right and walk north 0.1 mile to MP 284.5. Trail goes into woods on left (west) side of BRP.

34.4 Cross BRP to where trail enters woods on east (right) side. It climbs ridge, goes through rhododendron thicket, and follows switchbacks to creek crossing. Ascend hill. Friends trail workers call this section the "enchanted forest."

35.3 Come out of woods at private driveway. Cross drive and continue into woods. At pasture, turn left and walk inside split-rail fence. A large home sits atop hill on right. A third of way through pasture, watch for sinkholes. At end of fence, jog left through fence, turn right and walk shoulder of BRP north for 240 feet to MP 283.2. Cross BRP; trail goes left into woods.

35.8 Trail crosses bridge and goes to Don Hayes Rd. at MP 283. Turn right on road; walk through tunnel that goes under BRP. Walk 355 feet and turn left to cross bridge leading into woods on east side of

MST through the woods near Thunder Hill Overlook
Photo by Charles Register

BRP. At BRP, turn right and walk north 0.35 mile to MP 282.3. At end of wide cleared area on right, trail goes right into woods.

36.8 Walk north on east (right) side of BRP. Cross ridgeline, through switchbacks down and over Elk Creek Rd. Cross road onto dirt/grass service road paralleling BRP. Follow service road to pasture at top of hill. Before entering pasture, trail goes left into woods.

37.4 Walk north on BRP for 0.7 mile and go past Grandview Overlook on right (MP 281.2). Walk 800 feet north of overlook to where trail goes right into woods. Ⓟ

38.1 Walk in woods about 600 feet to service road. You pass a heritage apple orchard in this section. Turn left on service road, walk 225 feet and go through gate to BRP. You can see Parkway Elementary School across BRP. Turn right and walk 650 feet on shoulder. Turn right into woods on east (right) side. After 838 feet, trail crosses open area near Old US 421 and continues north. Trail comes back to BRP near speed limit sign. *Note:* For food, access Old US 421 and travel right (north) for 0.15 mile to Blue Ridge Diner, open 11-8 Monday through Friday. 🍴

Camping Lodging Ⓟ Parking Food Restrooms Supplies 💧Water Picnic

Goshen Creek
Photo by Shelton Wilder

38.9 At BRP, turn right and hike north. After hiking past two pastures on left, trail goes left into woods at MP 279.6.

39.8 Trail goes through small glade and uphill to landscaped driveway after 600 feet. Turn left on drive and walk 97 feet to road (Wildcat Rd.). Cross road onto another driveway and go 83 feet to right turn onto service road entering woods. Service road goes uphill; turn right into woods as service road curves left. Trail goes downhill near BRP, then back up before descending again. The Wilder Bench is on trail as you head downhill to BRP.

41.2 Cross BRP and enter woods on east side. Go uphill to white pines, then down switchbacks and back uphill to BRP. Turn right and walk on shoulder for 472 feet to Osborne Mountain Overlook (MP 278). Ⓟ

42.0 At north end of Osborne Mountain Overlook, cross to west (left) side of BRP and go into grassy field and then uphill into woods. The next 1.25 miles follow switchbacks to the ramp at US 421 on the west side of the BRP. Parking space is available in flat grassy area on

🔺Camping 🛏️Lodging Ⓟ Parking 🍴Food 🚻Restrooms 🏬Supplies 💧Water 🪑Picnic

BRP 0.2 mile south of entrance ramp. Leave the woods on the west side of the BRP, just south of bridge crossing over US 421.

43.3 Cross bridge, walking left along the west shoulder of BRP, facing oncoming traffic. Cross BRP at "Roanoke" mileage sign. Trail goes uphill into woods on right side.

43.6 Trail goes steadily uphill for a gain of 650 feet in elevation, but trail through hardwoods high above BRP is well graded.

45.3 Cross BRP diagonally and enter woods on west (left) side. This level section comes back to BRP across from sign for E.B. Jeffress Park (MP 274.1).

45.6 Just north of sign for Jeffress Park, enter the woods on the east (right) side of BRP and begin short ascent. This section is an easy walk with moderate elevation changes. Come out of the woods at Tomkins Knob parking area.

47.2 Enter woods at north side of parking area, near the BRP. It is 75 yards to the Cool Springs Baptist Church and the Jesse Brown cabin historic area.

47.3 Go back into the woods at the north side of the historic area, just to the left of the sign about Cool Springs Baptist Church. The trail goes downhill slightly then becomes level before reaching Cascades Recreation Area (MP 271.9).

48.0 At the north end of the recreation area, enter the woods following the signs to the cascades. After a few yards on the trail, take the left fork of this loop trail. The trail goes downhill and follows a stream. After crossing a log bridge, turn left going uphill to follow MST. If you go straight, it is a short walk downhill to the waterfall, which is well worth the detour.

48.4 Trail goes through woods until it reaches the BRP. Cross the parkway. Go around the chain across the road and walk 40 feet to turn right to follow MST. This part of the trail travels high above the BRP. You can appreciate the difficult construction work that allows this section of the trail to hang on the side of the steep hillside yet still makes it an easy walk as the path follows the ridgeline.

49.5 Come out of the woods and walk down across a pasture. Walk north on the west shoulder of BRP past Phillips Gap Rd., which goes west. Be sure to face oncoming traffic because of narrow shoulders and

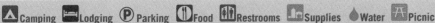

short sight lines. Phillips Gap is the crest of the Blue Ridge at 3,221 feet.

50.2 Come to the section of Phillips Gap Rd. that turns gravel and travels east. There is a parking space a few yards down the eastern segment of Phillips Gap Rd. (MP 269.8). Opposite this intersection, the MST goes uphill into the woods before leveling off.

50.5 Come to pasture. Cross it, going downhill. Keep near the tree line on the right, heading toward BRP.

50.6 Cross BRP diagonally. Look north for the MST sign at the end of the pasture where the woods begin. The sign is close to the BRP.

51.1 This section goes through a nice woodland. Cross a brook coming out of a stone culvert. This section of the trail is below the BRP, with a sharp drop-off on the right. 🟦

51.9 Continue walking through the woods until trail comes back to BRP, just south of intersection with Park Vista Rd. at Benge Gap (MP 268). Park Vista Inn can be seen from BRP. See "Lodging" for parking information. 🛏️ 🍴 Ⓟ 🟦

52.0 Cross BRP to west side. Turn right off Park Vista Rd., following paved Blue Ridge Church Rd. up the hill.

52.4 Pass the National Park Service maintenance yard on the right before arriving at Blue Ridge Baptist Church on the left a few yards beyond. The church cemetery is on the right.

52.5 Walk north of the cemetery and cross BRP. Walk 500 feet along the eastern segment of Blue Ridge Church Rd., which is now gravel. Turn left into the woods, following a creek. At top of the hill, MST makes a sharp left. *Note:* Don't be confused by the MST sign with arrow; that sign is for hikers traveling southbound. Keep walking up the hill to your left. A few yards up the hill, MST turns right. You are parallel to the BRP. 🟦

52.9 Walk through a stile into a pasture. Walk along the fence posts, noting the white dots on the posts periodically. You are on top of the ridge here and have an astounding view, with Grandfather, Sugar, and Beech Mountains to the south and Mount Jefferson in front of you. As you climb the hill, note large trees in the middle of the pasture will have MST dots and signs as the trail moves over to the center of the pasture. At the top of the hill, you will be opposite the

MST near Osbourne Mountain Overlook
Photo by Shelton Wilder

Mount Jefferson Overlook below. *Note:* If you park at the overlook, you can reach the trail by going to either of the stiles at the ends of the pasture. Continue downhill along tree line. A well-trod footpath begins closer to fenceline and white dots appear again on fence posts. Just past a pasture gate, go through a stile into the woods on your left. Ⓟ

53.7 The path goes through rhododendron thickets and woods, even though it is close to the BRP. The trail comes out of the woods and goes 150 yards outside the fenceline on the BRP shoulder before going back into the woods—still on the east (right) side of the BRP. Trail continues in woods along fenceline before going downhill away from the BRP.

54.3 Trail comes out of the woods at gravel road. This is once again Blue Ridge Church Rd. Turn left and walk on the road, which has little-to-no traffic. You will walk alongside scenic meadows for this section.

54.9 The gravel road reaches an intersection. Turn left (west) and go to BRP. Across the BRP, you'll see Calloway Gap Rd. Cross the BRP and follow MST sign a few yards north of Calloway Gap Rd.

Camping Lodging Ⓟ Parking Food Restrooms Supplies ◆ Water Picnic

55.0 Trail ascends to fenceline. *Note:* This fence is electrified! Trail comes out to BRP. Turn left and walk 600 feet on the shoulder. Trail goes back into woods along electrified fence still on west side of BRP.

55.5 At end of fence, trail enters laurel/rhododendron thicket then goes into forest with fern-covered floor. Trail goes up and down hills but steep ascents and descents never go more than 200 feet before leveling out. After switchbacks, trail comes into clearing. Trail crosses clearing going away from BRP towards the woods. Watch for white dots on trees. Trail passes Christmas tree farm with large pond on left. Trail ascends and makes sharp left turn near BRP. Trail descends 300 feet to wooden steps at switchback. It's 100 feet to open field.

57.1 It's 300 feet across field. You pass 2 MST posts placed at trail forks while crossing field; go right at first, left at second post. Enter woods and walk downhill about 700 feet. Trail is level for about 100 feet before descending for 0.4 mile. Come out of woods.

58.1 MST crosses BRP diagonally. This is Daniels Gap (MP 262.2). Look for MST sign at edge of woods to the north on the east side of BRP. The trail travels through woods for about 0.5 mile until it opens onto a grassy area under large power lines. Cross under lines and go back into woods. Trail comes to a gravel road; turn left. (*Note:* See Terry Mohn's entry under "Trail Angels" for camping.) Pass an iron gate; continue on road for 30 feet to where MST turns left into woods. Walk through woods to field that borders BRP. Turn right & walk along BRP to overpass over NC 16 (MP 261). Walk across the overpass on the shoulder. (Food & supplies 0.5 mile to left on NC 16. It is 13 miles to West Jefferson.)

59.1 MST goes back into woods across the access ramp on east (right) side. Look for sign northeast of stop sign. After 60 feet, turn left on grassy roadbed. Walk 40 feet to left turn back into woods. Blaze indicating turn may be faded, so look closely for this quick turn. After 260 feet, turn right onto old logging/service road. Walk 100 feet to where MST goes left back into woods. It's 0.2 mile to fork in trail. 100 feet to right is stonework overlook at Jumpinoff Rock; it's well worth the short detour. From the fork, MST goes left. It's 200 feet to bench on left. It's 0.2 mile to the Jumpinoff Rock Overlook parking area (MP 260.3).

60.1 From Jumpinoff Rock parking area, cross to west (left) side of BRP and enter woods to the north. Go 150 feet to gravel road. Turn right onto Doyle Bare Rd. Go 370 yards, pass gravel road on left (BRP is ahead). Before reaching parkway, just past the driveway, trail goes left into woods. Go on old logging road for 300 yards before turning right into woods. Come to and walk through field just below BRP. Go back into woods for 300 yards before coming back to BRP. Walk 220 yards on west (left) shoulder along split-rail fence. Come to Pony Farm Rd. (S.R. 1632).

61.9 Turn left on Pony Farm Rd., going away from BRP. Walk on gravel road that parallels BRP before going behind Northwest Trading Post to Trading Post Rd. You pass New River Inn & Cottages on the left. Glendale Springs is 0.5 mile to the left. Cross Trading Post Rd. and walk 150 yards east (right) on the north side of the road. Pass the Northwest Trading Post (MP 259) on the right. Sally Mae's on the Parkway gift shop is inside, along with sodas, sandwiches, and fudge. Ⓟ 🚻 🌢 🎋 🍴 🛏

62.6 Cross BRP and go left into woods just before Old Wilkes Rd. also goes off to the left. Walk about 950 yards before coming back to BRP. Turn right (north) and walk along east shoulder of BRP for 580 yards. Pass MP 258 on the way. Go back into woods on east (right) side. When you come out of woods, gate to Sam Miller Cemetery is on right; BRP on left. Cherry Hill Rd. is straight ahead. Raccoon Holler Rd. and Raccoon Holler Campground are across BRP. ⛺ 🌢 🏪

64.1 Continue straight on Cherry Hill Rd. for 800 yards. MST goes into woods on left. Trail comes out of woods at Cherry Hill Rd./Bare Creek Rd. intersection. BRP is on left; CH Coffeehouse Lane is across the BRP. Bare Creek Rd. is on other side of Cherry Hill Rd. Walk on Bare Creek Rd. for 150 feet. MST goes into woods on left. Trail comes out of woods at BRP and Bare Creek Rd.

65.6 Cross BRP to west side, staying on Bare Creek Rd. Go into woods north of Bare Creek Rd. Walk 660 yards back to BRP. Walk 125 yards north on BRP shoulder along fenceline. Go back into woods for 150 yards. Trail comes out at BRP (MP 256).

⛺ Camping 🛏 Lodging Ⓟ Parking 🍴 Food 🚻 Restrooms 🏪 Supplies 🌢 Water 🎋 Picnic

Climbing up from Deep Gap overpass
Photo by Shelton Wilder

66.2 Cross BRP to Don Bare Rd. Entrance to Mountain View Lodge and Cabins is at this intersection. (*Note:* See "Trail Angels" for information about free camping courtesy of Thomas & Theresa Haislip.) Walk 50 yards on Don Bare Rd., then turn left onto gravel Thistle Hill Lane. Walk 200 yards to left turn into woods. This is not well marked, so watch carefully for this turn. You can see a pond through trees on the right. Walk 150 yards to log steps leading down to small creek. Continue 0.4 mile to Roe Hunt Rd. (MP 255.3). 🛏️ ⛺ 💧

67.3 Cross to west side of BRP. Trail ascends gradually but steeply, then goes downhill for 0.8 mile to an interesting tree-root/rock area over a wet spot.

68.2 Still on west side, MST parallels BRP the whole way. It is 0.2 mile to switchback going downhill. It's another 0.2 mile of path meandering in woods to arrival at junction of gated side road and BRP.

68.6 Cross gated road and continue on west side of BRP. There is a short switchback before trail travels parallel below the BRP for little over 0.2 mile before starting steep but gradual downhill for 0.3 mile to a switchback. It is 200 feet to BRP.

69.2 Turn left to walk north along guardrail on west (left) side of BRP. Turn left uphill on gravel road leading up to Sheets Cemetery. You can see gate from the road. Go around gate and walk 65 feet to where MST goes right into woods.

69.4 MST winds through woods high above Sheets Overlook on BRP (no access from MST) before going steeply downhill to BRP.

70.2 Cross to east side of BRP. MST goes up and down before reaching gravel Cameron Mtn. Rd. Turn left on this private road and walk 180 feet past gate. Do not take road to right; MST goes right into woods near BRP. Jesse Sheets' log cabin (built in 1818) is on other side of BRP.

70.5 Proceed through young-growth pine stand. There is a moderate climb as trail winds around ravines before descending. Trail passes a cabin on the right before coming to dirt road. Turn left and walk 200 feet to go around gate. Continue 250 feet toward BRP. You are at Alder Gap. Turn right into woods just before BRP.

70.8 There is a gentle climb to ridgeline before a gentle descent back to BRP.

71.7 Turn right to walk 0.2 mile on BRP shoulder next to split-rail fence. You pass MP 251.

71.9 At end of fenceline, MST goes into woods on north side of Darnell Woodie Rd. There is a geological survey marker reading 3,008 feet elevation near MST sign. (*Note:* See Marc Arnsdorff's "Trail Angel" entry for camping.) You cross 4 small log footbridges in this section. Reach BRP at MP 250 and Hiram Bare Rd. ◆

72.8 Cross BRP to west (left) side at intersection with Hiram Bare Rd. MST goes uphill into woods on north side of dirt road. MST rises above BRP and makes several curves to skirt ravines and avoid steep ups and downs. Trail crosses creek about 100 feet before reaching gravel South Laurel Fork Rd. Turn right and walk 250 feet to BRP. ◆

73.9 Cross BRP to east (right) side and continue descending on curves of gravel South Laurel Fork Rd. Cross a small bridge; you'll see BRP on high bridge to your left. Walk about 50 feet and turn left onto old dirt/grass road.

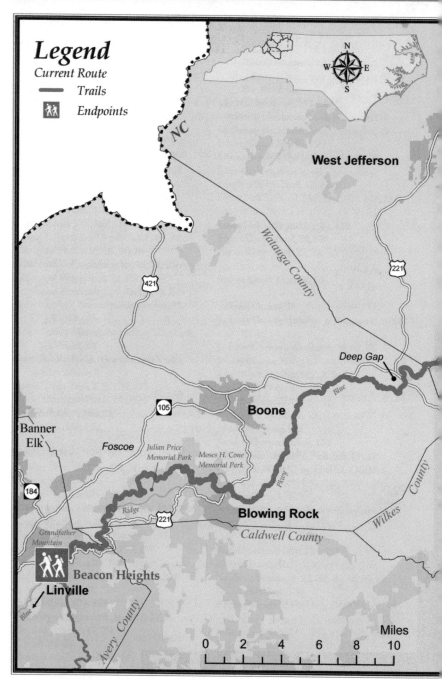

Map and elevation profile produced for Friends of the Mountains-to-Sea Trail by Curtis Belyea, 2016.

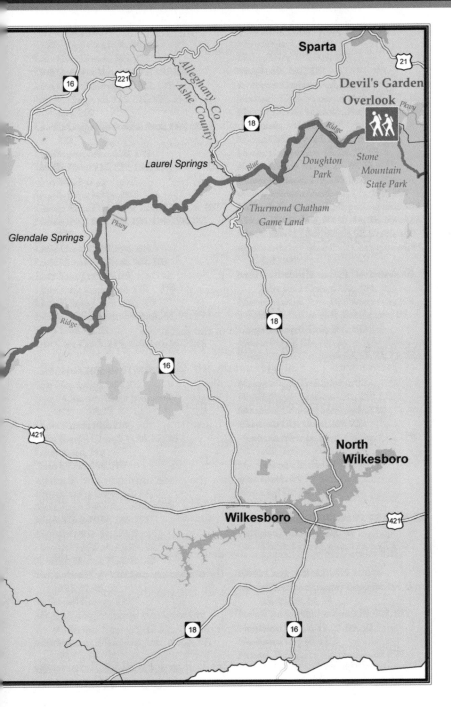

74.5 Approximately 100 feet on the road, the MST goes right up steps. You'll rock-hop one stream as the trail parallels the BRP before descending to come out of the woods just south of the BRP entry ramp to NC 18. 💧

75.3 Cross the BRP and walk along the shoulder as it crosses over the overpass. At the exit ramp, turn left and walk to the stop sign at NC 18. Turn right and walk west on the shoulder of NC 18.

75.6 You pass by or near restaurants, motels, campgrounds, and a small store (some are closed from November to April). Walk past Station's Inn and the general store on the right. Wild Woody's campground is on left past Freeborne's Eatery & Lodge. Turn right onto Miller Rd. 🍴 🛏 ⛺ 🛒

75.7 Pass Mountain Side Dr. on the left.

76.0 MST stays on Miller Rd. Pass Stillhouse Branch Rd. on right. Miller's Campground is visible uphill on left. ⛺ [closed Nov.–March]

76.2 Turn right onto Pruitt Cove Rd. Cross BRP to east side. MST goes uphill into woods on north side of the dirt road.

76.6 Reach the BRP and turn right (north). Walk 100 yards to the intersection with Elk Knob Dr. on the left. Cross the parkway onto Elk Knob Dr., then make a quick right onto Grassy Gap Lane on the right. Walk over small bridge and past old farmhouse on left. On right as you climb hill on the road, just before the gated private road, MST goes uphill to the right into the woods.

77.6 MST ascends through the woods. During the fall, trail may be difficult to follow at times but follow the grade until you find a white blaze. Pass buildings of district ranger's office down the hill to the right. After approximately a mile, there is a clearing with a hillside pasture on left. Look for white blazes showing right turn. BRP is uphill to the left now. Look for wooden steps leading up to the parkway in about 100 yards. The turn up the steps may not be well marked.

78.8 At BRP, cross to east side and walk left (north) beside stone wall. At end of wall, you'll be at Basin Cove Overlook (MP 244.7). In middle of overlook, look for break in the wall to find entrance to Bluff Mountain Trail (BMT) on left. ⓟ

78.9 Descend steeply for 300 feet to intersect with Flat Rock Ridge Trail, which goes right. Go left. Pass trail sign to stay on BMT, which runs

MST near Alder Gap
Photo by Carolyn Sakowski

conjunctively with MST for next 6.5 miles. This is an easy, gradual descent for about 0.5 mile to a footbridge, then 60 feet to an old stile to the right of the trail. Continue to another stile and go through it to join a fire road (part of Grassy Gap Trail). At this stile, turn left onto road.

79.9 MST goes off Grassy Gap Trail, downhill on the right, about 50 feet before reaching gate up to BRP.

80.0 The trail may not be well marked in this part. Soon after you turn into the woods, you'll see a concrete water trough at the bottom of the hill. Do not follow cowpaths leading to that trough; stay straight. Trail stays just below the ridgeline until you come to an open pas-

Camping Lodging Parking Food Restrooms Supplies Water 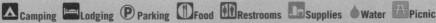Picnic

ture. At pasture, there are no signs. Turn right and you'll see a sign that reads "No horses" where trail re-enters woods.

80.4 Pass through a turnstile and walk around a bend to steps ascending sharply on left to Bluff Mountain View Overlook (MP 243.4). It's worth the short climb to the overlook to see the view. Ⓟ

80.6 Continue north from the overlook. After crossing a small stream, MST turns right as it ascends hill. 💧

81.5 Come to Alligator Back Overlook parking area (MP 242.3). Alligator Back's unusual outcroppings seen from here are geological features composed primarily of schists and gneiss. Ⓟ

82.0 Ascend 400 feet to top of Bluff Mountain. There are 5 sets of wooden steps before reaching an outcrop of rocks with spectacular views. Turn left and climb up the rocks to the ridge. Just past the summit, MST/BMT goes left toward the BRP. To the right is Bluff Ridge Primitive Trail. There is a 3-sided log-and-stone shelter a few yards down the right trail. The shelter is for viewing, not camping.

82.4 Descend toward the loop road for the Doughton Park picnic area (open seasonally), which you can see from the top of the hill. You are descending on BMT, so follow signs for that trail. Ⓟ 🪧

82.8 Cross the parking lot and ascend another knob where a lone tree stands in a meadow. Descend into a field and go through a stile; trail makes a sharp left. Ascend again and walk past restrooms (open seasonally) on the left. Bluffs Lodge (not open at this time) is on the right. You may want to take a short spur trail to Wildcat Rock. To reach it, go through the lodge parking area to the right end of the parking area. The Caudill Cabin is 800 feet below the overlook. To stay on the MST, stay left. 🚻 💧

83.2 Cross the road to walk past the Bluffs Coffee Shop (not open at this time). BMT/MST continues at north end of parking lot. Ⓟ

83.4 Cross to east (right) side of BRP.

83.7 Go through stile into meadow. Follow faint trail through the meadow before entering woods.

84.4 Trail descends to BRP and crosses to west side at Low Notch Gap.

84.6 Travel 800 feet as MST ascends to tent campground area. Follow signs for "Brinegar Cabin" as trail parallels the campground's paved road. ▲

85.6 Trail makes a right turn into the woods, away from paved campground road, then comes back to paved road later. Follow signs to Brinegar Cabin. When trail comes out of woods, turn right toward BRP.

85.8 Cross to east side of BRP (follow BMT signs). The trail goes 200 feet to a paved walkway. Follow white dots on pavement; you are in Doughton Park's RV campground area. Pass information sign on left. Go into woods at north end of campground. Still follow BMT and Brinegar Cabin signs.

86.1 Trail goes through meadows paralleling BRP before going back into woods.

87.0 Cedar Ridge Trail goes straight; BMT/MST goes left. Sign directs you to Brinegar Cabin. There is a Doughton Park trail information sign at this turn.

87.2 Descend out of woods to parking lot for Brinegar Cabin (MP 238.5). BMT stops here. Cabin often has live craft demonstrations in summer. Follow paved path that runs to left of cabin. At information sign labeled "A Mountain Home," turn left heading downhill where you will see a sign for MST going into the woods. Ⓟ 🔹 (seasonal)

87.4 Trail goes through several ascents and descents but none more than 200 yards long. You'll see several concrete USDI/NPS markers as trail travels along park-service boundary with Thurmond Chatham Game Lands.

88.6 Come out of woods and walk on shoulder of BRP as it crosses Air Bellows Gap (3,729 feet, crest of the Blue Ridge). Pass a ramp to Air Bellows Gap Rd. on right. (There is limited shoulder parking on that road.) Continue 50 feet uphill, going back into woods.

88.8 Trail goes through woods. Trail descends out of woods and crosses BRP diagonally to reach west (left) side.

89.2 Trail descends and ascends, paralleling BRP. You cross a small creek with BRP high above to right. Pass large rock field and see BRP stonework. MST descends to BRP. 🔹

90.3 Cross BRP to Devil's Garden Overlook parking area (MP 235.7) on east side. MST continues uphill at north end of parking area. You can continue north on BRP for 6 miles to US 21. Sparta is 7 miles north on US 21. It is 25 miles south on US 21 to Elkin and I-77. Ⓟ

🔺 Camping 🛏 Lodging Ⓟ Parking 🍴 Food 🚻 Restrooms 🏪 Supplies 🔹 Water 🪑 Picnic

Hiking Directions, Westbound

To help with directions, WB on BRP is going south; EB is going north. When going WB, east is on the left, west on the right. Going EB, east is on right, west on left.

0.0   Segment 5 begins at Devil's Garden Overlook on BRP (MP 235.7). This is 6 miles from the intersection of US 21 and BRP. Sparta is 7 miles north on US 21; Elkin and I-77 are 25 miles south on US 21. Cross BRP to west side and begin ascent. Trail descends and ascends, paralleling BRP. Pass large rock field and see BRP stonework. You will cross a small creek with BRP high above on left. Descend out of the woods to BRP. Ⓟ ●

1.1   Cross BRP diagonally to east (left) side and ascend into woods. Trail goes through woods. Trail comes out of the woods.

1.5   Walk along shoulder and pass the ramp on left leading to Air Bellows Gap Rd. (There is limited shoulder parking on that road.) Continue walking on BRP shoulder as the trail crosses Air Bellows Gap (3,729 feet elevation, crest of the Blue Ridge). Continue on shoulder; MST goes uphill back into woods, staying on east (left) side. It may be hard to see any white blaze indicating trail goes uphill into woods, but head uphill to an old road opening.

1.7   Trail goes through several ascents and descents but none more than 200 yards long. You'll see several concrete USDI/NPS markers as trail travels along park-service boundary with Thurmond Chatham Game Lands.

3.6   Descend out of woods to see Brinegar Cabin (MP 238.5) at top of the hill on the left. Walk toward the cabin and follow paved path that runs to right of cabin. Pass an information sign that reads "A Mountain Home." Reach the parking area (water fountain seasonal). Cabin has live craft demonstrations in summer. Ⓟ ● (seasonally)

3.8   Continue to south end of parking lot. Begin Bluff Mountain Trail (BMT), which runs conjunctively with MST for next 6.5 miles. Trail goes uphill into woods. Come to T-intersection. Cedar Ridge Trail goes left; BMT/MST goes right, going toward Doughton Park

Brinegar Cabin
Photo by Jonah Unks

campgrounds and coffee shop. A Doughton Park trail information sign is at this intersection.

4.1 Follow trail across meadow, paralleling BRP. Trail goes back into woods briefly, then enters another meadow before entering woods a second time.

5.1 Come out of woods at Doughton Park's RV campground. Head up-hill toward parking area. Follow white dots on pavement. Information sign for campground is on right. Follow BMT signs. Trail goes 200 feet across BRP to west side (tent campground). ⛺

5.3 Follow trail along left side of campground road. At trail sign, BMT/MST goes left into the woods away from campground road. ⛺

5.5 Trail comes out of woods, back to campground road. Turn left and continue back into woods. Trail goes through campground and begins descent to BRP at Low Notch Gap.

5.7 Cross BRP to east side and ascend into woods. BMT/MST comes into meadow, where it follows a faint trail.

6.9 Go through stile and cross to west side of BRP. Come to parking area for Bluffs Coffee Shop (not open at this time). BMT/MST continues across parking lot in front of the coffee shop. Ⓟ

7.1 Cross to east side of BRP. You may want to take the spur trail to Wildcat Rock (MP 241.1) on the left, which you can pick up at end of the Bluffs Lodge parking lot. It is worth the short walk to see Caudill Cabin, which is 800 feet below the overlook. Walk past Bluffs Lodge (not open at this time) on the left. Pass restrooms (open seasonally) on the right. Descend and go right to go through a stile. Ascend to knob where a lone tree stands in a meadow. There are outstanding long-range views here. Descend and cross parking lot. 🛉🛉 💧 (seasonally)

7.5 Ascend BMT/MST from picnic area (open seasonally) to top of hill. At ridge, BMT/MST goes right. To left is Bluff Ridge Primitive Trail. There is a 3-sided log-and-stone shelter a few yards down this trail. The shelter is for viewing, not camping. 🎋

7.9 The trail comes to a large rock outcropping with panoramic views. Descend on rocks but trail turns sharp right, going into woods before reaching ledge. Descend 5 sets of wooden steps and continue 400 feet before coming out of woods.

8.8 Reach Alligator Back Overlook parking area (MP 242.3). Alligator Back's unusual outcroppings seen from here are geological features composed primarily of schist and gneiss. Ⓟ

9.3 Walk past overlook and continue on east side until trail goes back into woods. Trail descends and makes sharp left turn at small stream. Trail continues to base of Bluff Mountain View Overlook (MP 243.5). It's worth the climb up steps to the overlook for the expansive view. Ⓟ

10.2 Continue trail around bend to turnstile. Trail enters woods.

10.4 Trail comes out of woods and enters meadow. There is no signage here, but walk in meadow along woods about 200 feet. Trail goes back into woods on the left. You will see an old concrete water trough downhill to the left of the trail. This section may not be well marked, so watch carefully for faded white dots on trees. The trail is ascending toward the ridgeline.

10.8 Trail joins old fire road, which is part of Grassy Gap Trail. Turn left and walk on road. To the right is gate just before reaching BRP.

10.9 BMT/MST goes right, uphill and around stile. Trail ascends gradually. Pass an old stile on left; cross footbridge. It is about 0.5 mile to trail information sign. Flat Rock Ridge Trail continues straight. BMT/MST ascends to right very steeply for 300 feet to Basin Cove Overlook (MP 244.7). Trail no longer runs conjunctively with BMT. Ⓟ

11.9 Follow paved walkway south and walk along stone wall on BRP shoulder. Cross BRP to west side, where steps lead back into woods.

12.0 Walk down steps and follow trail to the right. You will intuitively want to go left, but turn right. Walk about 100 yards through woods toward open field ahead. Just before reaching field, trail turns sharp left. Pass district ranger's office downhill on left. Trail comes out of woods at farm road.

12.8 Turn left onto farm road. There is a gate across private road on right. Walk toward white farmhouse. Pass farmhouse on right, cross small bridge. You are on Grassy Gap Lane. Short walk to intersection with Elk Knob Dr. Turn left for short walk to BRP. Cross BRP to east side. Walk 100 yards to where trail goes back into woods. ▲

13.8 Trail descends out of woods to Pruitt Cove Rd. Cross BRP to west side, staying on Pruitt Cove Rd.

14.1 Turn left onto Miller Rd. Pass Stillhouse Branch Rd. on left. Miller's Campground is visible uphill on right. ▲ (closed Nov.-March)

14.3 Continue on shoulder of Miller Rd. Pass Mountain Side Dr. on right.

14.6 Reach NC 18. Turn left and walk in front of Station's Inn (general store, restaurant, and motel). Wild Woody's Campground & Freeborne's Eatery & Lodge are across NC 18. Continue on shoulder of NC 18, walking toward BRP. 🍴 🛏 ▲ 🏠

14.7 Turn left and walk up ramp to BRP. At the parkway, turn right (south) and walk on shoulder as you cross over parkway overpass. Once across overpass, cross BRP to east (left) side. Walk through the grass, heading uphill to the woods.

15.0 Trail parallels the BRP. Rock-hop one stream. Trail comes out of woods. Descend steps to dirt/grass farm road. Turn left and walk approximately 100 feet to South Laurel Fork Rd. ▲

15.8 Turn right and walk on shoulder of South Laurel Fork Rd. Cross a small bridge. On the right, you'll see BRP traveling on high bridge. The road ascends through several curves before reaching BRP.

16.4 Cross BRP to west (right) side. Walk about 250 feet on gravel road to where MST goes left into the woods. Cross small creek. Trail ascends and makes several curves as it skirts the ravines to avoid steep ups and downs. Come out of woods at a dirt road. Turn left and walk to BRP. Cross to east side at this intersection with Hiram Bare Rd. (MP 250). 💧

17.5 Cross 4 small log footbridges in this section. As you come out of woods on north side of Darnell Woodie Rd., there is a geological survey marker near MST sign, which indicates an elevation of 3,008 feet. 💧

18.4 Cross Darnell Woodie Rd. and walk on shoulder of BRP beside split-rail fence. (*Note:* See Marc Arnsdorff's entry under "Trail Angels" for camping.) You pass MP 251.

18.6 At end of fenceline, MST goes back into woods. There is a gentle climb to ridgelines before easy descent that ends at dirt road. You are at Alder Gap. 🔺

19.5 Turn left and walk about 250 feet to gate. Walk around gate and walk about 200 feet before MST goes right. Watch closely for this turn. Trail passes a cabin on the left. There is a moderate climb as trail winds around ravines before going through young-growth pine stand.

19.8 Trail reaches gravel Cameron Mtn. Rd. Turn left on this road, going away from BRP. You can see Jesse Sheets log cabin (built in 1818) on other side of BRP. Walk past a private road going to the left; go past gate. Cameron Mtn. Rd. goes left, but MST goes off to the right. Come out of the woods and cross to west side of BRP.

20.1 MST ascends steeply as it winds through woods high above Sheets Overlook on BRP before coming to gravel road. (There is no access to Sheets Overlook from MST).

20.9 Gravel road continues right to Sheets Cemetery. MST turns left. Go around gate to shoulder of BRP. Walk south (right) along guardrail. Trail goes back into woods on west (right) side of BRP.

21.1 Trail begins a steep but gradual ascent for about 0.3 mile. It then travels parallel below the BRP. There is a short switchback before trail comes to road.

🔺Camping 🛏Lodging Ⓟ Parking 🍴Food 🚻Restrooms 🛒Supplies 💧Water ⛱Picnic

Fence along overlook at Doughton Park
Photo by Janet Pearson

21.7 BRP is to the left, but continue across gated side road. Trail goes back into woods, still on west side of BRP. After trail crosses an interesting tree-root/rock area, it ascends and then descends gradually but steeply back to BRP.

23.0 Cross to east side of BRP at this intersection with Roe Hunt Rd. (MP 255.3). Go back into woods on south side of Roe Hunt Rd. Cross log steps leading down to small creek. Come to gravel road. Turn right onto Thistle Hill Lane. You can see pond on left through the trees. It's about 200 yards to T-intersection with Don Bare Rd. MST turns right on that road, heading toward BRP. At the parkway, the driveway to Mountain View Lodge and Cabins is on the left. *Note:* See "Trail Angels" for information about free camping courtesy of Thomas & Theresa Haislip. 🛏 💧 ⛺

24.1 Cross BRP to west side. MST goes back into woods (MP 256). Trail comes back to BRP; walk south on shoulder along fenceline for about 125 yards. Go back into woods on west (right) side until you reach Bare Creek Rd. Turn left and walk to BRP.

24.7 Cross to east side of BRP. MST goes into woods on south side of Bare Creek Rd. Trail comes out of the woods at intersection with

Bluff Mountain View Overlook
Photo by Carolyn Sakowski

Bare Creek Rd. again. Turn right and go about 150 feet to intersection with Cherry Hill Rd. BRP is on right; CH Coffeehouse Lane is across the BRP. Go left on Cherry Hill Rd. to where MST goes back into woods on south side of that road. Continue through woods until trail comes to paved Cherry Hill Rd. Turn right and walk 800 yards on that road to intersection with BRP and entrance to Sam Miller Cemetery. Across the parkway, Raccoon Holler Rd. leads to Raccoon Holler Campground. ▲ 🏠

26.2 MST enters woods to right of gate to cemetery. Trail comes out of woods and travels 580 yards along the east (left) shoulder of the BRP. Pass MP 258. Trail goes back into woods at end of field.

27.3 Trail comes out of wood at T-intersection with Old Wilkes Rd. Turn right and walk toward BRP. Cross to west side of BRP at Northwest Trading Post (MP 259). Sally Mae's on the Parkway gift shop is inside, along with sodas, sandwiches, and fudge. Ⓟ 🚻 🍴 💧 🏠 🪑

27.7 MST continues past the trading post on Trading Post Rd. for 150 yards, going toward Glendale Springs. Turn left onto Pony Farm

Rd. (S.R. 1632) at New River Inn & Cottages. Walk on gravel Pony Farm Rd. as it goes behind the trading post and parallels the BRP.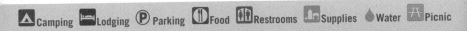

28.4 When Pony Farm Rd. reaches BRP, turn right (south) and walk along shoulder of parkway beside split-rail fence for 220 yards. MST goes back into woods on west (right) side of BRP. Come out of woods and walk through grassy meadow, which is just below BRP. Go back into woods for short distance until trail comes to old logging road. Turn left onto the logging road. MST comes to T-intersection with gravel Doyle Bare Rd. BRP is on left. Turn right and walk on shoulder of Doyle Bare Rd. for 370 yards. MST goes back into woods on left side, just after climbing a hill and just before road curves to the right. Go 150 feet before coming back to BRP across from Jumpinoff Rock Overlook parking area (MP 260.3). Ⓟ 🎋

30.2 Cross to east side of BRP. At south end of parking area, MST goes back into the woods. When you come to a bench on right side of trail, don't think the dirt path on the left leads to the overlook. Continue down trail for another 200 feet to the legitimate spur trail. It's only 100 feet to the left to a stone overlook with views of surrounding area. MST goes off to the right (south). Trail comes to old logging road; turn right. Walk about 100 feet to where MST goes left into woods again. Trail comes to grassy roadbed. Turn right and walk on road for about 40 feet to where MST goes back into woods on the right. Go about 60 feet before coming out of woods at ramp for NC 16/BRP (MP 261). (Food & supplies are about 0.5 mile to right on NC 16. It is 13 miles to West Jefferson.) 🍴 🏪

31.2 Walk along shoulder of BRP as it crosses the overpass. Trail goes uphill across the grassy area to go back into the woods. Trail is in woods for a short distance before coming to gravel road. Turn right onto road; pass an iron gate. (*Note:* See Terry Mohn's entry under "Trail Angels" for camping.) Trail then goes back into woods on right; look carefully for the sign. Cross grassy area under power lines and go back into woods. Trail comes back to BRP at Daniels Gap (MP 262.2). ⛺

32.2 Cross BRP diagonally, heading south. MST enters woods. Trail ascends, levels off, then ascends again. It comes to field. Walk across field. You pass 2 MST posts placed at trail forks in the field.

33.2 Trail re-enters woods. Come to wooden steps at switchback as trail ascends. Trail comes close to BRP at top of hill, then makes a sharp right turn to begin descent. Pass a Christmas tree farm with large pond on right. Cross a clearing with BRP visible to the left, but MST goes away from parkway to re-enter woods. Trail goes up and down hills but ascents and descents never go more than 200 feet before leveling off. Walk through a beautiful forest where trees tower over fern-covered floor. Trail then enters laurel/rhododendron thicket before coming to fenceline. *Note:* This fence is electrified. Walk along the fence before coming out of the woods.

34.8 MST comes back to BRP. Walk 600 feet on shoulder and re-enter woods. Trail comes out of woods at BRP.

35.3 Cross to east side of BRP. Calloway Gap Rd. is to the south of where you exited woods. Go a few yards down the road (Lump Rd.) on east (left) side of parkway before turning right onto Blue Ridge Church Rd. Walk along this gravel road past scenic meadows. There is little traffic on this road. MST turns right to go back into woods after 0.6 mile.

36.0 Trail ascends toward the BRP. You come out of the woods but turn left and walk along fenceline beside the BRP for 150 yards. Trail goes back into woods on left. It goes through woods and rhododendron thickets, although you are close to the parkway.

36.6 Go through a stile near a gate into a pasture. Walk through pasture going uphill near the fence posts. You will see white dots on some of the posts. Trail veers off towards woods. At the top of the hill, you can see large trees in the middle of the pasture; look for MST dots on the trees. You can see the Mount Jefferson Overlook below on the right. If you park at this overlook, you can access the trail through stiles at either end of the pasture. From the summit you have astounding views of Grandfather, Sugar, and Beech Mountains to the south and Mount Jefferson in front of you. Walk downhill, going along the fence posts. There is a stile at the south end of the pasture. Ⓟ

37.4 Go through stile and enter woods. MST turns left going downhill. Trail then turns right to parallel creek. It comes to gravel Blue Ridge Church Rd. Turn right and walk about 500 feet to BRP.

37.8 Cross BRP to west side, where you see Blue Ridge Baptist Church and its cemetery. Walk past the church and cemetery on paved road. Pass the National Park Service maintenance yard on the left.

37.9 Blue Ridge Church Rd. comes to a T-intersection with Park Vista Rd. Park Vista Inn is on right. Turn left and go to BRP.

38.3 Cross BRP to east side. You are at Benge Gap (MP 268). Walk south (right) on shoulder to where MST goes back into woods on your left.

38.4 This section of trail goes through a nice woodland. Cross a brook coming out of a stone culvert. This section of trail is below BRP. It has a sharp drop-off on your left.

39.2 Trail comes back to BRP. You cross to west side and walk uphill through a pasture. Walk along the tree line to find sign where trail re-enters woods.

39.7 Trail goes through woods before descending to BRP at Phillips Gap Rd. (MP 269.8). You will see the gravel part of that road across on the east (left) side of the parkway. Walk along right (west) shoulder of parkway with traffic past the paved section of Phillips Gap Rd., which goes west. Phillips Gap is the crest of the Blue Ridge at 3,221 feet.

40.0 On west side of BRP, walk uphill across a pasture. Look for MST sign showing where trail re-enters woods.

40.1 This section of trail travels high above the BRP. You can appreciate the construction work that allows this section of the trail to hang on the side of a steep hillside yet still makes it an easy walk as the path follows the ridgelines. Come to side road with chain across it. Turn left going toward the BRP.

40.8 Cross BRP to east side and re-enter woods. At a T-intersection, turn right on loop trail to waterfall at Cascades Recreation Area (MP 271.9), which runs conjunctively with MST. A short spur off to left to see the cascades is highly recommended. After seeing the falls, continue on MST. You cross a log bridge and then go uphill and follow a stream.

41.9 Trail comes out at north end of Cascades Recreation Area. Restrooms are on left. Ⓟ 🚻 💧 🏕

42.3 Walk across parking area and past picnic tables to where trail enters woods on south side of recreation area. Trail goes slightly uphill before coming out at Cool Springs Baptist Church and Jesse Brown cabin historic area.

43.0 Cross to south end of the historic area and go back into the woods. It is 75 yards to Tomkins Knob parking area. Ⓟ

43.1 Enter woods again at south end of parking area. This section is an easy walk with moderate elevation changes. When you come out of the woods, you will see sign for E.B. Jeffress Park (MP 274.1) straight ahead.

44.7 Cross BRP diagonally and enter woods on west (right) side of parkway.

45.0 Come out of woods and cross BRP diagonally to enter woods on east side. This 1.7-mile section of trail descends about 650 feet in elevation before reaching the US 421 bridge.

46.7 Trail comes out of woods on east shoulder of parkway near "Roanoke" distance sign. Cross parkway, walking south (left) along the west shoulder of BRP with traffic. You will have to walk along shoulder of the parkway from this spot all the way to the south side of the overpass over US 421. Be sure to walk on the right (west) shoulder with the traffic as the shoulder is narrow and sight line is limited on the left (east) shoulder.

47.0 On west side of BRP, just across from the ramp coming from US 421 to the BRP, MST goes uphill into the woods. Parking space is available in flat grassy area on BRP 0.2 mile south of entrance ramp. The trail goes high above the BRP for next 1.25 miles. Trail comes out of woods and downhill into grassy field. Cross BRP to Osborne Mountain Overlook (MP 278) on east side of BRP. Ⓟ

48.3 At south end of parking area, continue along shoulder of parkway for 472 feet. MST then goes downhill into woods on east (left) side of BRP. Trail descends then goes uphill through switchbacks before going through stand of white pines and then out of woods back to parkway.

Ferns in the mist in Ashe County
Photo by Carolyn Sakowski

49.1 Cross BRP to west side. You will see the Wilder Bench beside trail as you head uphill. Trail goes up and down as it parallels the parkway. Trail comes out at a service road. Turn left and follow service road downhill. MST turns left onto a driveway and goes 83 feet to Wildcat Rd. Cross that road and walk 97 feet on landscaped driveway. Turn right and walk downhill and through small glade for 600 feet.

50.5 Trail comes out of woods at MP 279.6. Hike on shoulder past large pasture on right, followed by pastures on both sides.

51.4 Cross to east side of BRP. Trail goes back into woods near speed limit sign. It crosses an open area near Old US 421, then goes back into woods for 838 feet before coming back to BRP. Turn left and walk on shoulder 650 feet. You can see Parkway Elementary School on the right. Turn left onto service road, go through gate, and walk

225 feet. Turn right into woods at signpost. Walk 600 feet through the woods; you pass a heritage apple orchard in this section. *Note:* For food, access Old US 421 and travel right (north) for 0.15 mile to Blue Ridge Diner, open 11-8 Monday through Friday. (⍾)

52.2 Come out of woods, turn left, and walk 800 feet south past Grandview Overlook (MP 281.2). Continue 0.7 mile on parkway shoulder. (Ⓟ)

52.9 Trail goes into woods and meanders up and down until it reaches a pasture and service road. Turn right onto dirt/grass service road, which parallels the parkway. Service road comes to Elk Creek Rd. Cross that road. (There is no MST sign here.) *Note:* Watch for traffic coming out of tunnel to right; sight lines are short. Continue on trail that goes uphill through switchbacks before strolling across ridgeline.

53.5 Trail comes out at BRP at MP 282.3. Walk on shoulder 0.35 mile past wide cleared area on right. Trail then goes left into woods, still on east side of BRP. This uphill section is a delightful walk. Trail comes out of woods. Cross bridge. Come to Don Hayes Rd. at MP 283. Turn right and follow road through tunnel under BRP. Turn left to follow trail into woods. You are now on west side of BRP.

54.5 Come out of the woods and cross to east side of BRP. Walk south on shoulder for 240 feet. At fence, jog right through the fence and continue walking through pasture on inside of split-rail fence. A large house sits atop hill on left. About two-thirds of way across pasture, watch for sinkholes. At end of pasture, trail re-enters woods for short distance. (This is not marked, so look for trail going into woods.) Come to private driveway. Cross drive and continue into woods.

55.0 Friends trail workers call this section the "enchanted forest." The trail descends below the parkway, crosses a creek at the bottom, then follows switchbacks as it ascends the hill. It then goes through rhododendron thickets as it comes down from the ridge.

55.9 Cross BRP to west side. Walk along shoulder before trail goes into woods. Trail comes out of woods. Cross BRP to east side and walk on shoulder 0.1 mile before trail goes into the woods. Trail comes out of the woods.

🅰 Camping 🛏 Lodging Ⓟ Parking ⍾ Food 🚻 Restrooms 🏪 Supplies 💧 Water ⛺ Picnic

MST by Blue Ridge Baptist Church
Photo by Chris Underhill

56.2 Turn south (left) and walk about 900 feet on shoulder to Boone's Trace Overlook (MP 285.1), where there is picnic table and trash receptacle. Cross to west side of BRP. Walk about 100 feet south on shoulder before trail goes back into woods. Ⓟ ⛱

56.5 Trail comes out of woods. Walk on shoulder alongside meadow on right.

56.8 Trail turns right into woods for short distance before coming to paved road. Turn left onto Bamboo Rd. It is 180 feet to intersection with Little Laurel Rd. Continue straight, staying on Bamboo Rd. For next 0.7 mile, walk on gravel road. You will see BRP paralleling on the left. Pass George Hayes Rd. on left. Bamboo Rd. becomes paved.

57.7 MST turns left and crosses a stile to reach pasture under Goshen Creek Viaduct high overhead. Cross pasture (you may have the company of a few cows). Cross a second stile and walk under the viaduct. MST follows a scenic creek. 💧

58.0 As you begin to climb away from the creek bed, you can see a footpath leading up to the parkway. There is a gravel parking area for a few cars here.

58.1 Continue on MST to impressive footbridge over cascading High Shoals Creek. *Note:* Excellent photo op here.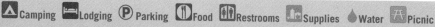

58.5 Come to creek crossing, which requires rock-hopping and may dampen your shoes. Trail then goes under large fallen tree. Trail winds across ridgeline, then descends to bridge. Climb steps up to George Hayes Rd.

59.5 Turn right and walk along shoulder of paved road for 0.46 mile to intersection with Sampson Rd. Turn right onto Sampson Rd. and walk 300 feet to BRP.

60.1 Cross BRP to west side, turn left (south), and walk 80 feet to where trail goes into woods. Trail crosses 3 bridges as it winds through woods and wetlands. Come to and climb over stile.

60.7 Cross pasture so you skirt the family cemetery near top of hill. At times, there are horses here; one horse may be aggressive to dogs. Walk downhill and stay near fence along BRP. Climb stile and cross Blackberry Rd. *Note:* Fence may be electrified.

61.1 Climb down steps and cross bridge before crossing over another stile. Climb uphill, keeping close to the fence parallel to the parkway. You can see cattle pens to the right. Ascend the hill and follow treeline until you come to stile on the left. Cross over the stile. Trail continues through the woods for 800 feet before coming out at BRP. Turn right (south) and walk 900 feet on the shoulder to the Raven Rock Overlook parking area (MP 289.5) (P)

61.5 At south end of overlook parking area, MST goes downhill into woods curving away from the parkway. You pass beside large outcroppings, then reach a log bench on right after ascending back up the hill. After descending another hill, take sharp left onto old forest road at bottom. Trail goes up and down hills. Trail goes sharply right and uphill away from BRP. Trail bears left going steeply uphill before leveling off. (This is Thunder Hill.) It's 450 feet downhill to side road just off the parkway.

Camping Lodging (P) Parking Food Restrooms Supplies Water Picnic

Thunder Hill Overlook
Photo by Charles Register

62.4 Cross side road, turn right (south), and walk along west (right) shoulder and then beside fence. Thunder Hill Overlook (MP 290.3) is across BRP. Ⓟ

63.2 Go through stile across from south end of parking area. Climb hill. After going over top of hill, turn left and cross meadow, going toward BRP. Go through stile and cross to east (left) side of BRP. Walk south 500 feet. Turn left onto Greenhill Rd. Walk 200 feet and climb over stile near farm gate and into pasture on right. Cross pasture heading toward BRP where MST goes back into woods.

63.4 Keep walking south until you reach an old farm road. Turn right and follow road out of woods into pasture. Go up the pasture toward the BRP and trail goes back into woods.

63.8 Go over stile at top of ridge and hike downhill through rhododendron thicket.

63.9 Come to another stile; continue into woods. Go through section of clearing, then cross 2 bridges. Trail travels along ridge across the pasture until it re-enters the woods.

64.3 Travel through woods near fence along BRP. Come into another pasture, where trail travels close to barbed-wire fence. Trail bears to the left and comes to another stile. Follow trail along hillside for 822 feet before it comes out to BRP.

64.7 Turn left and travel south along shoulder of BRP. Cross overpass over US 221/321 (MP 291.9).

65.1 Turn left and descend the exit ramp. To the right is a nearby shopping center and the town of Blowing Rock; Boone is 7 miles to left. Turn right onto shoulder of US 221/321 and walk 200 feet. 🍴 🛏 🏬

65.3 Turn right onto gravel Old Camp Catawba Rd. You are walking through a residential area with some traffic. MST turns left. You are now hiking on Watkin Rd., part of the Cone estate carriage trail system. Cross creek by rock hopping. 💧

65.5 You can see lake on left through the trees.

66.2 Come to intersection with Black Bottom Rd. Go right on Watkin Rd., following signs to the manor house.

68.3 At next intersection, turn right, still traveling toward manor house.

68.9 Just before reaching the manor house, turn right and follow road that goes in front of the carriage house. There are restrooms and water at the carriage house. There is parking here, but rangers discourage hikers from using it because it gets crowded on summer weekends. Continue through tunnel that goes under BRP. 🚻 💧 Ⓟ

69.1 At trail intersection, turn left going toward Trout Lake. Trail follows gentle switchbacks down to Flannery Fork Rd. Cross that road and continue on trail to Trout Lake. Turn right and walk alongside the lake. Turn left and cross over the dam. Continue to walk along the lake. 💧

70.2 MST turns right, following signs to Rich Mtn. You can continue on the trail along the lake to a right turn up the hill to a parking area. 💧 Ⓟ

72.0 Follow trail up to Rich Mtn. until it opens into a cleared area. You will cross 3 culverted creeks in this section. Turn right and go short distance to left turn, staying on Rich Mtn. Trail traveling conjunctively with MST.

72.6 You will see a large wooden stair-step stile on the left with MST sign. Climb that stile and head down a steep hill. The trail descends 500 feet in next half-mile. Trail descends wooden steps to Shulls Mill Rd.

Heritage apple orchard near Grandview Overlook
Photo by Shelton Wilder

As the road curves to the right, go left on the trail from the informal parking area and walk through overgrown pasture, then into woods.

73.1 Hike through woods until you reach logging road. Turn right and continue on the road.

74.0 Follow old roadbed. A side road goes off to right, but stay on main road.

74.4 Come to backcountry campsite with bench and firepit with grate but no amenities. Permit is required from Price Park campground office. Maximum of 6 campers allowed.

74.6 The trail goes downhill to the left, crossing over large boulder field for 75 yards. Bear right and walk downhill to cross Boone Fork bridge. On the other side of the creek, MST travels conjunctively with Boone Fork Trail (BFT). Turn right onto BFT/MST. The next 2 miles have numerous creeks where you can access water, but it should be treated.

74.8 Pass an old dam site on right.

75.0 Pass side trail to Hebron Falls on right.

Falling water near Bamboo Gap
Photo by Charlie Day

75.5 Pass a BFT milepost sign. Climb wooden ladder to get to top of rocks. Follow a stone walkway as it circles a large rock formation and goes downhill to continue on the trail.

75.6 Make 2 easy creek crossings. Cross metal bridge and pass a BFT milepost sign.

75.8 Climb down 3 sets of wooden steps. For the next 0.2 mile, you climb up and down hills, with a series of cascades in creek below on right. Cross creek using large boulders. Ascend steps and turn left to follow trail.

76.1 Cross a plank walkway. It is 100 yards to first of 4 creek crossings, some of which may require getting your feet wet. Climb down large rocks to third creek crossing. It is 30 feet past 4th creek crossing to another BFT milepost sign. About 100 yards beyond is metal bridge followed by crossing an old log bridge.

76.3 Make 3 more creek crossings.

76.4 Trail goes steeply downhill to the left to make another creek crossing. A 2nd creek crossing comes quickly followed by a bridge.

76.6 Rock hop 2 more creeks. Pass BFT milepost. Cross bridge

76.8 Rock hop 3 more creeks. Come to large rock. BFT/MST now turns to the left, heading uphill. Old trail straight ahead is closed off.

77.0 Climb uphill. Come out of woods into meadow. Follow trail uphill through meadow to summit, where there is another BFT milepost. Turn left to continue across ridge of meadow, heading toward the woods.

77.3 Tanawha Trail comes in from the right. It is 0.5 mile straight ahead to Julian Price Park Campground. Turn right and follow as MST and Tanawha Trail now run conjunctively for rest of this segment. ⓟ 🔺 🚻 💧

77.4 Cross bridge; pass stile on left.

77.5 Cross bridge and enter meadow.

77.9 Walk through meadow. At fork, stay left. Join old roadbed. Go through stile.

78.0 Travel on single-track trail until you reach old roadbed. Turn right onto roadbed.

78.1 Follow Tanawha Trail signs with single white feather as well as MST signs.

78.4 Go through stile to reach Holloway Mtn. Rd. A designated parking area is across the road. *Note:* BRP is 1.0 mile to left using Holloway Mtn. Rd. The intersection with BRP is 6 miles west of Blowing Rock. To the right, it is 1.0 mile to the town of Foscoe and NC 105. ⓟ 🍴 🛏 🛒

78.9 It is confusing as to what the official trail route is from the parking area. You can go across the pasture and go straight up the hill. The signs for the Tanawha Trail direct you to go left and circle that same hill. Either route arrives at the tree-sheltered area at the summit,

🔺Camping 🛏Lodging ⓟParking 🍴Food 🚻Restrooms 🛒Supplies 💧Water 🏕Picnic

where you continue to cross pasture on Tanawha/MST. On clear days, you have good views of Grandfather Mtn.

79.0 Go through stile and follow trail as it curves to left through a field. Trail then goes in and out of woods.

79.2 Trail comes out into pasture, then heads downhill. You should see trail markers on trees in the pasture. Downhill to the left, you see graveled Holloway Mountain Rd. Trail then goes off downhill alongside woods until it enters woods on right.

79.4 Leave woods and enter another field. Follow Tanawha Trail feather markers as trail veers to left and enters wood.

79.6 Come out of woods into another field. Walk about 50 yards and make left turn. You should see Tanawha Trail signs. Go about 50 yards to pass through stile going back into woods.

80.5 Rock hop 4 small creeks. Come to where trail to Cold Prong Pond parking area (MP 299) goes off to the left. You will also see Tanawha Trail information sign. Ⓟ ◊

80.6 Cross a bridge.

80.8 Cross another bridge.

82.2 Boone Fork parking area (MP 299.9) is 400 feet to the left. *Note:* Don't confuse this overlook with Boone Fork Trail near Price Park. Ⓟ

82.3 Upper Boone Fork Trail goes to left 0.5 mile to Calloway Peak Overlook (MP 299.7). Stay on Tanawha/MST. Cross Upper Boone Fork bridge. Asutsi Trail goes to left for 0.4 mile to US 221 (this is winter parking when BRP is closed). Just past Asutsi on the left, the Grandfather Mtn. State Park sign shows which campsites are in use and has permits to register for open sites located on Nuwati and Daniel Boone Scout Trails.

82.5 Nuwati Trail goes to the right. The 4 campsites described in "Camping" are on this trail. Stay left for MST. ▲

82.7 Daniel Boone Scout Trail goes right. Stay straight on main trail. Campsites are available 1.2 miles up the right-hand trail at Daniel Boone Campsite. ▲

83.7 Cross footbridge.

85.2 Side trail on left leads to Boulder Fields Overlook parking area (MP 302.4), but stay on main trail. Ⓟ

▲ Camping 🛏 Lodging Ⓟ Parking 🍴 Food 🚻 Restrooms 🏪 Supplies ◊ Water ⛱ Picnic

Bamboo Valley in the fall
Photo by Shelton Wilder

85.7 Cross Little Wilson Creek on arched footbridge. 💧

85.9 Trail to Rough Ridge parking area (MP 302.8) goes left. Stay on main trail. Ⓟ 💧

86.1 Walk along Rough Ridge boardwalk

86.5 Side trail on left goes to rock outcrop with good views. Continue right on main trail. Trail goes through field of large boulders for next 1.23 miles.

87.4 Cross bridge over Wilson Creek and continue left. Trail to Wilson Creek Overlook parking area (MP 303.6) is on left. Ⓟ 💧

87.5 Balanced Rock is on left.

88.0 Cross footbridge.

88.1 Side trail goes left for 60 feet to rock outcrop with good views of Linn Cove Viaduct, Table Rock, Hawksbill, and Pisgah Forest.

88.3 Bridge crosses Linn Cove Branch. 💧

88.6 Follow steps through large boulders and pass under viaduct.

Camping Lodging Ⓟ Parking Food Restrooms Supplies 💧 Water Picnic

Fallen Splendor
Photo by Chris Underhill

88.7 Come to Linn Cove parking area and visitor center (MP 304.4). Follow paved path around outside of parking lot. ⓟ 🚻 💧

88.8 Walk past visitor center. Storage buildings will be to right of trail.

89.0 Descend wooden and stone steps. *Note:* Some hikers may consider this section strenuous.

89.1 Cross bridge over Stack Rock Creek with waterfall on right. 💧

89.2 Ascend and then descend wooden boardwalk and stairway as they go around giant rock formation known as Stack Rock.

89.4 Stack Rock parking area (MP 304.8) goes 90 feet to right. MST goes to left and descends steps. ⓟ

89.8 Follow boardwalk next to parkway's stone retainer wall. Descend into area with large boulders.

89.9 Cross paved US 221.

90.3 Reach southern terminus of Tanawha Trail. Turn right and go 0.1 mile to Beacon Heights parking area (MP 305.2). Come out of woods and cross paved road to reach parking area. You can reach Linville by going north on BRP to first exit, which leads to US 221. At end of exit ramp, turn right and it is 2 miles to entrance to Grandfather Mtn. and another 2 miles downhill to Linville and intersection with NC 105. ⓟ 🍴 🏪 🛏️

Index